Women Preaching Revolution

Women Preaching Revolution

Calling for Connection in a Disconnected Time

Elaine J. Lawless

University of Pennsylvania Press

Philadelphia

Published by
University of Pennsylvania Press
Philadelphia, Pennsylvania 19104-6097

Library of Congress Cataloging-in-Publication Data
Lawless, Elaine J.
  Women preaching revolution : calling for connection in a disconnected time /
Elaine J. Lawless.
      p.   cm.
Includes bibliographical references.
ISBN 0-8122-3198-8 (alk. paper)
1. Sermons, American—Women authors.   2. Feminist theology.   I. Title.
BV4241.L38   1996
252'.0082—dc20   96-28701
                                                            CIP

Cover: The Rev. Kim Gage Ryan, Associate Minister, Broadway Christian Church-Disciples
of Christ, Columbia, Missouri, 1995. Photo copyright © 1996 Michael J. Hamtil. Used by
permission.
Figure, pp. vii, 219, from C. W. Leadbetter, *The Chakras* (Wheaton, IL: Theosophical
Publishing House, 1927), Fig. 7, p. 43. Reprinted by permission.

dedicated to all the women in ministry
I have come to know, respect, and love,
and to all those I'll never meet

and for Jessica
who insisted this one was "hers"

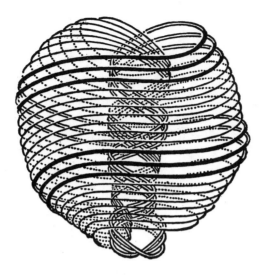

Spiral. 1. *Geom.* A continuous curve traced by a point moving round a fixed point in the same plane while steadily increasing (or diminishing) its distance from this. 2. A curve traced by a point, moving round and simultaneously advancing along, a cylinder or cone; a helix or screw-line. The *spiral* has sometimes been distinguished from the *helix*.

Spiral. To wind or move in a spiral manner; to form spiral curves.

Spirit. 1. The animating or vital principle in man [sic] (and animals); that which gives life to the physical organism, in contrast to its purely material elements; the breath of life.

Spiritual. 2. Of, belonging or relating to, concerned with sacred matters . . . .

Helix [a. L. *helix*, a. Gr. anything of spiral form]. 1. Anything of a spiral or coiled form, whether in one place (like a watch-spring), or advancing around an axis (like a corkscrew), but more usually applied to the latter; a coil, a spiral, a tendril, etc. . . . distinguished from spiral, which is applied only to plane curves.

Revolution.
I. 1. The action or fact, on the part of celestial bodies, of moving round in an orbit or circular course; **3.** a turn or twist; a bend or winding; **4.** the action, on the part of a thing or a person, of turning, of whirling around, or of moving around some point.
II. **5.a.** The action of turning over in discourse or talk; discussion.
III. An instance of great change or alteration in affairs or in some particular thing.

Revolve.
1. To turn (the eyes or sight) back or round, **2.b.** To bring round in course of time; **3.a.** To restore; to turn, bring, or roll (back into place); **11.c.** To wind spirally.
[Oxford English Dictionary]

Helix
1. *Geom.* A three-dimensional curve that lies on a cylinder or cone and cuts the elements at a constant angle. [Latin, from Gk, spiral, spiral object. See wel-[3] in Appendix.] wel-[3]. To turn, roll; with derivatives referring to curved, enclosing objects. 6. O-grade form *wol- in Germanic *wall-in: a. Old English *wiella*, a well ("rolling or bubbling water," "spring"): WELL[1]; 8. Extended form *welw- in: a. Germanic *walwon [note to ed. long o] in Old English *wealwian*, to roll; b. Latin *volvere*, to roll: VAULT VOLVOX, CIRCUMVOLVE, CONVOLVE, DEVOLVE, EVOLVE, INVOLVE, OBVOLUTE, REVOLVE; c. suffixed o-grade form *wolw-a [note to ed: long a] in Latin *vulva*, *volva*, covering, womb: VOLVA, VULVA; . . . 12. Suffixed form *wel-ik- in Greek *helix*, spiral object: HELIX.
[American Heritage Dictionary]

Contents

Acknowledgments

It would be extraordinarily difficult, if not impossible, to thank all the women who have helped to make this book possible. My eagerness to name each one is matched only by my fear of forgetting to name even one. Most important, I need to name the women who have continued to be helpful to me and supportive of my work over the years, many of whom speak in the pages of this book. Some of these women are Clare Austen, Martha Carroll, Sarah Cheney, Margaret Ann Crain, Maureen Dickmann, Coletta Eichenberger, Terri Gomez, Peggy Jeffries, Gertrude Lindener-Stawski, Moray Loring, Carole Lunde, Carol Millspaugh, Dianne Nunneley, Ashley Peak, Kim Ryan, Tamsen Whistler, Wendy Whiteside, ministers all. Friends, colleagues, and students who have read portions of this book and have generously given their time, energy, and wisdom include Tracey LeGrand, Lisa Higgins, Virginia Muller, Kristen Harmon, Marty Townsend, and Sharon Welch. I want to thank my mentors, Mary Lago and Wini Horner, who continue to provide support and encouragement for anything and everything I try to do and be. And I want to acknowledge the continued encouragement and faith in my work from Patricia Smith at the University of Pennsylvania Press.

I thank the University of Missouri Research Board for a year free from teaching to work on this book.

As for family, I have Sandy, Jessie, Kate, and Alex to thank—for sharing my life in many varied ways and keeping me safe and sane. I pray I never underestimate the importance of their collective embrace for my own well-being or neglect to tell them how much they mean to me.

Preface: *Spirals Within Spirals: The Helix as a Theological Model*

—In worship, you are there to listen to God's word and celebrate and focus.
—The focus is God and connecting with other people. It is more than only us.
—It is God's presence and us together.
—It is a circular effect. We have an experience and we have to test it against that which we know is true.
—It is spiral.

—The women in this book

This book grows out of, and extends, my work with clergywomen in central Missouri.[1] In 1993, I published *Holy Women, Wholly Women: Sharing Ministries Through Life Stories and Reciprocal Ethnography*, a book that explored clergywomen's life stories in relation to their ministries and introduced my use of what I call "reciprocal ethnography" as a feminist methodology that seeks to include the voices of the subjects in the study itself.[2] While *Holy Women, Wholly Women* focused on the personal stories of the women ministers and the relationship of their lives to their ministries, this book is a study of women preaching.

Although I did not fully comprehend my own words at the time, I closed *Holy Women, Wholly Women* with the following thoughts about women in ministry:

Quietly, they are invoking a new religious era.
Theirs is not a revolution but a re-volution,
a turning about the center, a spiral, a whorl toward the new center.[3]

Now, the words seem prophetic; indeed, they connect the two works. These words of invocation for a "re-volution," "a turning about the center, a spiral, a whorl toward a new center" invoke images of spirals, of curves. In this preface, I set the stage for the use of one spiraling metaphor, the helix. Throughout this book on women's sermons, I flesh out a natural evolution of the image, from the simple spiral to the complex genetic model of the double helix, and, finally, toward the expandability of a multi-stranded helix. Thus, I propose a visual image to inform our understanding of clergy-women's lives and their ministries, their sermons, and, ultimately, their perceptions of God.

Metaphors for women's lives, literature, and experiences abound in contemporary works that seek to recover, illuminate, and legitimate the creative, artistic, connected worlds of women. For example, the quilt, as an image and metaphor for the complex, intricate, but often pieced-together and interrupted aspects of women's lives, is widely accepted as a viable metaphor for women's experience.[4] Once associated only with domestic crafts, the quilt as a meaning-laden image has, in fact, far exceeded the boundaries of its traditional meaning in ordinary women's lives. The quilt has been accepted by the art community as a symbol of women's expression, especially in the ways it invokes notions of connection, pattern, layering, coding, and visual/tactile potential. The creative possibilities of quilting have been recognized beyond privatized women's spheres; the American gay community, for example, established its own commemorative quilt project that documents the lives of persons who have died of AIDS.[5] Feminist theory, literary criticism, women's history, and feminist theology have repeatedly turned to the image of the quilt as a way to talk about the expression, or coding, of women's lives, connections, collaboration, identification, thought processes, literary tendencies, acts of rebellion, and political statements (coded and not so coded).[6]

Other examples of women's needle and fabric art have also found their way into metaphorical thinking. Weaving, as a metaphor for the interconnectedness of women's lives and their spiritual or theological leanings, has been explored in a book of women's sermons[7] and is often used by literary critics eager to find an alternative to the long-accepted canonical pyramid of the literary Freitag model (introduction, rising action, climax, falling action) for plot and character development in women's literature.[8] Images associated with women's lives have also found metaphorical significance in critical endeavors. Paula Gunn Allen discusses the "Sacred Hoop" as an enduring natural symbol for women's lives and spirituality and finds in Native American women's writing an inclination toward the circular, the cyclical, the sacred, the spiritual.[9] Allen and others have likened the sacred hoop, or circle, to the spinning of the spider's web or the intricate patterns in the traditional "cat's cradle" string game, making strong connections between the complexity of the web and women's lives and relations.[10]

Building on these evocative images that connect with women's lives and their artistic and creative endeavors, the images I invoke in this study of women's sermons are the spiral and its double-stranded sister, the helix, particularly as these images are manifested in their expansion modes, that is, beyond the double helix to an ever-expandable, multi-stranded helix.[11] Consider the image of a helix with the possibility of innumerable parallel aspects that can also be intertwined or braided together as they form the various strands of the multi-stranded helix. Although the helix is perhaps not recognized as particularly or exclusively "female," I use it here as a richly contextualized female image. It is an image I seek to explore in all its complexities, a visual metaphor for how we might think about women's lives, relationships, connections, theology, spirituality, and, most importantly for this book, their sermon-making.

I draw the notion of the double helix as a metaphor for women's collaborative work from a lecture given by Kathleen S. Hurty during the Ecumenical Decade of Churches in Solidarity with Women (1988–1998); this source will take on a great deal of significance as the reader becomes familiar with what ordained women are trying to accomplish.[12] Hurty referred to the work of education specialist Helen B. Regan, who first proposed the double helix as a metaphor for women's leadership in school organizations, noting that the image provides a way to think about the strands and bonds that characterize the collaborative work of female administrators, which is generally recognized as not being competitive, not hierarchical, but collaborative: "intertwined, neither above the other, nor more valuable than the other."[13] I take Regan's image of the double helix even further by suggesting that the helix can work in a variety of visual capacities, but, particularly for this book, it is an image that best functions by enabling us to creatively imagine different aspects of clergywomen's lives, ministry, theology, and sermon making.

There are several reasons why the spiral itself provides a richly textured, expandable metaphor for a book on women's sermons. First, the spiral is not a fixed form but a malleable entity, expandable in many different ways. Like the child's Slinky toy, it can be pulled at both ends and infinitely stretched, vertically or laterally, or it can be joined at the ends to form a continuously woven circle. We can appreciate the fluidity of the spiraling image—the implication of process, of dynamic evolution, change, and transformation represented in the flow of the never-ending circles, the curves looping back always to remain in patterned concert with the ones before and anticipating those to come. Like a Slinky dropped from the hand, the spiral pulsates, bounces, moves with barely any manipulation. It is an image of life that seems actually to "breathe." It offers the perfected wedding of motion and consistent form, the spiral that has no beginning and no end, that perhaps spirals back onto itself. So, too, the image expands, in any direction; the ever-widening spirals can encompass, finally, the entire universe. However we might envision the spiral (and we are limited only by the imagined physical material of the spiral itself), we note that as the spiral is drawn ever and ever longer, the effect is to render the spiral itself tighter and tighter, smaller and smaller. Expandibility in this or any direction is limitless, and these experiments with form would not actually not alter the original spiral, yet each new configuration opens new creative possibilities.

If we can conceive of a single-stranded spiral and appreciate its possibilities for imagistic creativity, then we can easily envision the now-famous double helix: two perfectly parallel strands spiral around one another in the infinitely simple and yet complex natural form first illustrated by Francis Crick and James Watson as the visual representation for DNA. "We have discovered the secret of life," they cried, and the world heard them.[14] In this model for the genetic blueprint for all the cell's functions, the two strands remain at an equal distance from each other, folding around and around the invisible core, carrying with them all the genetic traits of all aspects of life that are passed on from generation to generation. If we take this image of the double helix and multiply the number of strands, we might, on the one hand, play with the metaphorical implications inherent *if* the strands remain parallel to and equidistant from one another, *or* we might, on the other hand, consider the possibility of the strands becoming braided together, spirals around spirals, as they twist and curve into the folds of the helix proper, making the configuration infinitely more complex and interconnected at each turn.

This multi-stranded helix as a metaphor for women's lives, ministries, and sermons is compelling on several levels. The first is the word's lexiconic connection with DNA, "the secret of life." What better image for our understanding of women's lives, thoughts, impressions, work, and theology than one well known as the metaphor for life itself? Moreover, natural connections link this image and other metaphorical images often associated with women's lives and literatures—the quilt, the web, weaving, and the circle. The circle predominates, and indeed, the metaphorical implications of circles, of weaving, of webs, and of hoops all pertain to concepts of interconnectedness, collaboration, intersection, overlapping, interweaving, complementarity, creativity, and complexity. Most compelling about the multi-stranded helix as a metaphorical image is its capacity to represent all life at the same time. I find the image appropriate to an examination of women's lives in ministry, theology, spirituality, and preaching, but the figure also weaves humankind, nature, and God into a comprehensible image useful for our attempts to understand and convey what women know about God and what they share with others. The Christian clergywomen in this study are concerned that theology take into account the actual stories of people past, present, and future, as well as the reality of the natural world and the way these stories and nature intersect with God. With feminist theologian Sallie McFague, they speak of connections between people, nature, and God as the collective, connected "body of God."[15]

Following the thinking and preaching of the women I have listened to in this study, I would like to suggest even further the metaphorical implications of how the center, or "core," of the helix may be explored as a space that embodies different perceptions of God. Conceiving the spiral and helix in spiritual and theological terms, we see that the restrictive stance of much of Christian tradition, including the exclusion of women and "others" from full participation in the church's activities, has pulled the spiral taut, eliminating the possibilities for expansion and providing only the most narrow, constricted space for the "core," hence limiting the possibilities for understanding God. This open-ness in the center of the spiral, however, suggests to me a space infinitely expandable, offering the possibility and the challenge for including all the different yet collective perceptions of who and what God is. The women in this book accept my interpretation of this image in relation to perceptions of God only as long as I make it clear that their concepts of God permeate the strands and reach far beyond the limits of the proposed image. That is, their perceptions of God are not limited to the core of this image. But if we allow ourselves the liberty of "playing with" this model, we can see that constricting the spiral and limiting the amount of space available in the "core" of the helix limits the possibilities of free-flowing, energized perception, while expanding the helix spacially creates a stronger configuration and provides more space at the center. At the same time, multiplying the strands of its composition increases the number of components that interact with each other and at all times "touch" (and are touched by) the core. "More is better" in this concept of building a bigger helix. The relationship of each encircling strand to the others and their simultaneous embrace of the core relates directly to the revolution in religion the women in this study are calling for. Theirs is a message for survival. In their insistence on the critical significance of connection in a disconnected time, women are striving to relate all of creation to itself and to God.[16]

In my perception of this configuration of the multi-stranded helix, the "edges" of the created form, as they loop back and forth in never-ending spirals, are actually defining and creating the essence of the center. There really are no "margins" in this conceptual model, only the curving strands of the organic matrix and the open center they create by their spiraling motion. There is no center without the encircling strands, and there can be no helix without a core.

Scientist Ruth Anshen's conception of *convergence* relates to my use of the multi-stranded helix as a metaphor for women's spiritual lives and their theology as examined in this book.[17] Anshen speaks of common bonds that link all of creation, people and nature, the universe and God/Energy; she suggests that the universe may be defined as a "living, dynamic process of unfolding," the study of which will lead us to the "comprehension of man's [sic] moral responsibility and participation in the totality, the organismic whole, of all reality."[18] Her vision corresponds in essence with the message conveyed in the sermons of the women in this book. In a rather unorthodox scientific treatise, Anshen claims the "outworn Cartesian, scientific worldview has ceased to be scientific in the most profound sense of the word, for a common bond links us all—man [sic], animal, plant, and galaxy—in the unitary principle of all reality."[19] In spite of the immense diversity of creation, Anshen proclaims, "a profound underlying *convergence* exists in all nature. And the principle of the conservation of energy simply signifies that there is *something* that remains constant . . . which we may call *energy*. We now do not say that the law of nature springs from the invariability of God."[20] Here she suggests, "Religion and science meld; reason and feeling merge in mutual respect for each other, nourishing each other, deepening, quickening, and enriching our experience of the life process."[21] Her "scientific" language strikes me as compatible with the image I am invoking for this study of women's sermons and with the call for a new perspective on theology.

The definition of "spiral" as a "continuous curve traced by a point moving round a fixed point in the same plane while steadily increasing (or diminishing) its distance from this" echoes the way I have been exploring the limiting and expansive capabilities of both the strands and the center. Note, too, the close lexiconic relationship of "spiral" with "spirit," defined as the "breath of life." Then, to find "helix" connected with e-volution, con-volution, re-volution, and vulva further endorses my adoption of the metaphor and my expansion of the spiral to the complexities of a multi-stranded helix. The helix is no artificial image, no invitation to a mere exercise in analogy or mind-play. The image of the helix can operate as a construct for our examination of the connections between the universe and God, as envisioned and articulated by women deeply engaged in the creating, learning, and sharing knowledge of God. It is a rich image that embodies the spiritually rewarding ways of living advocated by the women in this book—in close connection with all of creation and with God. Finally, the multi-stranded helix serves as a creative, evolving, and evocative model in this examination of the interconnectedness of clergywomen's lives, their theologies and spiritual realities, and the messages and structures of their delivered sermons.

I have listened to women preachers and have heard them talk about what it is like to "preach from the margins." On one level, this understanding of their place in the socio-cultural context is important to an understanding of their sermons; however, the development of the image of the helix enables us to reposition the margins! This approach will not be, once again, another case of "add women and stir" as Elizabeth Johnson has identified it, but an effort for a change so radical that it will change the system.[22] Women, men, and all of creation curve around each other and operate together as the various equal, multi-stranded aspects of reality that form the living spiral, which embodies at its core the collective perceptions of God. Perceived in *this* way, the new religious era signaled by women in ministry, both ordained and lay, sustains the energy for a revolution in religious thinking and enables us to conceive of relationship as the critical bond between the various interacting strands, and between those strands and the "core": God in and through revolution.

The term revolution (re-volution) has, itself, the possibilities for multiple meaning. Women in the contemporary pulpit are calling for a bloodless revolution in Christian thinking and living. Their re-volution is a gentle turning around, a recasting of the eye back to the roots of Christ's messages to the early church. We turn to Elizabeth Johnson, again, who has recovered the Greek word *perichoresis* to help evoke the cyclical, "co-inherence" of the trinity. The etymology of the word lies in the Greek word perichoreo "which signifies cyclical movement or reccurence." Johnson finds in this image "one way to portray the mutual indwelling and encircling of God's holy mystery." [23] Women preaching revolution invite the world to join them in a new circle dance; their hands reach out for new partners. To dance this dance of connection and inclusion, they would say, is indeed to learn the secret of living—with each other and with God.

Notes

1. For clarification, the reader needs to know that all of the women in this study belong to a regional "women in ministry" group that includes ordained clergy, Catholic sisters, and lay women. The primary focus of the sermon study is actually on the sermons of a smaller group of ordained women only, all of whom belong to the larger group.

2. *Holy Women, Wholly Women: Sharing Ministries of Wholeness Through Life Stories and Reciprocal Ethnography.* My interest in women preachers did not begin with that book, however. In 1988, I published *Handmaidens of the Lord: Women's Sermons and Traditional Religion*, a study of fundamentalist Pentecostal women's sermons.

3. Lawless, *Holy Women, Wholly Women*, p. 282.

4. See, for example, Cheryl B. Torsney and Judy Elsley, eds., *Quilt Culture: Tracing the Pattern*. Especially see Margot Anne Kelley, "Sisters' Choices: Quilting Aesthetics in Contemporary African-American Women's Fiction," pp. 49–67; and Cathy Peppers, "Fabricating a Reading of Toni Morrison's *Beloved* as a Quilt of Memory and Identity," pp. 84–95.

5. See Cindy Ruskin, *The Quilt: Stories from the NAMES Project.* Also see Van E. Hillard, "Census, Consensus, and the Commodification of Form: The NAMES Project Quilt," in Torsney and Elsley, eds., *Quilt Culture*, pp. 112–24.

6. See Pat Ferrero et al., *Hearts and Hands: The Influence of Women and Quilts on American Society.* See also Linda Pershing, " 'She Really Wanted to Be Her Own

Woman': Scandalous Sunbonnet Sue," in Joan Radner, ed., *Feminist Messages: Coding in Women's Folk Culture*, pp. 98–125, and Pershing, *They Tied a Ribbon Around the Pentagon.*

7. See Christine M. Smith, *Weaving the Sermon: Preaching in a Feminist Perspective* and *Spinning a Sacred Yarn: Women Speak from the Pulpit.*

8. Elaine Showalter, *Sister's Choice: Tradition and Change in American Women's Writing.* See also Showalter's "Piecing and Writing," in Nancy K. Miller, ed., *The Poetics of Gender*, pp. 222–47. For a contemporary explanation of the Freitag model as given here, see Sven P. Birkerts, ed., *Literature: The Evolving Canon*, p. 39.

9. Paula Gunn Allen, *The Sacred Hoop: Recovering the Feminine in American Indian Tradition*; also, Paula Gunn Allen, ed., *Spider Woman's Granddaughters: Traditional Tales and Contemporary Writing by Native American Women.*

10. See Theresa King O'Brien, *The Spiral Path: Essays and Interviews on Women's Spirituality.*

11. In my early drafts of this argument, I had wanted to alter our perceptions of the word "helix" by changing my usage of the word to he(r)lix, to not only connote a feminine use of the word but to expand its possibilities as a metaphorical image. The women in this book, however, felt this change was an unnecessary imposition on a perfectly good word, noting that if the *he-* in helix was bothersome to me that I might, instead, note the kinship of the word with *healing.* The intent of he(r)lix they did not find at all troublesome and, in fact, they liked it quite a lot. What they objected to was the constant use of the word he(r)lix throughout the book. I shall be quite happy, then, to rely on this endnote to alert the reader to the possibilities of a different way of perceiving the feminine helix.

12. Kathleen S. Hurty, "Collaborative Leadership in Chaotic Times, #3," delivered to the Arizona Ecumenical Council, Globe, Arizona, June 2–3, 1993. I want to thank Kim Ryan for sharing Hurty's lectures with me.

13. Helen B. Regan, "Not for Women Only: School Administration as a Feminist Activity."

14. For a fascinating look at the personal conflicts of the discovery of DNA, see James D. Watson, *The Double Helix: A Personal Account of the Discovery of the Structure of DNA.*

15. Sallie McFague, *The Body of God: An Ecological Theology.*

16. Jill Raitt calls this "relational theology" in her 1981 Presidential Address to the American Academy of Religion, "Strictures and Structures: Relational Theology and a Woman's Contribution to Theological Conversation." Rita Nakashima Brock, in her *Journeys by Heart: A Christology of Erotic Power* and Carter Heyward, in *Touching Our Strength: The Erotic as Power and the Love of God* both pose similar theologies based on connection and relationship, including the power of eros.

17. Ruth Nanda Anshen, "Introduction: Convergence," in Liebe F. Cavalieri, *The Double-Edged Helix: Science in the Real World.*

18. Anshen, in Cavalieri, *The Double-Edged Helix*, p. 8.

19. Anshen, in Cavalieri, *The Double-Edged Helix*, p. 2.

20. Anshen, in Cavalieri, *The Double-Edged Helix*, p. 9 (emphasis in the original).

21. Anshen, in Cavalieri, *The Double-Edged Helix*, p. 11.

22. Elizabeth A. Johnson, *She Who Is: The Mystery of God in Feminist Theological Discourse.*

23. Johnson, *She Who Is*, p. 220.

A Woman's Faith

TAMSEN WHISTLER
Calvary Episcopal Church
Columbia, Missouri
June 26, 1988

The lesson for this Sunday comes to us
from the Gospel of Mark:
"And one of the leaders of the
  synagogue named Jairus came
and when he saw him, fell at his feet and
  begged him repeatedly,
'My little daughter is at the point of death.
Come and lay your hands on her,
so that she may be made well, and live.'
So he went with him.

. . .

—Some people came from the leader's
  house to say,
'Your daughter is dead. Why trouble the
  teacher any further?'
But overhearing what they said,
Jesus said to the leader of the
  synagogue,
'Do not fear, only believe.'
He allowed no one to follow him except
  Peter, James, and John, the brother of
  James.
When they came to the house of the
  leader of the synagogue,

he saw a commotion, people weeping
  and wailing loudly.
When he had entered, he said to them,
'Why do you make a commotion and
  weep?
The child is not dead but sleeping.'
And they laughed at him.
Then he put them all outside,
and took the child's father and mother
  and those who were with him,
and went in where the child was.
He took her by the hand and said to her,
'Talitha cum,'
which means, 'Little girl, get up!'
And immediately the girl got up and
  began to walk about
(she was twelve years of age).
At this they were overcome with
  amazement.
He strictly ordered them that no one
  should know this,
and told them to give her something to
  eat." [Mark 5:22–24, 35b–43, NRSV]

The Gospel passage this morning
is a fairly straightforward miracle story,
particularly dramatic
because beyond healing,
Jesus raises someone from the dead.
A twelve-year-old is restored to life,
because of her parents' faith.
There's a pattern to miracle stories in the
    Bible,
and what we have heard this morning
follows the pattern pretty well.
Human resources are exhausted.
Jairus in desperation approaches Jesus.
Jesus encounters opposition in the
    pressing crowd
and the jeering mourners.
The miracle itself is private—
only parents and three disciples
witness Jesus' raising the girl.
Jesus both touches and speaks to the
    child.
Everyone is astonished
when she gets up and walks.
After requesting silence about the
    miracle
and making sure that the child eats,
Jesus leaves.

At issue here for us
in the twentieth century
is often the question,
"Is this really a miracle?
Did it really happen?"
But we can trap ourselves
so effectively
in the "Is it real" question
that we may not move beyond it
to the real issue,
the issue of faith.

Do we believe that God
can intervene in our lives?
Can we recognize God's action?

And there's another issue also,
which lies in the fact
that what the lectionary provides for us
this morning
in the healing of Jairus' daughter
is only *part* of the story.
You may have noticed in your bulletins
that what we heard a short while ago
were verses 22–24 and 35–43
of the fifth chapter of Mark.
Verses 25–34, which we did not read,
contain another story,
another healing miracle,
which interrupts the story of Jairus'
    daughter,
while providing an explanation
of Jesus' delay in reaching Jairus' house.
Let me read this passage.

"And a large crowd followed him and
    pressed in on him.
Now there was a woman who had been
    suffering fom hemorrhages for twelve
    years.
She had endured much under many
    physicians,
and had spent all that she had; and she
    was no better, but rather grew worse.
She had heard about Jesus, and came
    up behind him in the crowd
and touched his cloak,
for she said, 'If I but touch his clothes, I
    will be made well.'
Immediately her hemorrhage stopped;

and she felt in her body that she was
   healed of her disease.
Immediately aware that power had gone
   forth from him,
Jesus turned about in the crowd and
   said,
'Who touched my clothes?'
And his disciples said to him,
'You see the crowd pressing in on you;
   how can you say, "Who touched me?" '
He looked all around to see who had
   done it.
But the woman, knowing what had
   happened to her,
came in fear and trembling, fell down
   before him,
and told him the whole truth.
He said to her, 'Daughter, your faith has
   made you well;
go in peace, and be healed of your
   disease.' " [Mark 5:25–34]

An obvious question here,
of course,
is why did the designers of our lectionary
leave the woman with the twelve-year
   issue of blood
out of the story of Jairus' daughter?
We could get caught for a long time
in speculation about this,
and probably the explanation
is something simple like,
"The story of Jairus' daughter
stands on its own" or
"one healing makes the point as well as
   two"
or "the hemorrhaging woman is less
   tasteful
than the little girl."

It's apparently fairly clear
in the oldest Greek manuscripts of Mark
that the healing of the hemorrhaging
   woman
is written in better Greek
than the healing of Jairus' daughter.
So the writer of Mark
probably inserted the story to begin with.
Perhaps our lectionary designers left it
   out
because it began as an insertion.
Whatever the reason,
it's been left out.
But I think it's important that we
   consider it;
first, because the use of the "story within
   a story"
is fairly typical of the gospel of Mark,
but primarily because
the two stories together
offer us more about the nature of Jesus
and faith
than either story does on its own.
Without the story
of the hemorrhaging woman,
the healing of Jairus' daughter
invites us to concentrate
on the beautiful vision of a child lost,
now restored to her parents.
It is possible for us to talk about
the great spiritual meaning
of the child's return to life
without giving much thought
to the physical—
beyond the touch of Jesus' hand
and his command
that she be given something to eat.
We can be thrilled
that Jesus has acted

in such a dramatic way,
and we can recognize that children,
as well as adults,
are recipients of God's grace.
But we can stand outside the story
and watch.
And we can speculate
about the reality of miracles.
We can sidetrack ourselves,
while we admire the great spiritual
    revelation
of the child's return to life.
If we consider the healing
of the hemorrhaging woman
in the context of the healing of Jairus'
    daughter,
we find powerful contrasts.
The hemorrhaging woman
is not somebody we'd want to be around.
She's drained and desperate.
She's spent all her savings
seeking a cure,
and she's only grown worse.
For twelve years—
as long as Jairus' daughter has been
    alive—
the hemorrhaging woman
has been denied access
to the practice of her religion,
because she's unclean.
Close contact
with another human by her
renders that other person unclean, also.
The woman is an outcast,
one to be avoided,
one for whom life
within the structure of a supportive
    community
is impossible.

She is unclean;
and no decent person
should have anything to do with her.
In her desperation,
the woman forces herself through the
    crowd
toward Jesus,
seeking only to touch his clothing
to heal herself.
But the healing comes from Jesus.
She touches his garment
and feels within her body
that she is cured.
And he feels within his body
that someone has touched him.
His disciples think he is silly
to seek a particular person
in a pressing crowd,
but he recognizes
that a particular individual
has encountered him,
and he looks for her.
Overwhelmed by the fact of her new
    wholeness,
the woman is frightened.
Nevertheless,
she goes to Jesus as he seeks her,
and she tells him her whole story.
His response to her?
"Daughter, go in peace.
Your faith has healed you."
Another miracle, to be sure,
but the two stories together
help bring home to us
that an encounter with Jesus Christ
on any level
involves both the physical,
concrete, world
and dialogue with Jesus Christ.

The reality of experience
is imperative,
in our relationship with God.
We don't simply encounter Jesus Christ
on some esoteric plane
separate from our daily lives.
Instead, we encounter God in Christ
in our physical being,
our life in the world,
and our death.
The encounter involves both touch
and conversation.
Without the dialogue,
between Jesus and the woman,
Jesus and the child
and the child's parents,
the miracles have little meaning.
Without the dialogue,
what happens simply happens
and there's nothing to allay
the resulting fear.
When the woman is healed,
she is frightened.
Jesus gives peace
by acknowledging her faith,
and that's a miracle
beyond the physical healing.
We are like the hemorrhaging woman
and the little girl
because we are embodied beings.
We will undergo physical and emotional
    pain;
and we will die.
We are like them also
in that we know the world
through our physical presence,
through our senses as well as our
    thoughts,
and we need both

for wholeness in our daily lives.
The physical aspect of our lives
is not somehow separate
from our spiritual development.
We have to live that development out
in our bodies,
in the world,
in the here and now,
in the decisions we make,
in our connections with those around us.
How do we participate
in God's healing action?
We touch each other;
we talk to each other.
We love.
These stories are given to us
that we might learn something about
    faith,
not that we get sidetracked
on the issue of whether they really
    happened,
whether they're really miracles,
but that we might focus on the issue
of how it is that we encounter God.
Do we believe in the resurrection?
How do we live that belief,
act it out in our physical lives?
Can we recognize that concrete action—
touch and dialogue—
are the way we know each other
and the Christ within us?
Body and blood,
word and action—
the miracle of faith
lies in the concrete,
the particular,
the physical,
our daily lives.
We eat and drink together

that we might more fully know
our connection with each other,
with the hemorrhaging woman,

the dead and living child,
the crucified and risen Christ.
Amen.

Sometimes You Just Gotta Break the Rules

KIM RYAN
Broadway Christian Church (Disciples of Christ)
Columbia, Missouri
March 14, 1993

The Scripture that is offered to us this
day
is from the fifth chapter of the gospel of
John.
Keep in mind as we hear these words
that we're about halfway through this
season of Lent,
the forty days leading up to Easter.
And as we go along through these days
the Scriptures guide us
and lure us
to understand the road
that Jesus took to the cross.
So listen for the conflict
and listen for the tension
that will begin to
propel Jesus towards his crucifixion.

"After this there was a festival of the
Jews,
and Jesus went up to Jerusalem.
Now in Jerusalem, by the Sheep Gate,
there is a pool called, in Hebrew,
Bethzatha,
which has five porticoes.

In these lay many invalids—
blind, lame, and paralyzed.
One man was there who had been ill for
thirty-eight years.
Jesus saw him lying there,
and knew that he had been there a long
time, he said to him,
'Do you want to be made well?'
The sick man answered him,
'Sir, I have no one to put me into the pool
when the water is stirred up.
And while I am making my way,
someone steps down ahead of me.'
Jesus said to him: 'Stand up!
Take your mat and walk.'
At once the man was made well,
and he took up his mat and began to
walk.
Now that day was a Sabbath,
so the Jews said to the man who had
been cured,
'It is the Sabbath;
it is not lawful for you to carry your mat.'
But he answered them,
'The man who made me well

said to me, "take up your mat and walk.' "
And they asked him,
'Who is the man who said to you, 'take it
    up and walk?' "
Now the man who'd been healed did not
    know who it was,
for Jesus had disappeared into the crowd
    that was there.
Later, Jesus found him in the temple and
    said to him,
'See, you have been made well.
Do not sin any more,
so that nothing worse happens to you.'
The man went away and told the Jews
    that it was Jesus
who had made him well.
Therefore the Jews started persecuting
    Jesus
because he was doing such things on
    the Sabbath.
So Jesus answered them,
'My father is working
and I also am working.'
For this reason,
the Jews were seeking all the more to kill
    him,
because he was not only breaking the
    Sabbath,
but was also calling God his own father,
thereby making himself equal to God."
    [John 5:1–18, NRSV]

In the verses that follow
Jesus claims this relationship of
God the father and he his son.

May these words be a blessing in our
    lives,
an inspiration,

a challenge,
and an opportunity for growth.
Megan and Josh went to visit their
    grandparents.
Megan is six and Josh is four.
It didn't much matter what they played
    that week,
in their games of make-believe and
    play-acting,
six-year-old Megan always set the scene,
and she assigned the parts.
If they played school,
Josh was the student and she was the
    teacher.
And if they played the wild west,
Josh was the deputy and she was the
    sheriff.
And when they played Ninja Turtles,
well, Josh could be Michelangelo,
but she was Master Splinter.
It went like that all week long—
Megan in charge.
Toward the end of the week,
their grandfather overheard them playing
    in the next room,
and he heard Megan say "Let's play
    church, Josh,
and you can be the minister."
Grandpa thought, well, that was a first—
first time all week ole Josh got to be top
    dog.
Megan said "You can be the minister,
    Josh,
And I'll be God."
[lots of laughter; Kim laughs with them]
Don't you love it?
That was not what their grandfather
    expected.
Expectations,

they play an important role in our lives—
And how we anticipate life,
and how we anticipate one another.
Challenging expectations,
running up against them or running
    through them
can be risky.
And it can even be dangerous—
Well, maybe not for Megan,
but it certainly was for Jesus.

Didn't we hear that
in the Scripture stories for us today?
Didn't we hear
some of the conflict
and tension
as Jesus moves on to what will be his
    death
on the cross?
Now on the surface of that story,
it seems as if we have one of those
exciting stories of Jesus healing a
    person,
a man who had been sick for many
    years,
who had been waiting and hoping
for the opportunity to be immersed
in amazing healing waters,
because at that pool they thought that
an angel reached down and stirred the
    pool,
and if you could get in,
if you could be the first one to get in,
while those waters were still stirring,
you'd be healed.
But he just couldn't quite ever make it
    first.
And then Jesus healed him
with a few words—

amazing,
transforming,
words:
"Stand up!
Take your mat
and walk"
And he did—[a whisper]
That's the story.

But the gospel writer then takes us
beneath the surface,
with one phrase,
"Now that day was the Sabbath"—
That day was the Sabbath
and that's a clue that the tension is
    increasing.
The Sabbath was a sacred day, a holy
    day.
And you didn't do any work on the
    Sabbath.
And for the Jewish people,
in their religious understanding,
there were requirements,
and there were clear designations of
    what you did do,
and what you didn't do,
on the Sabbath.
And one of the things that you did not do,
you did not carry your mat on the
    Sabbath.
Those in the know weren't rejoicing that
    the man was healed.

It has been told that this is one of the
    reasons
why Jesus would be persecuted.
He healed a man on the Sabbath.
That was work.

He told the man to pick up his mat
and walk.
That was work.
He broke the law.
He broke the rule.
Who did he think he was,
breaking the rules of the Sabbath?
Who, indeed! [in a whisper]
Jesus says who he is:
"My father is working
and I also am working."

And then we're told—
and this is why they thought all the more
   to kill him,
because he not only broke the rule of the
   Sabbath,
but he called God his own father,
and he implied some kind of a
   relationship,
an equality
with God
the father.

Megan's grandfather's surprise at her
   declaration:
"I'll be God,"
didn't hold a candle to the surprise,
the indignation,
that came to Jesus when he proclaimed,
"My father and I are working
on the Sabbath."
This wasn't make-believe;
he wasn't play-acting.
He called God his own father,
and he identified his work
with the work of the father.
Let's back away just a bit
from that Scripture,

and the story that is there for us,
and give some attention to that idea—
God—
the father.
That's not a new idea to us.
That's not a strange idea.
We've probably called God "Father,"
once, twice, five times,
in the time of our being together this
   morning.
That's not new for us,
and it wasn't even new for the Hebrew
   people of the day.
The image,
the understanding,
of God as father
was an image that was a part of their
   history
and a part of their faith understanding
and a part of their scriptures
right along with a great diversity of other
   images—
God as rock
and God as shepherd
and God as mother
and protector
and mountain
and lover
and friend.
It was one of many of those
   understandings of God,
but it wasn't the government's
   understanding.
In those times, trying to understand God
   and how God acted,
it was far more common to give God that
   highest rank of human imagery—
God was king
God was royalty

God was sovereign,
    powerful,
    judging from the throne of glory.
God was distant
God was demanding
God was making the rules
and enforcing the rules.

But Jesus veered from this dominant
    understanding,
and he selects one
of those other images
and claims it as his own—
and expands it
and stretches it
beyond expectations.
In the gospel of Mark when Jesus talks
    about God as father,
he uses the word "abba."
And they tell us that that word means
    "daddy."
And that maybe it even means more than
    that,
maybe it means "dear daddy."
And there is communicated in that
a relationship,
a relationship of intimate need and of
    closeness,
a relationship of nearness with God.
And that—
    that's a little unsettling—
    that's a little threatening—
God as parent,
God as father.
Think about that.

I remember the first time I became a
    parent—
the day after Gage was born,

I stood at the window of the hospital
and I looked out on that outside world
    going by and wondered,
"Don't those people know I just had a
    baby?
What are they doing going on with their
    lives?"
But I stood there and I looked out that
    window
and I had the most indescribable sense
    of joy
and of completeness—
I can't even put it into words.
I had never felt that before
and have never felt it since. [in a whisper]

And two days later,
they put me in a wheelchair,
and they handed me that little tiny bundle
    of life,
and they pushed me out into that outside
    world,
and I cried the whole way [voices rises
    for dramatic effect]
I did!
We've got pictures of it!
I cried because I realized
that I had not tried even once to be a
    parent.
Never in my life had I felt so vulnerable—
And I still do.
But it's a haunting thing about being a
    parent
of vulnerability. [in a whisper]
And I can't quite shake it off.
It's very hard for me to watch news
    reports about two-year-olds
separated from their mommy in a mall for
    two minutes—

[makes a face of grief]
I am vulnerable to love—
and vulnerable because of love—
as are any of us
who love deeply
in any of our relationships.

What if?
What if
Jesus' declaration of God as father
could mean the possibility
of a God who experiences that feeling
of amazing and incredible joy,
and also a God who feels vulnerable—
[in a whisper]
A God who feels a feeling
and a pain
and opens himself
to pain
and hears the hurt
for hurting children.

Could it be that the cross
is about a God
who is vulnerable?

Jesus called God "Father."
It makes a difference
who we understand God to be.
It says a lot about God
and it says a whole lot about us.
If God is king,
we are subjects,
trying to please and win favor,
instead of breaking the rules.
And we fear the king's punishment,
and we try to stay on the king's good side
and the king will be kind if we do,
if we're loyal subjects,

if we don't carry our beds on the
    Sabbath.

If God is father,
we are in a unique relationship with
    God—
we are beloved children.
Jesus proclaimed his nearness to God
and God's nearness to him,
and Jesus proclaimed that it was a
    nearness
that was possible for all God's children.
Sin isn't about breaking the rules.
Sin is about not valuing the relationships,
and not valuing our brothers and our
    sisters,
and all of God's creation.
It makes a difference
who we understand God to be—
and ourselves and others.
And the powerful witness of Jesus Christ
    is this:
The witness of Jesus Christ
is that we not allow ourselves
to get boxed into a single perspective
of understanding God.
Jesus challenged the prevailing
    perspective of God,
when he emphasized in his life
and his teachings of God
as father. [whisper]
God as daddy?

Jesus challenged the expectations
and it was risky.
Sometimes you've just gotta break the
    rules.
That was risky.

Thinking about today
and thinking about where we are
in our understanding of God—
probably for most of us God as father
is a prevailing image for us.
Certainly the Christian community
has adopted that imagery—like Jesus—
and have claimed that as our own.
That's how we understand ourselves
and who we understand God to be.
But you know that's not true for
  everyone.
Renee is a woman who lived in
  California,
and it's only been in the last few years
that she's been able to admit to herself—
and entrust to others—
that it's hard for her to call God "Father."
It's hard for her to relate to God as a
  father,
Because, you see,
she is a survivor of incest.
And when she tries—
and she really tries—
when she tried to understand God as
  father,
she just couldn't begin to embrace God
  or herself,
until she tried to look elsewhere.
So, she went to her Bible,
and she found there other images,
and other understandings—of God.
And finally, she was able to give herself
  permission
to claim some of those other images.
It's only been recently
that she's been able to call God, "Friend"
and "Mother."

And that has given her a new way to
  understand God
and to relate to God
than she's ever had before.

Well, Renee has a friend, Kathy,
and they talk about this understanding of
  who God is.
And even though Kathy understands
why Renee feels the way she does,
she can't and she won't let go of God as
  father.
Her father walked out on her family when
  she was a baby
and God as father is the only father that
  she's ever had.
God is father to her
and is known by her as the "Faithful
  Father."
She can't change that.

Is one right or wrong?
Both are women of faith,
and both are women who are affirming
  God,
in their lives—
in seeking a relationship
of integrity with God.
Jesus offers us that example.
Jesus gives us that witness
of expanding our understandings of God
and letting us understand
the reflections of the best relationship
  possible.
Expanding my understanding of God
came home to me in a very unexpected
  way.
Did you notice the picture

as you came in the sanctuary,
the picture that's on the wall here?
That's not usually there, usually it's in my
  dining room.
But I brought it this morning.
It's one of my very favorite pictures,
it's a Jan Vermeer print
of this Dutch painter's work from the
  sixteen hundreds.
I've had it for twelve years,
and it's been in every dining room I've
  had
in those twelve years.
If you didn't see it,
let me describe it real quickly.
Then take a look when you go by it.
It's a print of a woman
who is standing at a table by a window,
and on the table are some pieces of
  bread—
and she's pouring milk from a pitcher into
  a bowl
and the light is shining from the
  window—
and shining on her peaceful face
and on the table.
Well, a few years ago,
when we were eating breakfast,
Gage, who was then four years old,
and had seen that picture
every day of his life said to me
"Mom, is that a picture of God?"
And my answer—"Of course not"—was
  just right there—
"Of course not."
[pause]
But it couldn't come out—
it was stuck.

And instead I said to him,
"Well, what do you think, Gage?"
And he looked at that picture
and said, "Yeah, I think it is.
What do you think, Mom?"
[grimaces]
I wasn't off the hook. [smiles]

And I looked at that picture with a new
  eye,
and saw what I had never seen in that
  picture before.
And I said to him,
"Well, I think it is, too."
And it felt like we were breaking the
  rules.
And I half-expected Dean Berry,
his Sunday school teacher, to call me
the next week and say,
"What are you teaching your child?"

And I would have had to have said,
it's not what I'm teaching my child,
it's what my child is teaching me. [in a
  whisper]

Being open
to expanding
our understandings of God,
beyond the expectations.
Expanding understandings
of who God is
and who we are—
and for one another.
Jesus lead the way.
Will we follow?
Will we follow? [whisper]
Amen.

Introduction: On Ethnographic Responsibility

The Writer as Author/ized Storyteller

So your question is—"have I heard you correctly?" Is that it? Well, when you tell a story it isn't necessarily "heard" by the listener, who is trying her best to hear it, but after all you come from your frame of reference and I come from mine and she comes from hers, so we don't always "hear" the stories that are told. So, what I hear you saying is that you want them to really be *heard* and not just refracted through you.

—Gertrude

In Mario Llosa's remarkable short book, *The Storyteller*, the narrator recounts his uneasiness as he gradually learns how his good friend Saul, a Jewish intellectual, has "gone native" in the Peruvian jungles.[1] Not only has his friend "become" a Machiguenga, a fact bothersome to the narrator, he has also become the traveling tribal storyteller, the native bard, the revered one entrusted with the ancient myths, legends, and holy mysteries of The People. The narrator is both fascinated and repelled by what he views as this impropriety on Saul's part. How could the unlikely Saul, his close friend, be offered, or take on, this most noble, this most potent, this near-priestly role? And how could the natives endure this intrusion, this claim to *their* history? I quote from Llosa:

Where I find it impossible to follow him—an insuperable difficulty that pains and frustrates me—is in the next stage: the transformation of the convert into the storyteller. It is this facet of Saul's story, naturally, that moves me most; it is what makes me think of it continually and weave and unweave it a thousand times; it is what has impelled me to put it into writing in the hope that if I do so, it will cease to haunt me.

Talking the way a storyteller talks means being able to feel and live in the very heart of that culture, means having penetrated its essence, reached the marrow of its history and mythology, given body to its taboos, images, ancestral desires, and terrors. It means being, in the most profound way possible, a rooted Machiguenga.[2]

Unlike Saul, I have not become a convert—I have neither "converted" to any particular denomination represented by the clergywomen in this study, nor have I become an ordained minister. But much like the narrator who cannot forget the story of Saul, I think of their stories and sermons "continually and weave and unweave them a thousand times." I want to talk the "way a storyteller talks," knowing it "means being able to feel and live in the very heart of that culture, means having penetrated its essence, reached the marrow of its history and mythology, given body to its taboos, images, ancestral desires, and terrors." I want to present myself to the reader of this work as an author/ized storyteller, one endorsed by those in the study, entrusted and authorized to tell their story. I put this in writing, as well, in the hope that if I do so, "it will cease to haunt me."

I am going to tell you a *story* about a group of women who are preaching and about my interactions with them over a period of time. This book is my story about them. It is a story about my ongoing endeavor to study the lives and ministries and sermons of a group of women who are ordained ministers in various Christian denominations. Since 1983, I have been tape recording women's sermons in mid-Missouri with the intention to write this book. When I discovered one particularly cohesive group of clergywomen, I focused my attentions on them. I have been attending their churches, accompanying them to various activities, visiting with them in their homes, having lunch with them, talking with them on the telephone, and meeting with them in my home, for nearly ten years. We have been convening, dialoguing, arguing, sharing, loving, agreeing, disagreeing, converging, and separating during this time. In seeking an appropriate "voice" in this ethnography, I must talk about myself with *them*, even though I am critically aware that naming *them* as an "other" distances and distinguishes *me* from *them*.[3] But I am not a member of the clergy; therefore, in a most fundamental way, I am not one of *them*. As a participant in our lives and work together, however, I am a full member and participant of this group of women seeking to know and learn. In fieldwork methodological terms, then, I am an observer of their ministries and their sermon making and performances. I am also a participant in our work together to interpret and understand their ministries, their preaching, and their collective impact on religion in the postmodern context, which more and more is revealed as a time of crisis. My story includes both the moments of observation and the moments of participation, which occasionally fuse. This book is an ethnography, a record of my involvement with a group of women and their own involvement with each other in living their various Christian ministries.

Some of the "book work," as the women have come to call our work together, included here is collaborative work. However, by acknowledging that this is my story, I am admitting that I know it is not actually a "collaborative ethnographic narrative." I have written this account. They have not.

They have worked on it with me at my invitation and at their insistence and desire. Perceived and desired ends have been shared, but ultimately I am the one writing the account. I claim it as my story because it may not be — indeed, cannot be — the story any one of them might have written, for I stand at a different place from any of *them* in my relationship to their lives, their ministries, and their sermons. I do nevertheless believe that my ongoing dedication to reciprocal ethnographic research and dialogue with the women in the study about the story I want to tell "author/izes" me to tell this story about them.[4] I have been vested, then, with a responsibility to tell a story they trust and, to some degree, endorse. They have not censored my work, silenced my pen, or diverted my attention in any way that I can discern; I have told them the story I want to tell, and they have helped me frame it, mold it, and flesh it out, until it is a story they are pleased to have me tell. In my quest, I am reminded of some rather unexpected words from scientist Ruth Anshen. Anshen admits that "scientists can no longer confront the universe as objective observers. Science recognizes the participation of man [sic] *with* the universe. Speaking qualitatively, nothing happens in man that does not have a bearing on the elements which constitute the universe.[5] She and some of her colleagues, then, seek to "expose the error which creates an unreconcilable dichotomy between the observer and the participant, thereby destroying the uniqueness of each . . . by neutralizing it. For in the end we would know everything but *understand nothing*."[6] We are "homeward bound," she claims, "because we have accepted our convergence with the cosmos. We have reconciled observer and participant."[7] Like Anshen, I seek to reconcile the observer and the participant.

The women who appear in this book have for several years lived in one rather small geographic area. They are all ordained ministers, pastors and associate pastors of local congregations in a fairly small town or chaplains at local hospitals and retirement centers, with the exception of one participant who is retired and two who have moved away but continue to interact with the group on a limited basis and send me tapes of their sermons. Like most dutiful ethnographers, I began this study in a traditional manner, by attending services and recording women's sermons, intending to write a textual study. Because texts are finite, it is easy to conceptualize them, type them, read them over and over, study, dissect, deconstruct them, reconstruct, rearrange, and reassemble them. We treat them as a "thing" separate from their makers, and their receivers. But the harder I tried to write a textual analysis of these orally performed texts, the more I resisted and rejected such an approach. I determined, therefore, to distance myself somewhat from the actual texts (at first) and to try to ground them more sensitively in their created context(s). An attempt to de-center the text in a sermon study may seem a ridiculous effort, but it is precisely what I hope to do in this ethnography. Actually, I want to de-center the sermon texts while simultaneously recognizing them as an integral part of the study. The result is a story that conveys, I hope, the collective nature of sermon making by this group of contemporary Christian women who envision alternatives to dominant notions of ministry, sermon making, and community building.

One way I seek to accomplish the task of de-centering both the text and the writer is to develop a creative model, based on the helix, that visually illustrates the way all aspects of women's lives, sermons, families, relationships, biblical Scriptures, congregations, and natural surroundings intersect with each other and with God. As I explain in the preface, I have chosen the multistranded helix as the basic foundation of this creative model. Early in my study, one of the women noted that she perceived her sermons to be like "spirals," moving around several key points rather than taking the expected, more traditional three-part sermon form. She is right; they are. This image not only works in terms of the sermon texts but also helps us to visualize all aspects of the women's lives that come together to create a theology based on experience and spirituality. The helix further serves to include me and my story as two of the strands interwoven with them and their stories, as both writer and as participant in our quest for understanding and meaning.

I must backtrack now (as every good storyteller must) to tell you more about the groups of women represented in this story.

First, a regular but totally informal bimonthly lunch meeting of "women in ministry," a group totaling perhaps twenty-five members. Rarely do all members attend on the same day. This fluid, ecumenical group crosses lines of race, class, age, and level of ministry involvement.

Second, a smaller liturgical group, also fluid and informal, derived from the bimonthly group. They meet weekly to share lunch, go over the readings offered in the Common Lectionary (see below), and begin a dialogue about sermons on these readings, an effort that continues through the week as members share ideas, other sources, old sermons, and other collaborative efforts. These "liturgical lunches" generally begin with the question, "So, what did you end up doing [in last Sunday's sermon]?" The group review the creation and performance of each other's sermons and work toward the sermons for the following Sunday. This ongoing dialogue shows how this intimate group of women collaborate in developing the messages they offer their congregations, even though they never actually hear each other preach.

Third, a regular group composed of all the women in the second group as well as several members of the bimonthly lunch group, who meet with me on a regular basis to talk about this book and my work in general. Early in our work on my previous book, *Holy Women, Wholly Women,* this group came together, based on whether they had the time, energy, and inclination to work with me; they drew in some new members as some women moved away and others developed an interest in the project. I have had some input into the formation of the group, but have largely allowed it to regroup naturally and select new members based on the women's interest in working closely with me on our "book work" or on members of the group suggesting to other women that they join us. The result is an eclectic, thoughtful, representative group of different denominations, whose members are very comfortable with each other and with me and very interested in the work we are doing together.

Fourth, and finally, a group from among these women who are also close, personal friends and who see each other on a regular basis. They also see each other at many city and regional denominational and ecumenical gatherings. Several of them are currently serving on Care Teams for the Regional Inter-Faith AIDS Network and other socially conscious organizations with which they are variously associated. As a group, they are faithful friends to one another. They share church, family, social, regional, and national concerns on a regular, often daily, basis. Nevertheless, they are a diverse group. Some are married with grown children; some are not married and probably never will be; one is widowed; some have newborn children or children in elementary school; one is retired, remarried, and with grown children; two have moved away but keep in touch with us. They represent a diversity of religious views—from Episcopalian to Disciples of Christ to Unitarian and Unity to United Methodist. Perhaps because of this denominational diversity, perhaps in spite of it, this group never debates doctrinal tenets. They speak openly and thoughtfully about their different theological points of view, even making jokes about and parodying these differences, but denominational or theological differences never enter our dialogue in competitive or disruptive ways. I remain convinced that they regard these differences as inconsequential. Regardless of official church affiliations, the women in this book have strong affinities for the same kinds of theological foundations; their beliefs, practices, and dedication to a new, revolutionary future for Christian life bind them together.

Women's Dialogue with Other Women

The ethnographic aspects of this project focus on one group of clergy-women in a fairly small geographical area. These women all preach on a regular basis in the pulpits of their respective denominations. They rarely, if ever, hear each other preach. Most had never seen any sermons from their "sisters" until I began to share their transcribed sermons with them as a group.

My fieldwork, at first, was isolated and consisted of meeting with the women individually for interviews, attending their church services, and tape recording their sermons over a long period of time. As outlined in *Holy Women, Wholly Women*, however, I eventually learned about the bi-monthly lunch meetings they were holding in one of their churches. After some discussion, I was welcomed into this group and have been attending the lunches, off and on, for about five years. Like the other women, I feel I can attend on any Tuesday when I can make it; I feel welcome when I attend; I catch up on all their news at these lunches and am free to share my own concerns and joys with them; and I can listen to their various dif-ficulties and successes in their individual churches. It is a perfect "check point" for my work. Through the regular lunches, I can determine where the women stand emotionally and professionally, what they are doing, what the concerns are in each of their churches, and I can let them know that I am still writing about them and concerned about their lives and their min-istries. Those who attend are from the regional area, including the small towns in the nearby vicinity. The women at these lunches call themselves the "Women in Ministry" group, and welcome clergywomen, lay chaplains, and Roman Catholic sisters in pastoral ministry. The lunches have been going on for more than ten years and obviously serve a deep need for the women who attend. The group continues to function in a totally unstruc-tured way. There is no leader, the meetings are always held on the first and third Tuesday of every month, and whatever happens and whoever attends is acceptable. The only "format" for these lunches that I have observed is that everyone present gives a short "report" on her life, work, or week in an orderly fashion around the table. I have occasionally seen turn-taking facilitated by each woman passing a small object (endowed with meaning—explained to the group by whomever brought it) to the woman next to her in the circle around the table. It is the shared perception that the lunches serve a purpose and that the women attend because they want and need to; they receive the kind of support and care from other women that they seek and desire when they attend. If someone does not appear for some time and no one in the group can report on her well-being and activities, then someone may very likely volunteer to call her during the next week to check on her. Their ties are flexible but tenacious. They want and need to know how the others are doing.

My methodology for *Holy Women, Wholly Women* emerged from these lunch gatherings. A smaller group of women from the regular lunch group wanted to participate and work more closely with me in what I called "dia-logue sessions," where we discussed various aspects of their ministries that were of concern to me as I tried to envision and write *Holy Women*. As it turned out, their life stories became the pivotal axis for that book and for the way I approached a presentation about their lives and their ministries. We worked together closely to examine several aspects of women in con-gregational ministry, using what I call "reciprocal ethnography." I would bring them the chapters I was writing and the transcriptions of their own life stories. In small group sessions in my home, we discussed their stories, my ideas, the conclusions I was drawing, the inferences I was making, the analyses I was writing. I would tape record these discussions and then incorporate their responses to and critical examinations of my work into the book itself. In *Holy Women, Wholly Women,* I tried to preserve all our voices in our collective *process* toward seeking meaning and understanding. In that book their voices are clearly distinguished from mine; our discussions and disagreements are left in evidence. I did not rewrite my "conclusions" to incorporate the discussions and disagreements; I chose to leave sections of the process intact, allowing the reader to see how my "conclusions" had been altered by the input of the women. The work was an attempt to offer a polyphonic, multivoiced, multileveled analysis that recognized the position of all of the participants and of the ethnographer/writer (me). I had intended also to include their sermons in that book. It became clear, however, that the sermons deserved an examination of their own, separate from the work on life stories that we had done for *Holy Women, Wholly Women.* Thus emerged the idea for this book.

I set out at first to do a rhetorical analysis of women's sermons. Parts of this book will be just that, and will focus on all the traditional aspects of rhetoric one might expect to see in such an examination. The longer I tried to write a rhetorical study of sermons, however, the more I resisted. Not only did a solely textual analysis seem limited and acontextual, but I knew that the approach would leave out some of the most fascinating and probably even more significant aspects of this pulpit phenomenon. For instance, no rhetorical analysis could capture the importance of the *performance* of the sermons in the living context of the churches in which they were delivered. Although a rhetorical approach certainly recognizes "delivery" as one aspect of the orally delivered speech, the performance of the sermon within its social, cultural, and religious context strikes me as much more pertinent to our understanding of women's sermons than an analysis that foregrounds and highlights the sermon text over its context.

Moreover, a strict rhetorical analysis would not enable me to explore the performative aspects of how the women in this book were actually developing a revolutionary discourse together, one that would and is disrupting the dominant discourse of much of contemporary Christianity. Although I instinctively thought this hypothesis might be true, I had to determine how to support such a claim. I could not argue that women are developing a re-volutionary approach to religion each on their own, separately, *because* they are women. But I do want to argue that they are developing such a revolution collectively, bringing to the endeavor the singular, separate experiences they have privately encountered and publicly have shared with each other—the praxis where private experience becomes collective experience because they have each experienced much the same thing.

Doggedly, I began to explore their ministerial lives again. I knew about the lunches; I sometimes attended them. I was always invited to their private Christmas party and shared in the flow of joy and love at that season with them. I continued to attend the services in the churches where they worked, and to record their sermons. Chapter 1 is a kind of tour from one service to another. I invite the reader to travel with me to the homes and the churches of women in this book. What would you hear from these pulpits on any typical Sunday morning? As I traveled from church to church, I began to learn some new things. Many of the women had become actively involved with support-team training and other aspects of a regional AIDS support project. I talked at length with one clergywoman who had come to view her ministry as being located in the local Planned Parenthood organization, where she works on a full-time basis.

In both the regular lunches and the smaller "lectionary" gatherings, the dialogue about sermon making was central. New dialogues were introduced and honed as well: dialogues with the Scriptures and anticipated dialogues with congregations. I knew I had found what I was looking for — evidence that the revolutionary language I was identifying in the women's sermons was being collectively imagined, shaped, and developed. Here I could see evidence of the dialogue between the women and the social and cultural milieux in which they interacted and the denominational and religious frameworks that determined some of the lenses through which they perceived the world at large. And I recognized that they were also in dialogue with me.

The inspiration for Chapter 2 came as I realized how these various encounters connected the sermons of the women who went their separate ways and preached to different congregations each Sunday. There were nearly visible threads linking the sermons they preached with the discussions of Scripture, life, meaning, and ideas. The threads pulled the women into the next week but also kept them connected to the previous week and the sermons they had just preached. Lunch, then, was generally the time to talk about last Sunday. "So, what did you finally do yesterday?" and "Well, how did it go?" or "How did you feel about it?" or "Did anyone *say* anything?" After these initial inquiries, each would in turn explain what she had done the Sunday before, especially relating her sermon to their previous discussions and being careful to note how a particular idea or story from another woman at the table had helped her finally focus on her topic.

It was especially interesting for me to note how differently they had each responded to the guidelines of their denominations with respect to the Scripture lessons to be read. The norm in the Episcopal church, for example, is that the Old Testament, New Testament, and Gospel lessons and psalm from the lectionary be read, and that the sermon be based on one or more of these. Other denominations expect more flexibility in the choice of lessons to be read, or in choosing to preach on a different selection altogether. All the women in the group at least read the lectionary first to see what the recommended passages were and to decide from there which ones they would read or have read at the upcoming service. Even more interesting was how the women decided which particular aspects of the given verses to focus on and how to make connections between the verses and the concerns and needs of their respective congregations.

Not only did a dialogue develop between the women and the biblical texts, but an anticipated dialogue emerged with the members of the separate congregations. As they "heard" this dialogue and shared it with each other, the clergywomen could also "hear" the dialogue their congregations were having with the sociocultural world(s) in which they were all struggling—individually and collectively. In a sermon, this sense of having overheard the dialogue could take the form of the preacher's observation that "I know what you're going to say" or "I know what you're thinking"— a simple form that belies the complexity of the multiple levels of dialogue interacting in the heads and lives of churchmembers at any given moment. The clergywomen might know, for example, that the teenagers in their congregations were hearing many different dialogues concerning sexuality, condom use, and the threat of AIDS, and they might become concerned about how the dialogue with the Scriptures and the dialogue between the Scriptures and the congregation would intersect with those other very loud dialogues. Or they might know that the dialogues about death and dying in one particular household were intersecting with dialogues among the congregation members and with the pastor at the same time. In the lectionary discussion, the minister would, then, wonder aloud how to present a sermon that would intersect with those other dialogues—and make a difference to the persons listening. The lectionary conversations convinced me more than ever that these women preachers were not mainly interested in the well-honed sermon as an admirable *text* but that they perceived their sermons to be yet another voice in an ongoing dialogue that was constantly in focus and constantly shifting as they and their congregations wound their way through the various and often confusing, trying, despairing, unfathomable, joyous, rich, and full aspects of their lives.

Chapter 2 offers a very personal ethnographic account tying two sermons to the lectionary lunches that connected them. I have never asked to tape record these lunches. I feel honored to be allowed to come to these meetings and recognize that a great deal of personal and private information is shared here, information that I know is not intended for my consumption (or that of my reading audience). I have, however, tried to give a true ethnographic description of the lunches without sharing information or details that should be kept private. The sermons included in this book, however, are verbatim transcriptions of the performed sermons delivered in the context of actual church services.

When I first began my work with ordained women preachers, they told me they believed women did not preach "like men." They recounted stories of their seminary experiences and the (often) required homiletics and preaching courses. By and large, they had been disappointed with these courses. Classical approaches to homiletics, the art of the three-part sermon, instruction on how to "insert" anecdotes effectively often seemed to miss the mark for them. They sought out new courses in feminist and liberation theology and the exciting new offerings by teachers like Rosemary Radford Ruether, Letty Russell, and Lee McGee and found these courses to be, as one woman put it, "like a breath of fresh air. Like oxygen!" Importantly, the women in this book believe that women preach differently from men. Thus, how and why women preach differently—and if they actually do—became two of the central foci for this book and for my inquiry. Chapter 3 briefly examines homiletics and places the sermons of the women in this book within an historical and creative perspective.

Interspersed throughout the book are examples of sermons delivered by women in their home churches. Most of these sermons were delivered between 1989 and 1994 in central Missouri. A few samples, however, are considerably older, delivered years ago when the authors were in active parish ministry elsewhere or were in a different ministerial position. Some sermons were delivered by women who had left the Midwest (but continued to send tapes of their sermons to me for the book). The selection of sermons in this book represents less than one-tenth of the sermons I have transcribed and that have helped me to write this book. The interweaving of texts, theirs and mine, represents my attempt to bring the spiraling helix into play; the different texts are strands that curve around each other, intersecting, relating, and collaborating in the book as a whole. Their presentation in these pages is "ethnopoetic": I have "lined-out" the sermons based on breath pauses, as they were delivered orally from the pulpit. The sermon texts are actual verbatim transcriptions of sermons, not written texts (with the exception of one, where no tape recordings were available to me). I have used only minimal kinds of voice modulations and performance registers—bold for loud, italics for whisper or emphasis that is not loud, a dash (—) for a kind of trailing off or thought unfinished. I have added punctuation and capital letters because these literary devices aid in our "reading" of the oral texts. Since we cannot "hear" them here on the printed page, standard literary conventions will perhaps help the reader "hear" the woman's voice better than would a continuous, unbroken line of words. Thus sentences are maintained as the speaker spoke them. I accept full responsibility for the addition of these conventions to "unbroken" speech patterns.

I am also interested in the formal, rhetorical aspects of women's sermons, which include structure, imagery, use of narrative, repetition, tropes,
point of view, and so on. In various ways throughout the book these characteristics of women's sermons are examined and interpreted. As the sermons
are presented and examined, the reader will be better able to see patterns
and characteristics as they emerge in the study. The formal analyses of the
sermons appear primarily in Chapters 3 and 4. Chapter 3 is an overview of
the characteristics of women's sermons; Chapter 4 is an in-depth critique
of one sermon—an artistic text that provides an opportunity to examine
in detail the way women's sermons are conceived, constructed, and performed.

I explore also the messages of women's sermons. What is the content?
How is it shared with the listeners? Is there a collective message or messages
that emerges from the study of many different women and their many different sermons? Potentially, what kind of impact could women's messages
have on the church as a whole? Women are delivering challenging messages from their pulpits, messages of tolerance, inclusion, and connection.
The message they bring is one of holistic religion, one cognizant of how
religious belief and knowledge of God *must* stem directly from human experience, relation, connection, inclusion, and collaboration. Such a recognition demands a radical rethinking of *whose experience this knowledge is going
to be based upon.* Traditional religious constructs have been based on male
experience; hence the church liturgy, scripture, and imagery have all been
formulated out of the life experience of males holding the power and authority to decree that all participants would share in the knowledge of God
based on their experiences. All "other" persons, then—women, children, persons of color, differently abled, homosexuals—have been expected to *know*
about God based on someone else's experience and perceptions. As long as
only men were in the pulpits and holding positions of power and authority
in the world's churches this narrow-mindedness could persist. No more.

From these women's voices in the pulpit comes a new, different, challenging, revolutionary message, based on the life experiences of women,
but seeking to validate and invite the experiences of all persons. Chapter 5
examines the heart of this new message and the implications for Christian religion at large. Speaking for those who have been relegated to the
margins for so long, these women speak the new voice of the "bystander"
who has found her voice—and her voice is helping to reshape religion and
redefine the "margins." Their sermons convey messages of vulnerability,
pain, exploration, and reimagining, of critical rethinking and renaming.
Their voices frame challenging messages because they have been so long
absent and ignored they are recasting their position in the margins as a
privileged one, because from there they can speak to, and for, others in
similar circumstances. These women and others are invoking a vision of

the world as a different and better place for all creation in this time. The appeal of their vision informs my story about these women preachers.

Notes

1. Mario Vargas Llosa, *The Storyteller*.
2. Llosa, *The Storyteller*, pp. 243–44.
3. For discussions of "reflexive anthropology," see James Clifford and George E. Marcus, eds., *Writing Culture: The Poetics and Politics of Ethnography*; James Clifford, *The Predicament of Culture: Twentieth-Century Ethnography, Literature, and Art*; Jay Ruby, ed., *A Crack in the Mirror: Reflexive Perspectives in Anthropology*; George E. Marcus and Michael M. J. Fischer, *Anthropology as Cultural Critique: An Experimental Moment in the Human Sciences*; Stephen A. Tyler, *The Unspeakable: Discourse, Dialogue, and Rhetoric in the Postmodern World*; Vincent Crapanzano, *Tuhami: Portrait of a Moroccan*; and Dennis Tedlock, *The Spoken Word and the Work of Interpretation*. For a cautionary look at the use of reflexive ethnography by persons already in power positions, see Frances E. Mascia-Lees, Patricia Sharpe, and Colleen Ballerino Cohen, "The Postmodernist Turn in Anthropology: Cautions from a Feminist Perspective." For feminist critiques of the danger of speaking of the "other" in our work, see Judith Stacey, "Can There Be a Feminist Ethnography?"; Lila Abu-Lughod, "Can There Be a Feminist Ethnography?"; and Trinh Minh-Ha, *Woman, Native, Other*.
4. See my "Women's Life Stories and Reciprocal Ethnography as Feminist and Emergent," and "'I was afraid someone like you . . . an outsider . . . would misunderstand': Negotiating Interpretive Differences Between Ethnographers and Subjects."
5. Ruth N. Anshen, "Introduction: Convergence," in Liebe F. Cavalieri, ed., *The Double-Edged Helix: Science in the Real World*, p. 1.
6. Anshen, in Cavalieri, *The Double-Edged Helix*, p. 11.
7. Anshen, in Cavalieri, *The Double-Edged Helix*, p. 11.

Making Connections

MAUREEN DICKMANN
Rockbridge Christian Church-Disciples of Christ
Columbia, Missouri
September 5, 1993

Our Scripture today
comes from the eighteenth chapter
of the Gospel according to Matthew.
This is directly after Jesus has told them
    about
the good shepherd,
the shepherd who goes out
after the one lost sheep
and leaving the ninety-nine because
God doesn't want anyone to be lost.
This is spoken by Jesus according to
    Matthew:
"If another member of the church sins
    against you,
go and point out the fault,
when the two of you are alone.
If the member listens to you,
you have regained that one,
but if you are not listened to,
take one or two others along with you
so that every word may be confirmed by
    the evidence of two or three witnesses.
If the member refuses to listen to them,
go to the church,

and if the offender refuses to listen
even to the church,
let such a one be to you
as are the Gentiles and the tax
    collectors.
Truly, I tell you,
whatever you bind on earth
will be bound in heaven,
and whatever you loose on earth
will be loosed in heaven.
Again, truly I tell you,
if two of you agree on earth,
about anything,
whatever you ask will be done by God.
For, where two or three are gathered in
    my name,
I am there." [Matthew 18:15–20, NRSV]
Amen.

During the course of this week,
I talked to so many members of our
    congregation
who were telling me they were going to
    be away this weekend.

You know, Labor Day is kind of the last
  gasp of summer,
so many of our regular folks are gone,
and as I looked at what our lectionary
  readings were,
I thought, well,
"where two or three are gathered"
may be just the right thing for this
  weekend,
with so many gone.
But as it turns out,
I'm very happy to see so many of us here
  today.

The gospel of Matthew
in the eighteenth chapter
is one of Jesus' discourses
where he is teaching the disciples
about something.
And between this week and next week,
Jesus is teaching about how
we can live together as a church—
the corporate life we Christians lead,
maintaining the church's fellowship.
And the overriding theme of this
is the interrelatedness of everything.

Now next week,
the gospel will focus on the issue of
  forgiveness,
which is very essential to the Christian
  story.
But this week, preceding his treatise on
  forgiveness,
we hear about what to do,
when someone offends in the church.
It's about how to restore someone who's
  strayed.

It's, remember, right after the lost sheep
  story,
and how God just won't give up on
  anybody.
God doesn't want anyone lost.
And, I think the implication is,
God depends on us to do some of the
  shepherding.
So if there's someone that offends you in
  the church,
then Matthew lays out the formula of
  what should be done.
It's not to be talking about each other
and going behind each other's back,
and the kind of tensions that are easy to
  happen
when you are in any kind of community.

Let's look at Matthew's formula.
First off, notice that the offended one
has to take the initiative—
the person who's been hurt—
the person who's been sinned against
is encouraged to take the initiative.
And that's very important, I think.
We can't always avoid being a victim in
  life,
or hurt, or being upset,
but we can avoid a victim mentality—
that is, every time we're hurt,
we withdraw to collect our thoughts,
and let others know.
In this case, Matthew is encouraging us
to go out,
reach out,
to this other person.
Confront this person directly
and with respect.

You respect that person's privacy,
and that's why it begins with just the two
of you,
alone.
Now, if that doesn't work,
they don't want you to give up,
there's too much at stake here.
Look at that lost sheep,
there's too much at stake.
So witnesses are called in,
two or three elders of the church
can come along.
But it's important that all of those
witnesses
are there for *both*—
the accused and the accuser.
It's not to really gang up on this person,
but it keeps it from becoming too
personal.
Then, if that doesn't work,
we'll bring it to the church.
So you go through these stages,
trying to seek reconciliation.
Then if that doesn't work,
we have this incredible statement—
that doesn't sound like the Jesus we
know:
"If that person doesn't listen to the
church,
then let that person be as a Gentile and
a tax collector."

Now, at first glance we think,
wow!
Here we are in the gospel,
written by the tax collector.
Supposedly Matthew is the one
who was called by Jesus from his tax
collecting table, right?

Here we are at the gospel
that ends with Jesus telling his disciples
to go out into the world to all the nations.
And here it sounds like,
they're all backsliding into some sort of
insular type community
where there's usury and greed.

But I wonder if that's the case.
Is it really that the person is to be
shunned?
Or can we look at how Jesus, in fact,
in his life,
treated Gentiles and tax collectors?
How did he treat them?
Did he shun them?
No, he ate with them,
he welcomed them,
he taught them,
healed them,
and fed them.
He did.
He continued to welcome them,
and he continued to seek them out.
If we look at how Jesus treated "Gentiles
and tax collectors,"
then we say with him,
we never give up,
we do not ever give up.
Even if that person isn't listening to the
church,
you continue to reach out.

All of this is meant to emphasize
the interrelatedness of us all.
We are all connected,
and we're all responsible for each other.

Of course, this is a very critical topic for
these days.
If any of you have been to a movie in the
last year in Columbia,
you've seen that "trailer" about the third
planet from the sun.
It's a very well done piece.
As the camera pans,
this voice is telling us—
they show people all over the world and
talk about
our fragile ecosystem and how life is the
same—
it starts out the same—
all over the world,
and then it concludes with
"and whatever we do to the Earth,
we do to ourselves."
And some kind of big tractor drives by
and throws all this dust in the camera's
face.
It's a very effective message about this
very thing—
the interconnectedness of all creation.
There's no real separation,
nothing is separate from anything else,
we're all connected.
I don't know if any of you have heard this
butterfly theory
that has been talked about recently.
I've heard it a number of times,
and I can't begin to explain it,
or understand it,
but I guess physicists tell us
that a butterfly flapping its wings in
Peking
will have some kind of effect on the
weather in New York
at some point.

It doesn't really make a lot of sense
to me,
but I get the point
that everything eventually touches
everything else.
I think that it was put very well by Martin
Luther King,
who said—
it was Christmas Eve 1967—
when he said,
"It really boils down to this,
that all life is interrelated.
We're all caught in an inescapable
network of mutuality,
tied into a single garment of destiny.
Whatever affects one directly,
affects all indirectly.
We're made to live together,
because of the interrelated structure of
reality.
This is the way our universe is
structured.
This is its interrelated quality.
We aren't gonna have peace on earth,
until we recognize this basic fact—
the interrelated structure of all reality.
Everyone is connected."

There's a novel called *The Spire*, by
William Golding,
and it's a story about a dean of a
cathedral
who wants to build this four-hundred-foot
spire.
It's a big, big spire.
And at the end of the story,
the spire is in place above the cathedral,
but it's been built at the cost of wrecked
lives,

the arrogant manipulation of people,
leaving behind a trail of death,
and infidelity between spouses.
And as this dean's life flashes before
  him,
he says,
"If I could go back,
I would say that God
lies between people
and is to be found there."*
The idea that God is actually between us
in our relationships,
that God is actually present between
  people—
is to be found there—
is emphasizing the interrelatedness of all
  creation,
the way it was made by God.
Nothing is more important
than right relationship between persons.
For we experience nothing less
than the very presence of God
in those relationships.
It's all connected.
Now, go back to Jesus at the end of this
  verse saying,
"Where two or three of you are gathered
  in my name,
I am there with you."

I one time saw a cartoon about this:
In the first frame,
you see a preacher standing before a
  congregation,
calling it to worship with this very phrase,
"Where two or three are gathered in my
  name,

there I am in the midst of them."
When you looked at the second frame,
the preacher has raised his eyes
from the printed word on the lectern
and looked out at the congregation
to announce the first hymn.
But something has stopped him in
  mid-sentence.
For there in the fifth row,
surrounded by familiar faces,
is Jesus,
at least the familiar artists' conception
of what Jesus looked like.
The last frame then shows the preacher
  lying prone,
behind the lectern,
in a dead faint.
What I think this cartoon
is trying to get at,
in a sort of irreverent fashion,
is how much do we really believe
Jesus Christ is with us,
as we gather here right now—
as we gather at any time?
How much do we really believe that?
Of course Jesus isn't present
in the way the cartoonist is showing him
  to us.
But his presence is no less real.
He is no less alive
because he is not sitting there
in some kind of cartoonist's pose.
The truth of the matter is
that a Christian fellowship survives
the strains that are placed upon it by
  human failures,
you know we have some,
because the risen Lord sustains us.

*William Golding, *The Spire* (New York: Harcourt Brace, 1964), p. 210.

It's the only way we can continue to be
the church,
even with all our faults,
and all our shortcomings.
We do so because there is a Lord
who sustains us
and who makes it so important
that we do all that we can
to keep our relationships running and
healthy.
Because it's in the midst of such
relationships,
such communion,
that God is so very close to us.

This power of people,
two and three together,
gathered in the name of Christ,
who can make amazing things happen.
God lying between people,
Jesus in the midst.
This is enough to strengthen weak
hands,
make firm feeble knees,
and lift up faint hearts.
It's the power of that presence
in even the smallest of groups,
that can truly change the world.
Amen.

Making Sense of Primal Stew

MARGARET ANN CRAIN
Peachtree Road United Methodist Church
Atlanta, Georgia
September 5, 1993

"Come unto me, all ye that labour and
   are heavy laden,
and I will give you rest.
Take my yoke upon you, and learn of me;
for I am meek and lowly in heart:
and ye shall find rest unto your souls.
For my yoke is easy, and my burden is
   light." [Matthew 11:28–30, King James]

If you were planing a church service
for Labor Day weekend,
what biblical quotation would pop into
   your head?
Probably many of us are thinking this
   one.
"Come unto me, all ye that labour and
   are heavy laden,
and I will give you rest."
Such a familiar Scripture,
so familiar, and so comforting—
it's certainly part of the good news that
   Christ offers to us.
But like so many familiar passages,
when I got to thinking about it some
   more,

it began to raise some questions for me.
The assumption behind that particular
   passage
seems to be that work is heavy and
   wearying,
something to escape from in rest.
And that's really not the way I
   experience it,
do you?
I find that work gives my life meaning,
work is what anchors my day.
Without work I don't need recreation.
Work is something to celebrate,
for without work we wonder at our value
   to the world.
I know when I go on vacation
and go to one of those lovely places
where a person comes in to make the
   bed in the morning
and pick up the towels
and wipes the counters,
everything is just beautiful
and you're waited on hand and foot.
But it usually doesn't take more than a
   day of that

before I'm dying for some work to do.
I know you stay in a little condo and you
    think
"Oh good, I can wipe the kitchen counter,
it will make me feel better."
Work is welcome,
constant leisure is a bit hard to take.
And I remember so well my Uncle
    Bruce—
he's gone now, but he was a man who
    loved to work—
he found his meaning for his life in his
    work,
and when he retired he went into a
    terrible decline.
He became so depressed
without work to go to,
he had no structure in his day.
He wouldn't sleep at night,
he had no sense of any importance for
    his life.
Work is important and good.
But the other side of that coin comes
    when we,
like my Uncle Bruce, get addicted to our
    work.
As you probably know,
a key symptom of addiction is denial.
The alcoholic or otherwise addicted
    person
will often maintain very stoutly,
"Oh, I don't have a problem,
I can quit any time,
I can control it."
The strange thing about our work
    addictions, though,
most of us brag about them.
About how many hours we had to work
and how late we stayed.

We boast about our addictions.
There's a name for that addiction,
workaholic.
I hear that word rather a lot lately.
Evidently we all know what it means,
we recognize the syndrome and we
    celebrate it,
I'm afraid,
with books like *A Passion for Excellence*,
by Peters and Austin, it came out just a
    few years ago.
Listen to what they say.
It's appalling—
This is a quote out of the book:
"Even a pocket of excellence
can fill your life like a wall-to-wall
revolution.
We have found that the majority of
    passionate activists
who hammer away the old boundaries
have given us family vacations,
little league games,
birthday dinners, evenings, weekends,
    and lunch hours,
gardening, reading,
movies, and most other pasttimes.
We have a number of friends
whose marriages or partnerships
    crumble
under the weight of their devotion to a
    dream.
There are more newly single parents
than we expected to find among our
    colleagues.
We're frequently asked if it's possible to
    have it all,
a full and satisfying personal life,
and a full and satisfying hardworking
    professional one.

Our answer is no;
the price of excellence is time, energy,
    attention and focus.
Excellence is a high cost item."*
Indeed the cost is high,
the cost, I believe, is death.
In fact, I learned that the Japanese
    culture
has experienced so much early death
    from overwork
that they have a special name for it.
They call it the Kuroshi syndrome.
In their book, *The Addictive
    Organization,*
Anne Wilson Schaef and Diane Fassel
    warn that
work is a trick addiction,
because when workaholics are most into
    their disease,
they feel most alive,
even though it may be killing them.
In their interviews with workaholics,
they have found that the surge of energy
these people *think* they feel,
and that they identify with "feeling alive
    and energetic,"
is actually the addiction, the stress.
Unfortunately, they don't get that same
    surge on a family vacation
or a night out with friends;
therefore, they actually experience a
    let-down
and encounter depression
when they are not at work or thinking
    about work.
Does that sound familiar to you?

Does it fit your spouse?
or your son? or daughter?
or maybe yourself?
I don't know about you
but I get a little bit squirmy with this kind
    of talk.
Maybe the shoe fits just a little bit?
Or you might be sitting there getting kind
    of annoyed with me.
And that's all right too.
This is Labor Day.
Aren't we supposed to be honoring
those who labor?
We have gotten into the habit of honoring
    work and labor,
by spending the weekend, I've noticed,
in this sort of frantic search for leisure.
People jam the interstates
trying desperately for one last trip to the
    beach
or one last round of golf.
This, it seems to me, only perpetuates
    the myth
that labor is unpleasant and to be
    escaped from
and only perpetuates the addiction to
    frantic activity.
The headline in Friday's *Journal and
    Constitution* read:
"Wanted, jobs with freedom."
Perhaps you read that article.
A five-year study
of the American work force
has come up with findings

*Thomas Peters and Nancy Austin, *A Passion for Excellence* (New York: Warner, 1985), pp. 495–96, quoted in Anne Wilson Schaef and Diane Fassel, *The Addictive Organization* (San Francisco: Harper and Row, 1988), p. 24.

that most working people know only too well:

many feel burned out by the end of the day;

they don't have enough time with their families;

and they fear they'll be laid off or have to retire early.

The study paints a portrait of a nation of hardworkers

who feel burned out from balancing work and family,

yet care intensely about performing well on the job.

At the end of the workday

42 percent of employees feel used up.

And 40 percent feel tired

when they get up for work in the morning.

Hmm.

I do think there's a way out of this dilemma.

And please understand that I preach to myself;

if this means something to you that's fine,

but I'm always preaching for myself.

Both the Bible verse I mentioned a while ago,

that is, "Come unto me all ye who labor and who are heavy-laden

and I will give you rest,"

and the passage that I read from Romans today

are germane to the question.

Both Scriptures help us to think more holistically

about work and leisure in our lives.

To begin with

I'd like to suggest we substitute the word vocation

for the word work.

I'm talking about vocation as our human vocation,

the job of being human,

the whole of what we are,

that means our work,

our leisure,

our family,

our roles,

our interests,

our talents,

our God-given gifts.

In order to construct a full picture of who you are,

you might try to see your life as a narrative,

a story in progress.

At times you find yourself especially aware

of that need to decide on the story of your life.

For instance,

when you chose the person you would marry,

or when you decided what to major in in college,

or when your children leave home

and you readjust the household,

or when you retire.

Those times you are intentionally,

and consciously,

writing your story.

But when we tell our story

often it helps us to make sense in hindsight

of our past

and what it means for the future.
One well-known author,
her name might be Phyllis Rose says it, I
    think very powerfully,
here are the words she used:
"Questions we've all asked of ourselves
    such as:
why am I doing this?
or the even more basic,
what am I doing?
suggest the way in which living forces us
to look for and forces us to find
a design within the primal stew of data
which is our daily experience."
Primal stew,
all that stuff that happens to us,
that we do and that is around us all the
    time.
I want to invite you this morning
to sift through that primal stew
that makes up your daily experience
and constructs the narrative
that tells of your vocation.
A weekend like this is a prime time for it,
if you haven't gone rushing off to the
    beach,
which obviously none of you have.
You have the luxury of a three-day
    weekend
to take an extra breath,
to ask:
who am I?

One of the interviewees that I met in my
    own dissertation research
answered the question this way,

She said,
"Life is important.
Life is the only hope you have.
If you're alive,
you still might get to know God better.
We don't even know what life is;
only God gives life,
only God can take it away.
So we need to make sure
people have a good life.
I have a family.
If I turn out two good human beings,
maybe that's enough."
That's how she answered it.

Or if I were answering the question,
I'd say something like this:
"I am one who searches for the meaning
    of life,
both in my work and in my leisure.
All my life is beginning to fit together
like a patchwork piece,
a patchwork of relationships,
and projects,
which attempt to answer the question,
what does God mean for this world to be,
and how do I, Margaret Ann, contribute
    to that vision?"

Another writer, Frederick Buechner,
speaks of vocation,
as the place where the heart's deep
    gladness
meets the world's deep hunger.*
I love that.
I think that's so meaningful.

*Frederick Buechner, *Wishful Thinking: A Theological ABC* (New York: Harper and Row, 1973), p. 95.

The woman I quoted above has really
done that;
she's a mother raising two children,
trying to honor the ultimate value of life
and her heart's deep gladness in
motherhood—
is meeting the world's deep hunger for
humans
who care about others.
Vocation then is not to negate your
special gifts and graces;
vocation is not giving yourself away
in such a way as to ignore the gifts
that God has given you,
but giving your gifts away
in partnership with God's work in the
world.
We play out that vocation
in a drama or a narrative;
the narrative that comes out of that
primal stew
of life experience,
and like any good drama
we're not the only characters in this
drama.
Listen to how another writer, James
Fowler,
who is a professor at Emory,
describes it:
he says,
"The prime creator, God,
is in some sense simultaneously
theater owner, producer, first author,
director,
and fellow participant in the action.
In the whirl,

in the stirring of subplots and
counterplots
we find places in relation to others
who story about the larger story
which forms our movements
and gives us clues to the larger action
in which we try to fit the motions
of our days and years.
To be in vocation
seems to develop the talents and gifts
one has been given
for the sake of enriching and moving
the whole drama dance
toward the climactic fulfillment,
envisioned by God's script.
To be in vocation means to know and
trust
that the actor/director is also present
in masked or hidden form,
sharing,
bearing,
and working to redeem the whole
creation
to the goals of the larger play."*

That was Fowler's metaphor of the
drama.
And I want to invite you this morning
to explore that metaphor of the drama
as you sort through the experiences of
your life
which make up that primal stew.
Who are the other main characters in
your drama?
What are the special gifts you've been
given?
Who's playing the small parts,

---

*James W. Fowler, *Becoming Adult, Becoming Christian: Adult Development in Christian Faith* (San Francisco: Harper and Row, 1984), p. 138.

the walk-ons? in your drama?
Should they have larger roles?
What are the creative contributions
your life makes
to the vision of the playwright, God?
Watch out for your tendency
to downplay your own value.
Each of us has special gifts
and special roles to play in the big drama
for which God has set the stage.
Remember the words of Paul:
"I appeal to you therefore, brothers and
   sisters,
by the mercies of God
to present your bodies
as a living sacrifice,
holy (and wholly [spelled out w-h-o-l-l-y])
   and acceptable to God,
which is your spiritual worship.
For as in one body we have many
   members
and not all the members have the same
   function,
so we, who are many,
are one body in Christ,
and individually members one of another.
We have gifts that differ
according to the strengths given us."

Let us pray:
Dear God who has created us
and who has gifted us,
help us we pray to make sense of our
   lives.
Some days seem to go by in a chaos of
   unfinished tasks
and unsatisfied relationships.
We feel out of control.
It's hard to keep the house orderly,

the shopping done,
the memos written,
the accounts productive,
the staff content,
the lawn mowed,
the church solvent,
the car running right.
Even more difficult is to take the time to
   listen
truly listen to our lives,
for your voice,
your voice calling us to wholeness.
But this morning we pray for whole lives,
lives lived in harmony with your will, oh
   God,
lives that are not numbed by a steady
   round of work
but alive with the depth and breadth of
   experience,
lives that are productive,
but whole and balanced,
lives that include space for friends and
   family,
through whom you teach us about your
   grace and love,
lives in the vocation brought forth
by the gift you have given us.
Help us, beginning this day
and this hour,
to live whole lives,
through which we are present
to the needs of ourselves,
our families,
our community,
our church,
and our world.
This we pray in the name of your son,
Jesus the Christ.
Amen.

Musings from a Hot Blackberry Patch

GERTRUDE LINDENER-STAWSKI
August 1983

This sermon is reproduced by permission from Gertrude's sermon in written form. I did not record it, and therefore have not attempted to render it in any ethnopoetic form.

One of the blessings of this summer has been time for reflection. Away from the usual round of tasks, a different kind of thought rises to the surface. I'd like this morning, with your indulgence, to take you with me into that other world.

I want to share not the traveling, full and satisfying as that was. Rather it is to that most familiar place, the farm, I take you to. We have had a long, demanding relationship with it, comprising care and worry, sudden surprise, frustration, and joy. Sixty acres it is, of poor pasture and thin oak woods. On the farm are half a dozen beef cattle, a few geese, a vegetable garden, and a barn.

The blackberries were full this summer. My mother always made blackberry jam for us. The summer days roaming in the woods, reconnoitering creeks amid the buzz and drone of insects, were also times of bringing back berries from that wondrous world out there, berries which magically turned into rows of dark matched jars of jam under her knowing hands.

This summer I was going to make blackberry jam. I would re-enact the old ritual, this time by my own efforts. The lightness of childhood would be reincarnated in all its innocence. Living would return to purity and simplicity. The childhood fields would be brought back and made one with the pastures we worked in now.

The morning was still and hot. Fool that I was, I waded into the thicket armed with shorts, sneakers, and a large bucket. There, in the insane tangle of sawtooth briars, sudden sneaking poison ivy, and grass, the berries hung in scattered clumps. I finally bore them back to the car in triumph, a whole gallon and a half of them, though I was scratched, torn and exhausted by the time I was done. The berries went into the freezer—whatever we could not eat.

Determination of a kind overcame all hesitation once the berries had been tasted. The free, wild harvest of the coming few weeks had to be ours. I returned again, armed this time with long sleeves, heavy trousers, hiking boots, wide-brimmed hat, and a pair of pruning shears safely in my pocket. The plumpest and juiciest berries were down behind the dam where the bushes are thickest and the footing treacherously uneven. There, swaddled in sunlight and insect buzz, a timelessness took shape. Drops of perspiration trickled down my neck into my shirt. I learned to move slowly, carefully, outwitting the sea of thorns by deliberateness of movement. Berries high up were sweet and warm in the sun. And thus body, feet, eyes, and balance were caught up in the picking and concentrated wholly in a rhythmic struggle of oneness with the thorns, the heat, the simple taking of the food. It was a lovers' combat with earth and self and the distant trees.

And then I saw it—the skeleton of our old gray gander. There, among the blackberries, picked clean, a heap of dried sinews and bone stuck with feathers, he lay. Unmistakable was the rounded goose's bill, the long neck. Some fox or coyote had gotten him.

The fox had evidently been very hungry. Long he must have worked over that carcass, his agile tongue feeling between the tiny latticework of bone for every attached shred. After him would have come varied insects, picking microscopic bits clean. And then the drying sun. Perhaps that fox had not had a good meal for days. The sudden leap and grasp, a brief skirmish with desperate struggling wings, the alarmed honking of the other birds, would be only his manner of getting a plate out of the cupboard for dinner. He would have eaten hungrily, possessively, watchfully, as all animals do.

Here lay the tough old gander who had tyrannized and protected his little family and its space—all too ineffectually—against us and all comers. Every magnificent goose egg of the spring had been stolen from behind his honking and posturing. He lorded it over the younger males unmercifully, chasing and pecking, while the little chicks wisely cowered out of the way in a corner. Such a harridan had he been that we had had to separate him and his consort from the remainder of the flock to preserve some peace by taking them to the lake. Such a stubborn old coot he was, he would not stay at the lake. Three times he returned to the barn, limping, nearly dead of thirst and exhaustion, before he was willing to accept splendid exile at the pond. Later we moved the whole flock down to the water. And now he lay, a rounded tangle of bones, dried masses, feathers. He would have been fierce in his death as he was in his life. I turned away from the bones and back to the berries.

In the timelessness, many thoughts flowed, unaccustomed in the normal round. This bounty of berries here was free. The rising swell of juicy rounds in the buckets was there for us without planting or pruning or watering. They would still be there in spendthrift abundance even if I did not pick them. How long since I had enjoyed something not planned and organized and purposefully brought to pass? How long since I had simply sucked the gratuitous nourishment of the world without a care? This arrangement, this time was not a tit-for-tat transaction. No bargain was made and carried through, no purchase paid. There was no sowing and weeding to pay the harvest. It was simple bounty like divine grace—unmerited and good. I thought to stand in the timelessness forever, plucking berries, the drops of sweat teasing my neck—one with the sun, the motion, the black bounty.

But had someone else been picking my berries? Was the grass matted down where I had not gone, berries missing where Tuesday's observation had indicated they would be black and full today? Poachers perhaps had been here, the same shadowy figures who left their traces around the pond when sometimes they fished uninvited? Did the interlopers need to be outwitted if we were to have jam and with it the return of innocence? These were *our* bushes. It was *our* careful expectations that had ripened the berries for the ritual of the jelly jars. My childhood of old carelessness and innocence, the womb of simplicity, had been ripening slowly on those vines. The imagination that waited for its completion had guarded its fruition. And now it had been stolen.

Who was that thoughtless, careless person, who picked so randomly only where the best berries were? What right had they? Could he not see there were fences, signs? Probably it was someone who sponged off society for other things, too. If I met the intruder in the early dew of some morning—should I lie in wait for him?—what should I say if I surprised someone in the thievery? "Who do you think you are? We've spent all summer getting these berries to ripen so that we could make jam. There was no crop last year. Two years we have been waiting for these. Go pick berries somewhere else . . ."

Or was it, maybe, the neighbor who helped us when the cow got out, scouting the meadows as she had done since childhood for the summer's harvest—as I had done in my childhood on other people's farms. Jars of her strawberries sat even now on our shelves, a wedding gift of summer sun and kitchen labor telling simply of country generosity.

Shame flooded over me at the anger and possessiveness that my expectations had wedded to the efforts of picking. The blackberries were not "mine," even though I joyed to be one and alone with their timelessness. The bushes were their own masters. They fought with me, and with the neighbor, and with the raccoons, and with the sun and the rain for the precious seeds they nurtured. They had done so since time immemorial, and would do so long after I was gone. They in their silent stubbornness would outwit cows and bulldozers and would slowly one day give way to the shade of whatever trees came there in the long cycle of forest building. They were not mine. I was ashamed.

So I thought about possessing and about being possessed, and about eating and being eaten. In the ending cycle of summer it is hard to find an unmarked leaf anymore. They are pitted and scarred and nicked in their long fighting to be alive, to do living against and with the sun, hail, insects, cankers, rust, rabbits, woodchucks, chewing, eating, wind, dust, mowing. We are all survivors. Annie Dillard writes of this in *Pilgrim at Tinker Creek*:

> Is this what it's like, I thought then, and think now: a little blood here, a chomp there, and still we live, trampling the grass? Must everything whole be nibbled? Here was a new light on the intricate texture of things in the world, the actual plot of the present moment in time after the Fall: the way we the living are nibbled and nibbling—not held aloft on a cloud in the air but bumbling pitted and seered and broken through a fragile and beautiful land. . . . I learn this lesson in a new way every day. It must be, I think tonight, that in a certain sense only the newborn in this world are whole, that as adults we are expected to be, and necessarily, somewhat nibbled.*

Here in Columbia the woodchucks and moles, the yellowstriped beetles and little flying moths are also living in my world. They are hungry for the young leaves on rows of carefully planted beans, for grubs under the sod, for my woolen sweaters. It is them or me. I fight them off, sometimes with poisons which poison my own air and soil. But I am sad as I do so, and hungry, and angry. Is this what it is, this eating and being eaten, I as well as they? Are we all finally one, locked in a vast parasitical symbiosis?

I have to acknowledge it is so—and that rightly it should be so. In that moment's folly when I have imagined my world space might be serene and polished, paved and safe, I had been inviting only desperate nonexistence in an unreal world. It is better the ceaseless round of beauty and nibbling. We are locked in the embrace and terror of living with large and small creatures, for precious moments until the darkness returns us to itself. In trying to be lords over life, we lose the priceless gift of living.

The Great Spirit is terrible and good. So be it.

---

*Annie Dillard, *Pilgrim at Tinker Creek* (New York: Bantam Books, 1975), p. 244.

Chapter 1
Claiming the Pulpit

Hearing Women Speak

There is a model of the male minister. There's a definite model of that person. [But] there's not a model for a woman minister. [And] yes, there are some similarities among us, but there is also a diversity among us, and that's something that I hope we will lift up as well, because of the very fact that we don't have those models and we don't have those scripts.

We are writing our own scripts, and they're definitely coming out differently. There are some parallels, but there's also that openness and freedom and flexibility for something new.

—The women in this study

On any given Sunday in central Missouri, you can attend religious services in a wide variety of denominations and hear a woman preach. I do, almost every Sunday. Across town at the Unity Center, in the Episcopal church, in several Christian Church-Disciples of Christ churches, at the different hospital chapels, at the Second Baptist Church, at several of the United Methodist churches, as well as in the outlying areas in the smaller congregations in the rural towns or dotting the landscape in the farming communities that surround the larger towns, simultaneously, probably in twenty-five or more settings, women don their robes and adjust their collars or stoles, walk into the worship space and take their place, survey the congregation, and contemplate the worship service to come. Most of them admit to some apprehension about their sermon and its delivery; some confess that they are rather terrified every single Sunday. Some of them read the sermon they have carefully written out, others use only notecards or outlines to guide their presentation, a few speak extemporaneously.

How typical is this scenario? Although most people are surprised to hear me relate just how many women are actually preaching in the pulpits of contemporary religious contexts in the American Midwest, I suspect what I have described is quite typical. Ordained women are taking posts as pastors and associate pastors in a wide variety of denominations across the country. Although it is still the case that women are less often the rectors or senior pastors at the larger, more prestigious churches that boast the largest congregations and the best salaries, they are, nevertheless, entering the ranks of the pastorate at a steady rate.

I have already noted that these women rarely, if ever, hear each other preach. How could they? They each have that Sunday morning obligation to face in their different and various churches. They stand before their own congregations, seemingly alone. Only *I* have had the enormous pleasure of hearing all of them at different times. *I* can choose which one I want to hear on any given Sunday morning. Deciding which church to attend is never easy, although at this point in my field research I have developed a solid relationship with a great many of these women preachers, and often, now, they call me when they want to invite me to hear and record a sermon about which they are feeling particularly confident or excited. Each preacher, in her own way, captivates me with her style, her imagery, her delivery, her manner, her sincerity, her faith. As I wrote this book, I shared with them my own experiences in their churches, and I shared their sermons with the other members of this community of ministers. They listened to each other for the first time on the tape recordings I made and read each other's sermons in the transcribed form that I duplicated for this book. In our discussion sessions, we listened to the sermons and worked together to determine what, if anything, could and should be said about women's sermons to an interested reader. Even though, apart from our work together, these women do not hear each other preach, it is possible to identify and speak with authority about the important shared characteristics of their sermons.

What, then, would you hear if you went to a church where one of these women was preaching the sermon? I offer here a selection of excerpts from sermons I have transcribed over the past decade. Most of them were preached by women within an approximately twenty-five-mile radius of Columbia, Missouri.

*   *   *

If you had walked into the sanctuary of the Broadway Christian Church-Disciples of Christ in Columbia with me on February 3, 1990, you would have heard Kim Ryan preaching about Jonah. In this sermon, Kim re-tells the story of the wildly raging storm and the reluctance of the crew to throw Jonah overboard, even when he tells them that God is angry with him and that he (Jonah) is the cause for their dilemma. Of course, eventually, they do throw him overboard in order to calm the seas and save themselves. Later, after being saved from the belly of the large fish, Jonah pouts because God saves a city Jonah did not particularly want saved, for he considered it "the enemy." Kim tells the congregation:

The Jonah story is told
with the hope
that the listeners would see
in that reluctant and disgruntled prophet
a reflection of themselves
and hear God's question—
the confrontation with Jonah,
as the question of confrontation to them.

We are invited to enter this story
to see perhaps ourselves,
to allow this biblical message
to raise some questions for us
    in our own time.
    Such questions as:

Am I avoiding God's request
    to be a light for others—
    to be a voice of invitation
    for others into God's love?
Am I a voice of invitation
    to the one that I might call enemy?
Am I
    sleeping safely
    while a storm rages around me?
Am I really secure in my own escape
    vessel
of pride,
prejudice,
and disapproval?[1]

In March of that year, on a cold and rainy day, you might have traveled with me to two small United Methodist churches not far from Columbia. These two small congregations are both charges of Peggy Jeffries. She preaches to one congregation in Hallsville, then travels fourteen miles on small winding roads between milo and corn fields to the other, even smaller, church to preach the same message again to another small gathering of believers at Red Rock. Had you accompanied me, you would have met Peggy at her parsonage and joined her as she went about her typical Sunday morning routine. You would have met her husband, Bruce, who is also a pastor, at another, larger church in town. We would have sat around the kitchen as they fed their two small boys and laughed with them as they tried to get all the orange juice off their faces and their hair combed, ready for church, one to go with Daddy, one with Mama. In the car, we would have talked with Peggy as her one-year-old son babbled in the car seat beside her.

You might have marveled with me as I watched Peggy enter the church with her large Bible, notes, robes, diaper bag, bottles, binky, and baby all clutched in her two strong arms. You would have smiled as I did as several women standing around the small sanctuary came to her to relieve her of the baby and the baby necessities, ready to take care of him while Peggy put on her robes and prepared to begin the service. It would have further surprised you to see this mother/woman/pastor go to the piano and begin to play exquisitely beautiful music, then call out the number for the first hymn and lead the congregation in the songs, her own lyrical voice noticeable above the others in its strength and clarity. By the time Peggy stood in the pulpit to preach, you would have realized with me that this woman had done all the tasks involved in leading a church service singlehandedly, with a smile. She begins to talk with them about how the young David was chosen by God to be the next king:

And he brings in David
and Samuel says,
"This one.
This is the one
whom God wants to be anointed.
This is the one who will be king
over Israel."
And joining Sarah in laughing,
you can almost hear the folks around the
    synagogue,
around the temple,
laughing as Samuel gets out the oil
and begins to anoint the youngest of
    eight children.
The youngest.
The little one who goes out and plays
    with the sheep.
Who sings.
[pause]

And he anoints David.
[pause]
"For my ways are not your ways," God
    says.
"You look on the outside.
You look at people
the way that your society has come to
    accept them,
the way that your society deems things
    to be.
You go with your traditions
but your traditions may not be the way I
    need for it to be.
For my ways are not your ways."
Don't concentrate on what's outside.
See what's inside.
Look at the heart,
the soul,
the spirit of the person.

On another Sunday, at the smaller church, you might have remembered Peggy praying the following prayer:

Strong God,
when we are weak,
your strength empowers us.
When we would shut our eyes
and our ears to the cries of those who
    need us,
your spirit breaks forth,
opens our eyes,
opens our ears,
and then grants to us the gifts,
the talents,
the abilities,

that we need
to minister to your people.
May we be branches that grow strong
and firm
and new
and that go forth to bear fruit.
For it is in our bearing fruit
that you are glorified
that your essence begins to be seen
here on this earth.
Amen.

I heard Margaret Ann Crain, standing in a United Methodist pulpit, preaching on April 11, 1990, from the Gospel of John. As the liturgical year approaches the story of Easter, Margaret Ann does not preach about the death of Jesus but retells the story of Thomas's doubt. She relates how, like that of Thomas, believers' faith develops at its own pace—different people will develop their faith in different ways and times. She asks the congregation:

Which camp are you in?
Do you need to see
in order to believe?
Or are you able to count yourself among
   those few blessed ones
who have not seen and yet believe?
You may agree
about how hard it is
to accept the story of the resurrection,
especially with our twentieth-century
   eyes,
but you may also agree with me that
there is something there.
Something great happened,
something that changed
the entire course of history.
We simply cannot dismiss it.

She suggests that in our world today we equivocate on issues of critical importance in our lives, like the health of God's environment. She tells her congregation:

It may seem like a long jump to you
from Thomas—
to Earth Day,
but perhaps it's not.
I remember Earth Day, 1970,
the first one.
Some of you were around then.
I was a student at the University of Iowa
and I was sitting on the campus
and the campus was full
of seething movement
and action
and violence.
There were daisies everywhere,
the symbol of the Earth Day.
I was about to give birth to our first
   daughter
and I was a graduate student.
So I stood somewhat apart
and I watched
as the students rebelled against
   institutional authority
and against the Vietnam War
and the many other things
disturbing us all then.
We seem to need
to touch the wounds of the earth
to believe.
What I want to suggest today
is that we are wary
because we know that commitment
or belief
brings with it the responsibility
to bear others' burdens.
Caring isn't enough.
We must bear each other's burdens.

Margaret Ann then concludes her sermon by reading a "modern parable" about a "Rag Man," a story that, she says,

picks up this idea of bearing burdens,
but more than that,
it has taught me the meaning
of Christ's sacrifice for us.

It has helped me to understand what that phrase,
"He was wounded for our transgressions,"
what that means.

At the conclusion of her sermon, she prays:

Rag Man, Christ,
remove our inertia
replace it with faith
and energy

that we may believe
and be made new by that belief.
Amen.

On another Sunday in April 1993, in that same Methodist church, Margaret Ann tells the congregation (see pp. 198–205 for full text of sermon, "What Should I Do?"):

John's gospel tells us, "In the beginning
was the word and the word was with
    God,
and the word became flesh and dwelt
    among us."
So, we begin always with God's actions.
The whole
of the biblical witness testifies to that.
. . .
God is there before us,
from creation to the present.
And what do we do to Jesus?
We crucify him.
. . .
"Now wait a minute," you say to me.
"I didn't crucify Jesus. I wasn't there!
I didn't have anything to do with that
    action!
You can't blame me for that."
. . .

In an ambiguous, I admit,
roundabout, impersonal sort of way,
I am guilty.
I crucified Jesus.
Even more, I think,
I crucify Jesus every day
as I make choices
which are not really consistent
with God's will for the earth
and for creation.
I crucify Jesus
when I use more than my share of the
    world's resources.
I crucify Jesus
when I don't hear the cry of my family
    member
who is hurting and needs a hug.
The good news is that even in the face of
    our active resistance,
God is greater than we are.

God continues to act first.
So what should we do?

. . .

Do something,
which clearly puts God first in your life.
And number two,
is to reflect on that action.

. . .

I mean critical reflection.

. . .

Because to reflect theologically
is simply to tell our stories.
In the telling,
we discover God's presence.
That's what theology is.
"Theo" meaning God,
"logy" meaning word,
theology,
God-talk.

. . .

Our stories
are probably our most accessible
  resource

for coming to know God.

. . .

What we hunger for, I think,
more than anything else,
is to be known in our full humanness,
and yet paradoxically
that's probably what we fear the most as
  well.
What we can do for each other as
  Christians
is to offer to listen to each other's stories.
And we listen with awe,
and respect,
for these are sacred stories,
stories which reveal God's actions
and God's presence.

. . .

Our repentance,
our turning around
requires that we know our stories
for they tell us who we are,
how God is present in our life,
and thereby direct us into the future.

And her concluding prayer:

Creator God,
you know our stories often better than we
  do ourselves.

. . .

surrounded by your light,
and open now to the mystery,
we pray that we may be found by

  wholeness,
surprised by recognition,
and transformed by healing,
trusting in your grace
we pray,
Holy One.
Amen.

If you had traveled with me in September 1993, across town to another Christian Church-Disciples of Christ church, you would have heard Maureen Dickmann speak to the congregation about the interrelatedness and connected relationship of all things (see pp. 13–19 for full sermon, "Making Connections"). You would have heard her quote Jesus as saying, "If that person doesn't listen to the church, then let that person be as a

Gentile and a tax collector." Maureen points out just how incongruent, harsh, and uncaring this advice seems, coming from Jesus:

But I wonder if that's the case.
Is it really
that the person is to be shunned?
Or,
can we look at how Jesus, in fact,
in his life,
treated Gentiles and tax collectors?
How did he treat them?
Did he shun them?
No.
No, he ate with them;
he welcomed them;
he taught them,
healed them,

and fed them.
He did.
. . .
If we look at how Jesus treated "Gentiles
   and tax collectors,"
then we see again,
we never give up,
we do not ever give up.
. . .
All of this is meant to emphasize
the interrelatedness of us all.
We are all connected,
and we are all responsible for each other.

Maureen then quotes from William Golding's novel *The Spire*, in which a character states: "If I could go back, I would say that God lies between people and is to be found there." She words it another way:

The idea that God is actually between us
in our relationships
that God is actually present between
   people—
is to be found there—
is emphasizing the interrelatedness of all
   creation,

the way it was made by God.
Nothing is more important
than right relationship between persons.
For we experience nothing less
than the very presence of God
in those relationships.
It's all connected.

She then reminds her congregation of Jesus' words:

"Where two or three of you are gathered
   in my name,
I am there with you."
. . .
God lying between people,
Jesus in the midst,
This is enough to strengthen weak
   hands,

make firm feeble knees,
and lift up faint hearts.
It's the power of that presence
in even the smallest of groups,
that can truly change the world.
Amen.

On November 21, 1993, Kim Ryan preached on the Twenty-Third Psalm (see pp. 118–24 for full text of sermon, "Scraps from the Table"). At the beginning of the sermon, you would have heard Kim admit that she had not wanted to preach on this psalm, that when she first saw it listed in the lectionary it seemed so time-worn and "not relevant," overused and too familiar. After working on her sermon off and on all week, however, Kim tells us, her thoughts inadvertently kept returning to the passage about peace, quiet, and relaxation, about "still waters and green pastures," finally convincing her that she *should* focus on the well-known psalm in her sermon:

Psalm 23 says again,
"Got any still waters?
Got any green pastures
on your list?"

"Who is your shepherd, child?"

And suddenly those old,
familiar,
words of poetry,
became quite challenging
and provocative.

I hear my friends say,
"I'm so sorry to call you,
I know you are so very busy.
I promise I won't take much of your time;
I'll really be quick."
Now obviously I do not appear
to be following the shepherd
of still waters.

And I heard my twenty-one-month-old
    say
as I headed out the door,
again,

"Don't leave, Mama."
. . .
And what difference would it make
if before we planned the social activities
for our children,
we said,
"The Lord is our shepherd."
What if
Psalm 23
were a way of life,
instead of a send-off into death?

Ask yourself,
what are you going to do?

"The Lord is my shepherd,

I shall not want." [in a whisper].
. . .
Who *is* your shepherd?

What *are* we going to do?
Amen.

If you had traveled with me during the last ten years, you would have heard sermons similar to these every Sunday in different congregations, different denominations, urban and rural, large and small. You might have come to look forward to the sermons because the women who preach them are vibrant, sincere, talented speakers. You might have remained somewhat awed, as I have, by the prospect of a woman in long black or white robes, with religious insignia on her stole, perhaps with a collar, rise from her seat, approach the pulpit, clasp its edges with her sure hands, survey her audience, and speak with authority, clarity, and conviction of her God and her faith, guiding her listeners to an appreciation of religion and spirituality appropriate for their daily lives. I find women in the pulpit to be disarming in their presence and their delivery simply by their presence. None of the women in this study preach loudly; none of them chant their sermons; none of them leave the pulpit to wander around the altar area or walk the aisles as they speak; none have chosen dramatic presentation styles; they do not pound the podium, march, shout, or sing during their sermons. Their delivery is open, direct, and soft-spoken but certainly clear enough to be heard by all in the audience. Often the women choose particular rhetorical devices for emphasis. They might, for example, whisper for one effect, or use a dramatic pause for another. They are great storytellers and their sermons are rich with stories, often based in their own experiences — stories about their families, their children, their friends. They often choose to retell biblical stories dramatically, bringing the familiar stories alive for their audiences. They sometimes choose dramatic readings to include in their sermons and on occasion they do a bit of dramatic "acting out" of a story. But, by and large, their sermon texts contain their "message," and the preaching performance is keyed toward the import of the spoken word.

The excerpts I include in this introductory chapter typify the kinds of sermons that I have heard over the past ten years and that I have been systematically tape recording and transcribing over the past five years. The passages are striking for their lyrical beauty, their passion and intensity, and the richness of their metaphoric imagery, language, and rhetorical delivery. These sermons contain examples of repetition for effect, analogy, alliteration, assonance, imagery — in fact, all of the poetic devices we recognize as essential in fine poetry.

It would be nearly impossible to discern from this small sampling whether these sermons are similar in any way, whether their delivery was similar, whether the underlying themes in these sermons were developed along the same lines. What you can sense, perhaps, in a first reading, are the women's concerns about the dangers of prejudice, about the power and necessity of including the reality of *all* lives, about wholeness, about love and caring for all persons, about acceptance and discernment, about coping with expectations gone awry, about understanding the various aspects of God and what God-talk, or thinking theologically, means, about how God is in evidence in relationships and in the way we treat the earth's body, about how all of God's creation is interrelated. You may have heard the women's voices in these short passages speaking from their own experience, using that experience as illustration, analogy, and metaphor. You might have noticed, too, that in none of these sermons is God gendered. The women speak often of God and of Jesus Christ, but God is most often referred to as Creator God, Holy One, Strong God, or simply, God. We do not hear in these sermons many references to God as Father, King, Sovereign, Almighty, or Lord. In several of these sermons, the preacher intentionally aligns herself with her congregation members who might be asking the questions, "Are we like that?" "Do we do that?" "Does your faith grow at a different pace from mine?" "Do you need to see in order to believe?"

I noted early in this chapter that these clergywomen never have the opportunity to hear each other preach and that they stand alone before their own congregations. I want to probe my statement further, for in fact it emerges that these women have developed a close community of exchange and collaboration, and it only *appears* that they stand alone. True, the ordained women in this particular geographical area do not all attend ecumenical meetings designed to foster preaching exchange, and they never hear each other preach. An outside observer might well assume that they do not collaborate in their sermon making. In unofficial circles established and sustained by the women themselves, however, they collaborate in a variety of ways throughout the week in preparation for their Sunday sermon presentations.

Women have a particular style of sermon creation. I do not mean to suggest that they all preach in the same manner or deliver the same messages in their sermons. I do, however, assert that women's preaching shares certain characteristics, which I illustrate here by presenting data collected through first-hand observation and experience of women preachers on a nearly daily basis and from their own words on this subject in regular dialogue sessions.

Certainly there are women who will never preach in the ways outlined in this book. The women in this study do preach in similar ways, however, and I believe they preach similarly for three defensible reasons: first, because they are in close contact and connection; second, because of their shared experiences as middle-class white women educated in reputable seminaries, ordained and preaching in recognized contemporary denominations in this country in the past decade or two; and, third, because of their experiences as women. I fully recognize that the first two reasons will appear more defensible than the third, but I am not afraid of being labeled an essentialist. At the outset, I might note that the women themselves believe deeply that they do preach from the position of their sex and gender. We have discussed this issue from several different aspects, and they are convinced that both women's biological realities and experiences and their gendered experiences as women in American culture and society affect and mold who they are personally and professionally. As preachers who are striving to preach from an authority based on their own legitimate life experiences, they argue that their sermons reflect a reality of femaleness and the life experiences of women. This stance is *never* expressed in simplistic ways, by aligning women with morality and men with sin or by assigning women to the sacred and men to the secular, or vice versa. In fact, the women in this study are adamant about *not* framing the issue in competitive terms. Indeed, they are convinced that many men can help to legitimize women's experiences and preach from a more holistic, inclusive point of view. There are, they insist, men who are doing just that and who are thus aiding in the effort to make the church a more embracing, grace-filled, nurturing environment. What they insist upon and what I continue to strive to achieve in my own discussion is a point of view that emphasizes and legitimizes a woman's point of view, experience, and voice. Thus I do not try here to make a point-by-point comparison of women's and men's sermons; I present and celebrate women's creative, artistic, and sustaining powers as evidenced in their sermons.

Notes

1. At times in this book, I emphasize alliteration and repetition in the presentation of the sermon text on the page. Typing the sermons in different ways allows for their visual appearance on the page to alert the reader to the various poetic and rhetorical strategies of the speaker.

Bearing Fruit (I)

PEGGY JEFFRIES
Hallsville United Methodist Church
Hallsville, Missouri
May 1, 1994

From the Gospel according to John
in the fifteenth chapter:
"I am the true vine
and my father is the vine grower.
He removes every branch in me that
    bears no fruit;
every branch that bears fruit,
he prunes to make it bear more fruit.
You have already been cleansed
by the words that I have spoken to you.
Abide in me as I abide in you.
Just as the branch cannot bear fruit by
    itself
unless it abides in a vine,
neither can you
unless you abide in me.
I am the vine
you are the branches.
Those who abide in me and I in them
bear much fruit,
because apart from me you can do
    nothing.
Whoever does not abide in me is thrown
    away,
like a branch and withers.

Such branches are gathered
to make a fire and burned.
If you abide in me,
I will abide in you.
Ask for whatever you wish
and it will be done for you.
My father is glorified by this
that you bear much fruit
and become my disciples."
    [John 15:1–8, RSV]
Amen.

"Whoever does not abide in me
is thrown away like a branch and
    withers."
That's a scary thought.
The one who doesn't bear fruit is cut off
and thrown away.
That's not something designed to make
    us feel very good.
You know yourselves,
as you go out in the spring
and you look at trees,
and you look at the bushes around,
and you look at the various things

that are growing around you,
those that are not flowering,
those that aren't bearing fruit,
you know yourself,
after those strawberry plants
get to the point where they're putting out
little nothingnesses,
you dig them up
and you start new strawberry plants.

What Jesus has said here
is that if we become
like those strawberry plants
and don't bear fruit,
we get dug up and thrown away.
If we become a branch on a tree that
    may have leaves
but has no apples,
we get cut off,
because there is something wrong
    with us,
we are diseased,
we are not bearing the kind of fruit
that God needs from us.
If we are not bearing fruit,
Jesus says,
we are worthless to God,
and God cuts us off
and throws us into the pile with the rest.
That's a scary thought!
I don't know about you,
but the idea that if I'm not bearing fruit,
if I'm not doing what God asks of me,
if I am not the kind of disciple that Jesus
    needs,
that I will be cut off at the roots and
    thrown out
is kind of frightening.
Jesus also says something else

that's not very encouraging,
if you take it at least to
its logical conclusion.
He says that God is the one who
    prunes us.

I have a very lovely rose bush in front of
    my house—
most of you know the rose bush—
and as the legend goes Rose Williams
    planted that rose bush.
Now, this rose bush
has, I think, developed into two rose
    bushes.
I don't know enough about rose bushes
    to be able to tell,
but I think I have two of them.
But in looking and trying to decide what
    to do with the rose bush
and how to keep it living,
and growing,
and bearing roses,
I discovered something—
in reading about roses—
you have to cut them back.
You can't just let them bloom
and then let the blooms die,
and let the stuff fall off,
and then let more come up,
because more will come up.
I've discovered that.
But if you—
after that rose is finished—
if you cut it back down to a certain place,
and you cut it off,
not only do the roses that keep growing
grow stronger,
but you get more of them.

You know about this.
You know about pruning plants back.
You know about what happens with that,
you make a cut and two come where one
  was.
You know all about this.
But Jesus says that this is what God
  does to us
that maybe it's not that God inflicts
difficulty upon us,
but rather that God at least
uses the difficulties that come to us,
to make us stronger,
to make us better able to bear fruit.
The Scripture also calls on us,
when the difficulties in our lives are over,
to not just draw into ourselves,
but it calls us out,
it calls us out,
to bear more fruit,
to be stronger flowers,
if you will,
than we were before.

I watched this morning
the ABC morning news show.
They are running,
starting today,
a series on worship in America in the
  nineties.
And this morning they started off
with a report on megachurches.
Megachurches are churches that are
  huge—
well, the Missouri church, for example,
  would be small—
But what they were talking about in these
  megachurches
is that one of the reasons that people

like to come to them
is that they don't do very much asking for
  money;
they're not very socially active or socially
  conscious;
they don't ask time of the people,
and they don't require people to,
say,
teach Sunday school classes,
or cook for smorgasbords,
or any of the other myriad things
that we typically do in our churches.
Now, I'm sorry,
but just going into a church,
sitting down,
and having somebody preach at me,
and then going home,
is not what church is all about,
is not what God called us to
is not about the good news
we are called to share.
The man who was doing this report
also pointed that out
that they don't ask the people to be
  socially conscious,
which is one of the things that Jesus did
  in the gospels.
He said, "Go out into the world
and teach them,
and baptize them,
and give clothes to them,
and visit them in their sickness."
And I'm sorry,
but to my mind,
if they're not doing what Jesus asked us
  to do,
then they're not really a church.
They're just a nice place to go
and hear somebody say something nice.

A church
calls us out of ourselves,
challenges us,
feeds and nourishes us,
so that we can go
and bear fruit
and be disciples.
For Jesus didn't say,
"Go out into the world
and feel good
and don't be challenged."
Jesus said,
"Go out into the world,
teach,
and baptize,
and share the good news,
and feed those who are hungry,
and clothe those who are naked,
and visit those who are scared,
and sick,
and imprisoned."
That's what church is about.
That's what it is to be a Christian.
That's what it is to be a disciple,
not going home
and feel good
and get on with your life as it always was,
and then pat yourself on the back and
   say,
"Yes, it's o.k.,
I'm going to church,
God bless me."
To be a Christian,
to be a disciple of Jesus Christ
is to bear fruit,
and fruit is not just the number of people
who sit in the pews.
It's making sure that the hungry are fed,
and the naked are clothed,

that those who need someone to visit
   and care for them
are visited,
that those who are hurting
have someone come and share the love
   of Jesus Christ
with them.

"When we all get to heaven,"
the song says,
when we all get to heaven,
Peter isn't going to say
what church were you a member of?
Peter's gonna say,
"What did you do?
Did you feed?
Did you clothe?
Did you visit?"
They're not going to ask about your
   church membership.
That's not the most important thing.
It's what you did
with your faith.
That's what's going to be important.
Coming to church,
it's important,
it's one of the ways that we stay fed
and nurtured and nourished.
Jesus said he is the vine and we are the
   branches.
And if we stay attached to the vine,
we stay strong.
Coming to church,
and coming to worship,
and coming to Sunday school,
and coming to Bible studies,
and coming to weekly meetings,
and all the myriad of things we do
   together,

are all ways that we are fed
and nurtured and nourished,
and empowered to then go forth,
and bear fruit.
Because if we're not in church,
and if we're not reading the Bible,
and if we're not praying,
and if we're not doing any of those things
that Jesus has instructed us to do,
then we're cut off from the vine,
and we can't bear fruit anyway.
But even if we're firmly attached to the
    vine,
if we're not bearing fruit,
then we are not worthy,
we are not worthwhile,
we are not being good disciples.
We are a branch that deserves to be cut
    off
and thrown into the fire.
Jesus calls us to bear good fruit,
to be in ministry
with those outside our own community,
with those outside of our own
    congregation.
Yes,
the congregation needs to be strong,
because that's where we are nourished,
but we can't stop there.
We have to go out
into the community,
out into the county,
out into the state,
out into the country
and halfway around the world.
Jesus said, "Go into all the world,
and bear good fruit."
Bear fruit that is befitting
with the gospel of Jesus Christ.

Just coming
and worshiping
and filling in a place in the pew,
just doesn't do it.
You have to go out from this place
and bear that fruit,
and be disciples of Jesus Christ.

The good news is
that by coming to worship on Sunday
    morning,
by participating,
by spending time in prayer—
and I don't mean long flowery prayers
that go on endlessly with the "thee's,"
and the "thy's,"
and the "thou's" all over—
however, if that's the way you pray that's
    perfectly fine—
but even just saying,
"God,
I don't know what to do here,
help me."
Just that counts as a prayer.
It's the matter of talking to God
that's important.
And as we come this morning,
we come to the table of God
which nourishes our souls—
it doesn't nourish our bodies too much—
you don't partake of it for physical food—
but it nourishes our spirits,
and empowers us,
and keeps us firmly attached
to the vine which gives us life,
and enables us
to go out into the world and be good
    disciples.

Let us pray.
Strong God, when we are weak,
your strength empowers us.
When we would shut our eyes and our
    ears
to the cries of those who need us,
your spirit breaks forth and
opens our ears,
opens our eyes,
and then grants to us the gifts,
the talents,
the abilities,
that we need
to minister to your people.
May we be branches
that grow strong,
and firm,
and new,
and that go forth to bear fruit.
For it is in bearing fruit
that you are glorified,
that your kingdom begins to be seen
here on this earth.
Amen.

Bearing Fruit (II)

PEGGY JEFFRIES
Red Rock United Methodist Church
Hallsville, Missouri
May 1, 1994

From the gospel according to John
in the fifteenth chapter:
"I am the true vine
and my father is the vine grower.
He removes every branch in me that
    bears no fruit;
every branch that bears fruit,
he prunes to make it bear more fruit.
You have already been cleansed
by the words that I have spoken to you.
Abide in me as I abide in you.
Just as the branch cannot bear fruit by
    itself
unless it abides in a vine,
neither can you
unless you abide in me.
I am the vine
you are the branches.
Those who abide in me and I in them
bear much fruit,
because apart from me you can do
    nothing.
Whoever does not abide in me is thrown
    away,
like a branch and withers.

Such branches are gathered
to make a fire and burned.
If you abide in me,
I will abide in you.
Ask for whatever you wish
and it will be done for you.
My father is glorified by this
that you bear much fruit
and become my disciples." [John 15:1–8,
    RSV]
Amen.

This is a great time of year
for this particular Scripture
when we have been able in the cool fall
to get out into our yard.
This is the time of year
to prune away the extra growth.

We have,
between our house and our neighbors,
we have this huge
hedge row of some sort
and down at the end of it
is this sort of a bush

that is
completely
overgrown.
It's beginning to hang out into the street.
We can't see whether our neighbors are
    coming,
and they can't see whether we're pulling
    out.
We desperately need to get in there
and take care of some of that.
The problem is
that it's right by the ditch
and the ditch has this much water in it
[gestures about two feet].
Ever since we got
to where we realized it needed to be
    pruned,
oh, like sometime in July [laughs],
we've been saying
we're going to get out there
and take care of that.
[pause]
But we all know
that one of the things that happens
when you prune back something like
    that,
is that it has a tendency
to grow even stronger,
unless you are very careful with where
    you prune.
That fascinated me with roses,
you know.
Do you think that if you just let them
    grow,
then they would go ahead and grow,
but if you cut them back,
they grow even stronger;
they grow even bigger;
they grow more roses even.

We now have a rose bush
in front of our house
that seems to have developed into two
    rose bushes.
It seems to have done that
because we've been careful about
    pruning.
We've been careful about cutting back on
    it a little bit.
We also know that when we do
do that pruning around our houses,
that when we cut off that branch,
it's going to die,
unless we find some way to
to restart that branch,
it's going to die.
And all we're going to wind up doing
    with it
is setting it out for the people in the trash,
or putting it over into the neighbor's yard
where they kind of have
a heap of things like this,
or we're going to wind up burning it.

When something is not bearing fruit,
you cut it off.
When something is not being helpful.
When a branch,
or when a plant,
is not bearing fruit,
when it finally gets to the point
where there's no fruit coming out of it at
    all,
it's time to be done with it.

When we first moved to Missouri
we lived in a house
that was a hundred and some years old,

and the women who used to live in this
house
were sisters who had never married.
They were into their eighties
before they gave the house to the
parsonage.
When they were still able to get out and
around,
their favorite thing to do
on a Sunday afternoon,
was to get into their old beat-up heap of
a car
and go driving through the countryside.
And what they would do
when they drove through the
countryside,
one of them would see something pretty,
a tree,
or a flower,
or a plant,
and they would stop the car—
the stories that people leave behind them
in that area
are legendary
from these sisters
who'd be out driving around—
they'd stop [claps loudly] the car,
right where they were,
get out of the car,
go over to the side of the road,
and dig up whatever it was
and bring it back and plant it in their yard.
And there were two
good-sized flower beds.
There was a grape vine,
there were peach trees,
and there were untold numbers
of unknown things

that would grow up around all the
buildings.
There were a couple of outbuildings,
and then this huge house,
and up close to all of these buildings
things would grow profusely.

We were the fifth family
to live in this old house,
after these elderly women,
and there were still things coming up.
Every family had tried
to bring some kind of
sense to the nonsense,
to try to tame the jungle
that was around this house.
But there was no taming of this jungle.
And in part
it was because of the idea
that if you prune something back,
it grows stronger the next time.
There had been at least three families
that had tried to get rid of the grape vine,
because there was this huge grape arbor
outside.
And then they had gotten old,
and then decrepit,
and then it really wasn't giving much in
the way of grapes anymore,
and so people would cut it back.
Two families before us
had chopped this thing down
to absolute roots!
There was nothing there at all!

And Ron, our friend, made wine
off of that grape vine.
[pause; congregation laugh with her]

Which gives you an idea of how well,
they were able to kill that grapevine.
He was living there just before us,
and by the time we got there,
the grapevine had grown that strong.
But if you cut off
a piece of that grape arbor—
every year we had to do that—
every year you had to kind of trim it back
    a little bit.
So when you cut it off,
it died.
By the time we got there
the grapes weren't worth a whole lot,
you couldn't even make jelly out of them.
And it's gone now
a little piece of it tries to come back
every now and then,
strong,
stubborn,
courageous,
still attached to the roots,
still attached to the roots which are
    strong.
No matter how often that grape arbor has
    been cut back,
those roots still struggle
to put forth vines
that bear fruit.
[pause]
Jesus said
he was the vine,
we are the branches.
Jesus said he was the vine,
the strong and sturdy vine,
from which the branches receive their
    sustenance.
He says that God may
prune the branches back a little bit,

may occasionally have to prune them
    back.
There may come things in our lives
that we struggle against;
there may come difficulties
and trials and tribulations in our lives
which according to Jesus
are there to make us strong.
But he says that if the branch
is cut off from the vine,
the branch withers
and dies.
We need the strength
of being attached to that vine.
We need the strength that comes from
    that connection,
in order to bear fruit.
He also says
that if we do not bear fruit,
we're not worth living.
Now what's the best way
to remain attached to the vine?
The best ways to remain attached to the
    vine—
one of them you're doing this morning,
you're here.
One of the best ways to stay attached to
    the vine
is to be in worship,
to be in fellowship with other people,
because we strengthen one another,
we make each other strong.
Just like Billy can go out and help
    Michelle
as she is facing the struggles of her life,
that he's already gone through.
We can help each other,
when we struggle against the difficulties
    of life.

And so it is important
that we are in worship.
It is important that we are in worship
  because
we can hear the words
in maybe a different way.
We sing the hymns,
new ones that challenge us
and old ones that comfort us.
We can go home and read scripture.
We can go home—
the Bible is available to us,
it's in our homes.
A few hundred years ago it wasn't,
a few hundred years ago
the priests kept it all to themselves
and wouldn't allow
the people to read the Bible,
themselves.
We have that opportunity.
We also can pray.
We don't need to be in worship to pray.
we don't need to have somebody else
  leading us.
In fact,
we don't even have to say all the fancy
  words.
I can remember growing up
and trying to create a prayer for myself
and to talk to God with the "thee's" and
  the "thou's"
and the "thy's"
and all of the fancy language
that I was hearing in worship.
But it just never quite worked for me,
because I couldn't quite figure out how to
  get all those
pronouns where they needed to be,
until it suddenly occurred to me

that I could talk to God
as though God was just another person
sitting here beside me,
or I could use the hymns
and sing my prayers.
We can pray.
We don't need another mediary.
We don't need someone else to lead us
  or guide us in our prayer.
We can sit there and say
"God, I am confused,
or I am angry,
or I'm so snowed under
that I don't know what to do with myself."
"Or God,
where do I go now and what do I do?
I don't know what to do with my life.
Help me."
A prayer doesn't have to be fancy.
It doesn't have to start off
In one certain way
and ending in another particular way,
with a certain number of things in the
  middle.
Just a few words is enough.

Like those strange little branches
that grow out of that almost dead
  rootstock,
it doesn't take much to continue to keep
  us attached
to the vine which sustains us,
a few words can help keep us attached.

We come this morning to share around
  the table,
another good way of staying attached,
another good way of staying in touch,
not only with the vine that sustains us

but with all those who have gone
  before us.
We are in a line two thousand years old
of people who have come to the table
to receive sustenance,
to receive strength,
to receive nourishment.
So when we go out into the world,
we can bear fruit,
we can be strong,
we can be in ministry,
we can be the disciples of Jesus Christ,
because we have come to the table
and been nourished and sustained.

So we come to worship
for fellowship with one another;
we read Scriptures;
we pray;
and we come to the table for
  nourishment
of our souls,
of our spirits.

Jesus says that there is nothing else
by which God is more glorified
Than that we, the branches,
bear good fruit.
Strong is the vine which sustains us.
May we pray today
to bear good fruit.

Let us pray.
Loving and merciful God,
we struggle with what it means to be
  your disciples.
We struggle with who it is
you call us to minister to
and what you call us to do.
And yet, our opportunities for growth
are always present,
and we are grateful for that.
We pray for your guidance and your
  blessings,
for your nourishments as we come to
  your table.
Amen.

Chapter 2
Collaborative Praxis Against All Odds

My Journal Remembers

It's not that there are no successful women out there, it's just that there are so few, ever, who have gone on to actually become ministers, who have tried that route. So that, it is like you are reinventing the wheel every time it seems like. Seems to me that is why things like this group are so important because if we didn't have this, if I didn't have this, I would really be nuts. I think that just to know, hey, this feels weird and to hear other women say, yes, it does, it feels weird, that really helps.

—The women in this book

This chapter is based on the "lectionary lunches" that evolved from the larger group and included only five or six "regulars" besides myself. I have chosen a first person voice and a journal-like format based loosely on my actual journals at the time. I was a participant in the conversations and an observer of the collaborative sermon work. These lunches were never recorded, so the dialogue reproduced is only my personal recollections, and I have edited the more personal narratives and experiences. I have intentionally not named the participants, and the quotation marks do not indicate verbatim transcriptions. As a significant part of my story, however, this is a true account of what happened on the dates given.

November 22, 1993

I could never see very well when we stepped inside the campus Chinese restaurant, not very good but cheap and close to just about everything. We sat at a table for five, thinking the others might join us at any moment. We remembered it was the anniversary of Kennedy's death; we remarked on it, amazed it had been thirty years. Several women were already late; I wondered why, maybe the others were wondering, too, but no one asked. Finally, another woman arrived, puffing in, a bit out of breath, wearing a new slippery track suit in red, white, and blue. By the time she blew in, I could see much better. Obviously, she was having trouble seeing our table, coming in from the bright white sunlight of that cold November day. It's a good thing she got there when she did—one woman had already ordered, quickly checking her watch and saying she had to be somewhere. Then another came in late, too, moving easily in her eighth month of pregnancy, her clerical collar evident above her rounded body. She caught some eyes as she wound her way to our table ducking her head beneath the bright red lanterns and dodging the chairs. Someone had just asked me about my father as we sat waiting for everyone to gather. I told them he wasn't doing very well; in fact, I told them, he was probably dying. We were going down to visit for Thanksgiving and taking the girls and a huge roast turkey. I knew they cared and shared my pain.

The woman sitting next to me made a remark about how tough things were sometimes, a vague reference to my father, but then a hint at her own troubles. We all asked her, rather in unison, how her services went the Sunday before. "The services were great," she declared, "it's just my life that's complicated!" She talked at length about her concerns about a daughter who was ill and would probably face surgery in the near future. We all listened; some of the women offered her advice, but mostly what she found here were women willing to listen to her most personal difficulties and frustrations.

Her willingness to talk openly about her daughter seemed to prompt another woman to tell us about her mother, who was very ill and lived thousands of miles away, making it difficult for her to be involved with her care. We were all aware that she often flew out to help her sister deal with her mother's condition, but she now had a "condition" of her own and the doctors were telling her she could not fly any more. She'd already had two miscarriages, and she was nearly forty, and this baby was still considered high risk. She, too, found sympathetic and helpful listeners at the lunch table that day.

Eventually, the earlier comments about last Sunday's service being "great" brought questions from everyone. "What made it 'great'?" they asked her.

"Well, one thing that was real different," she began, "was that, as usual, on Friday I began writing out my sermon the way I always do. I had read the Scriptures again, and I selected the one I wanted to focus on and I began to write it out and I wrote a good deal of it. But I was dissatisfied, so I just put that sermon aside and I took up fresh sheets of paper and I did something I rarely do, I just wrote in kind of a free association style, just whatever came to my mind, letting my thoughts flow. And it was the Scripture, you know, about the ten lepers and the one, the only one, who comes back to give thanks for his healing. I've been doing a lot on lepers."

At this the others laughed and made light fun of her being stuck on the subject of lepers; apparently, she had preached on this topic before and it was a favorite of hers. She was undaunted and continued her story with a smile. "In the free association I took up the voice of one of the lepers and talked about *us* as lepers, how we manage, what we had to suffer (in those days) as lepers in the society. We were ostracized, shunned, ridiculed, pushed aside, and how all of that felt. I spoke in first person *as* one of the lepers—I continued this for some time and I could tell by their faces they were really listening during this portion where I took on the persona and made it seem really real. And then I talked about the one who came back to say thank-you for being healed. I explained that he's the only one who received a 'holistic' healing because returning to say thank-you to God provided him with a new relationship with the giver, whose new gift is a different kind of healing, one that makes for a complete, holistic kind of healing. The 'gift' he received is a new kind of relationship between the giver and the receiver of the healing. So, I said, we could all be the one who returns to say thank-you—see this was my Thanksgiving sermon—saying thank-you, giving thanks. And by giving thanks then it opens up the possibility for this new relationship with the giver. If we will just pay attention and go back and thank the giver. And I ended right there! But actually I'm getting them ready for another important message next Sunday, when I've asked the regional director of the Regional AIDS Interfaith Network [RAIN] to come to the Sunday morning service and give a message about our church becoming involved in the RAIN project. I want members of our congregation to consider forming a care team and going to the preparation workshops. I don't want to cause them discomfort. There are already too many people in my church who might hesitate to come if they knew I was going to do this. I'm pretty scared about it, but I know I need to do it. And you know what, about my sermon last Sunday, no one said one word about it! Not one! That's pretty unusual. I wonder what they'll do next Sunday; they might just get up and walk out. And so, last Sunday's sermon was really in preparation for this Sunday. I left it on that note—that they could be the one who comes back and tries for the holistic relationship, a new gift from God. But that's really in preparation for next Sunday."

Someone turned to me and asked where I had attended church last Sunday. I told them I'd been pretty busy, first attending one service at 9:30 on one side of town, then driving across town to attend a different one at 10:45. I had to leave the first one early, in fact, before communion; I told them I always hated to leave a service like that, it was embarrassing. But I told them that the service had seemed quite long, longer than usual, but the sermon was excellent. They asked which Scripture the pastor had used and I told them how deftly she had used the Twenty-Third Psalm to talk to her congregation about how so many activities and business in all our lives was, in the end, affecting us and affecting our marriages, our health, and our relationships with our children. It was a very powerful message, and I told them I thought her audience was really listening. I also told them that the pastor had told me earlier in the week that she intended to preach this sermon; she'd been thinking about it a long time and felt it was a really important sermon to preach, but that she was nervous about it because the other readings were all about giving unselfishly and Jesus saying "I was hungry and you gave me food, thirsty and you gave me drink" and how she saw her sermon as *very* different, focusing maybe on the fact that we are all already stretched way beyond any reasonable point and that we simply cannot do one more thing! She'd be preaching to herself, too, she told me, and I told the others about it there in the Peking restaurant.

The woman sitting across from me laughed and said she suspected I didn't cry during her sermon this past Sunday! She'd felt "flat," she told us, not quite able to rouse her own spirit. But it was a significant service in many ways, she knew, because her church was celebrating their anniversary, and hers. Charter members were identified and they were having a huge thanksgiving dinner together in the church after the service. What *had* worked well, she thought, was that her congregation had, from its beginnings, actually taken the scriptural passages that were in the lectionary, the "I was hungry and you gave me food," as their "charter" mission. So it was appropriate that these verses appeared on their anniversary day.

"But I might have had you in tears—or stitches—this summer," she laughed, recalling a different sermon, "if you had seen me lie down flat on the floor, my arms crossed over my breast, my eyes closed." (She demonstrated, there, in the restaurant, but sitting in her chair. She began to laugh with abandon and the others joined in. I was befuddled; I hadn't heard this story.) "I can't believe I haven't told you this story!" (One woman indicated she had some vague memory of it. Another laughed loudly, obviously in the know on this one.) "Oh, it was great," she howled. "I can't believe I was there lying on the floor, my robes on, the works, arms crossed. I was dead, you see. And we had this all worked out—dear friend, here, [she motions toward one of the other women at the table] had come out a couple of times to help us rehearse, it was actually her idea—but she only *told* the story, of course, in her church, me, I have to act it out! She'd gotten the idea at a conference she'd been to in Chicago. So, I'm lying there on the floor, but, of course, I really grab their attention first by moving the communion table and the pulpit over, clearing a big space, then lying down on it. I can't believe I actually laid down right there in the middle of the floor," she laughed and laughed. Her eyes were watering by now and her face was flushed with the pure joy of telling me this story. I was laughing already and could not wait to hear the rest.

"So, I have this elder ready. He's standing up there, standing over me, see, he's Jesus. Arms open, beckoning, and I get up. 'Hello,' he welcomes me, 'I'm so glad to see you.' So, I say, 'I'm dead, is that it?' 'Yes,' he says and points first to a sign to his right which reads "Heaven" and one to his left "Hell." 'Now,' he tells me, 'choose where you want to go.' 'Right,' I say, amused, 'I can just *choose* which place I want to go?' 'Right,' he says. 'It's very simple, just choose.' 'Oh, sure, I'm truly skeptical, I can just choose. So, don't you need a list of the things I've done in my life? Don't you need some kind of list?' 'No,' he says, getting slightly frustrated with me, 'just choose.' But then I really begin to get out of hand, claiming some sort of trick. He's trying to trick me and I won't have it. If there are no criteria for this then all the murderers and liars and all those despicable people would get into heaven. Now, he's getting really fed up with me as well and says, 'So just choose, already! Just choose, it's so simple. You're making it hard. Just choose. There are many others waiting to get in.' So, I stomp off toward hell mumbling that 'I'm not about to be tricked by this guy, I'll just go to hell, forget this noise.' And then he turns to the congregation and again holds out his hands and says, 'it's so simple, and so many choose hell over heaven. Time and again, they *choose* hell.'

"It was a hoot," she was still laughing. The others, too, were laughing, as was I. "So, then, I came back to the congregation," she concluded her story, "and told them that we only intended to get them to think about the issues and that as they thought about it we could talk about it. Some of them did. And they certainly commented on the service—it had, indeed, gotten their attention. But they didn't talk about the issue a lot, not as much as I wish they had. But I think it got to them. That's a sure-fire attention-getter, just lie down on the floor!"

We wiped our eyes and, just as quickly, the narrator of this story turned back to the woman who had just spoken about last Sunday's service. "So," she asked her, "how was last week's sermon just a teaser for this Sunday? What I mean is, how are you actually relating the lepers to next Sunday's sermon?" She was obviously trying to piece this all together. Her questions were sincere and probing; she listened, then, to her friend explain.

"Well, it does," replied her friend, eager to share her story, "both because people with AIDS are treated like lepers, and also because if we come back to give thanks for our healing all sorts of new possibilities and relationships are possible. If we give thanks then that opens the door for other, new things/possibilities to emerge. I haven't written that part of the sermon, yet. But I'll talk about it to some people and then turn it over and over, then share it."

"So, what can we do next Sunday?" They turned their attention to the possibilities for the following Sunday's sermons. One woman took the lectionary and began to read the appropriate scriptures for the following Sunday. I sat bemused by the faces around us. The waitresses who could barely speak English somehow sensed that this Bible reading was a bit unconventional, and the women serving us smiled discreetly as they poured us more and more tea. Somehow, the women who had been in a hurry earlier now seemed to have forgotten their appointments. They had settled into the easy repartee of the storytelling, and now turned to the serious collective consideration of the scriptures for the coming Sunday's sermons. The deep red and black of this Chinese palace seemed an unlikely place for a women's liturgical discourse, but here we were. The reader began to complain good-naturedly about the ominous "watch and wait" message of the Gospel in the lectionary. "Here's John moaning, the doomsayer. Sometimes I hate this stuff, don't you?"

The woman next to me was laughing in her teacup in response to the reader's blunt honesty: "You crack me up, when you summarize these Scriptures," she told the reader, "sometimes I can't even use them, or it can be hard, after I've heard you read them and give your running commentary." But she was laughing, as the others were. Her good friend read all the lectionary possibilities aloud—the psalms, the gospel, the Old Testament passages.

"I love Advent," one woman quietly admitted.

"Why?" I asked her.

"Somehow it is more quiet; I guess I see it more as anticipation, expectations of the Christ child. The music is quieter and then I love the candles and the purple."

"I love that, too," the reader agreed.

Now her friend was confused. "Do you love it or hate it? Make up your mind."

She shrugged and laughed. "Both, maybe. So what can I do with this?" She implored her friends to help her out, give her ideas.

"Well, if you love the candles, too," they seemed to say in unison, "why not see this as lighting your way into the Advent season? Light the first Advent candle that morning. In fact, no, it would be even better, light it at the end of the sermon to indicate you're lighting it to move into the Advent season."

She liked this plan. "That's great, that's what I think I'll do." They talked a bit longer about darkness and light and how we are all in darkness much of the time and how Jesus talks about a light, a small light in the darkness. You're still there, but there's a light.

"Ohhh," our narrator crooned, "I can turn down the lights like I did when I played dead on the floor, then turn them up after I light the candle. That will be good. I'll do that." We all smiled.

It was after 2:00. Suddenly, they all remembered they should have been somewhere already—the hospital, to pick up a child, to deliver communion to a shut-in, their list of things to do loomed up and pulled them out into the sunlight again. We all hugged there on the sidewalk with the local barbers looking on, across from the oblivious skateboarders who were gradually honing down the rough edges of the stone steps leading to the door of a corner church, where the drunks had set up housekeeping, their candles and lanterns providing no warmth at all from the bitter wind. I walked to my car filled with wonder at this unusual event I'd been witness to and knew some of the pulpits in Columbia would resound with a new kind of message this Advent, a message of hope and daring, one created and shaped by these thoughtful women in a dark Chinese restaurant, only one block down from the record store known as The Salt of the Earth.

November 28, 1993

I thought I was late as I hit the loose gravel leading up to the small, country church, white, complete with requisite steeple, side yard cemetery, and picket fences. This small United Methodist church sits just on the margins of a tiny unincorporated cluster of houses that could not even count as a town, a village, or even a hamlet. Typical of other such groupings of buildings in mid-Missouri, this collection sits not two miles from the interstate that runs east and west across the very heart of America. By incongruent contrast, right off the interstate, sits, in grand neon style, a truck stop which would make any state proud. The big rigs pull in here from all over the map and stay a while in the glitzy smear of restaurants, bars, barber shops, bowling alley, motels, flea market, groceries, lounges, massage parlors, and even a child-care center. No needs of the men or women of the road have been forgotten or overlooked. The entrepreneur who built this wheeler's heaven has expanded to an arena and exhibition center large enough to host a regional rodeo, a tractor pull, a demolition derby, or a three-ring circus.

But only one-quarter of a mile down from this manufactured extravaganza, the dirt road leads away from the rumble of the highway, curves down a hill, makes a sharp turn, then another, creeps past abandoned gas stations, past a general store long empty, its shelves bare and dusty through opaque glass, past several rambling clapboard houses with uneven porches swaying on three sides, where pick-up trucks parked askew here and there and a car which has not moved in twenty years rusts quietly, undisturbed, light years away from the business of the truck stop crowd.

From the way the cars are parked at the church, and the way they are all facing, it occurs to me that not all of them arrived here at the church via the truck stop and its madness, as I did, but arrived on roads which stretch away from the interstate and the world represented there. These folks greet one another with genuine warmth and the kind of companionship which comes only with years of meeting here at the church. Today, only one other person headed for the huge wooden door ahead of me, feeling, too, the blast of warm air from within, reminding me just how cold it was on the outside. I blew in with the cold air and was greeted warmly by the young woman handing out bulletins.

The people at this church remind me of my own family; it could be the church where my parents and my brother and his family have attended every Sunday for the past thirty years—the church I grew up in. The congregation members appear to be comfortable with their natural looks and casual dress. Children abound, held in tow by young parents, scrubbed and attentive, or grandparents doting with flourish and pride. The American flag adorns the corner, as prominent as the Christian flag and the Missouri flag. Last year the church added on a new section to house open-air Sunday School classes and meeting rooms. The space is large and airy, filled with children's drawings, posters, diagrams, blueprints of the extension, and photographs of "Our Church Family"—young couples with babies, obvious grandparents, extended families, families with five clean-cut teenagers, all smiles. I have become accustomed to these "family" touches; several other of the women's churches have in display these "Church Family" photographs. I am delighted when I recognize one of the families in the pews. The intention is, of course, for me to feel like I know them—it works! They smile and I smile in return. Pat and Alice, little Brittany, Jennifer, Todd, and Lisa sit down at the other end of my pew and open their bulletins in synchrony with me.

As I read the words printed before me, I try to glance at the faces around me as they, too, read what is in store this Sunday. I know, but they do not until they reach the second sheet, that this Sunday's service has a theme: "First Sunday of Advent, AIDS awareness Sunday." The Advent prayers and hymns look rather typical, but a "meditation" is listed under the name of the Executive Director of RAIN. Her "meditation" is entitled "Compassionate Care: HIV Ministry." Did Alice shift in her seat ever so slightly, or was I simply looking for it? Did she put her arm on Jennifer's shoulder and pat Todd on the head in some kind of protective or nervous gesture, or would she have done that even if the pastor's sermon had not been listed as "Jesus' Healing Touch"?

The pastor recognized the visitors, asking them to stand and introduce themselves. She asked me to stand, identifying me as her friend, telling them I had been there before and that I was meeting with several area clergywomen on a regular basis and was interested in writing about their ministries. She turned a pleased face toward me. I was welcomed, so happy she had introduced me as her friend. I beamed back at her across the heads of her attentive congregation members, sending her encouragement. I wanted her to know I was here for her, to support her in this endeavor. After last week, when she told us all at the lectionary lunch how she had tried to prepare her congregation the week before so that they might be open to a service on AIDS awareness and ministry, I'd asked her if I could come. I wanted to see the reaction to this endeavor. I wanted to see how she shared her deep concern about AIDS education and ministry with her flock.

Even before the RAIN director approached the pulpit to educate the congregation about AIDS awareness, my friend sat in her rich, deep purple robes at her low stool and gathered around her all the small children in the building for the "children's sermon." It took a few minutes to make certain all were seated around her. Some seemed to want to sit in her lap, edging closer and closer, sitting on her robes, pulling her sleeves, leaning over each other to peer at the book she was trying to hold so all could see, including the congregation, amused and interested. They could, after all, trust their prize possessions, these little ones, to their pastor and friend. But could I feel my pew partners stiffen again as she began to talk about the picture she was holding up?

"Who was in this picture?"

"Jesus," the children chorus back.

"That's right. And who else is in the picture?"

"A man."

"Yes. Who is this other man?"

"A poor man?"

"Yes."

"A blind man?"

"Perhaps."

"A crippled man?"

"Yes. Actually, this man is a leper. He has a disease which was common in Jesus' day, called leprosy. It was a really terrible disease. It caused people afflicted with it to go blind sometimes, and to be crippled, to be in pain, and to die. And many people who did not have this awful, dreadful disease were really mean to the people who did because they did not want to get the disease themselves. So they often shunned the persons with the disease or put them off on an island by themselves. But what is Jesus doing in this picture? Is he running away from the sick man?" The children answer together that he is touching the man.

"He's touching him, that's right. He's stretching out his hand and he is touching him. Does it look like he is afraid of the sick man?" The children, in unison, claim, "Nooooo."

"No. Why do you think he is touching the sick man? To make him feel better? To make him all better? To help him get well? To be nice to him? [All possible answers offered by the children.] That's right, you're all right. Now, how many of you have heard of a disease in our time called AIDS? [Most of the little ones hold up their hands; some do not; some cannot decide.] That many! Well, AIDS in our day is very much like leprosy was in Jesus' day. People who have AIDS get very sick and they die and lots of people who do not have AIDS do not want to help the people who have AIDS and even may blame them for getting the disease—so that only makes them feel worse, right? Now, if Jesus were right here in Missouri today, how do you think he would treat a person with AIDS? Do you think he would run away from the sick person?"

"Nooooo," they answer.

"Or make him feel bad?"

"Nooooo."

"What do you think Jesus would do?"

"He would love him and touch him like he's doing to the man in the picture."

"Yes. Love him and touch him. Don't you think Jesus would be afraid to touch the person with AIDS, afraid that he might get the disease, too?"

"Noooo."

"Do you think Jesus would try to blame the person for getting AIDS and make him feel worse?"

"Nooooo."

"Well, I don't either. I think Jesus would touch a person with AIDS and try to love them and care for them just like he did this man with leprosy. And if we love God and Jesus, then how would they teach us to treat a person with AIDS? To be nice to them. That's right. Jesus teaches us to love and care for persons who are sick, no matter what might be wrong with them. We should try to be more like Jesus. Right? Now, let's pray together. God, help us to understand how to be more like you and care for those who are less fortunate than we. Amen."

I glanced around. It was pretty quiet in here, I thought. Was it my imagination or were these folks getting pretty nervous with all this open talk about AIDS and caring for people with AIDS? Were they stunned to have their pastor talk with their children in this way and about this topic? Did they agree with her? I could not tell. But something in that room was nearly palpable, and there was more, much more to come.

The RAIN director was a strong speaker, but not forceful or strident, not angry or evangelistic in her manner or her message. She was thoughtful, direct, and careful. She neither lectured nor preached. She was there to plant some seeds, to ease some fears, to educate, to set the stage for action. She did not plead, cajole, threaten, push, or minimize her case. She was forthright: all persons who contract AIDS will die; there is no immunization now or in sight for the near future; most persons who die of AIDS die without a support system of friends and family; most people in the United States now have been touched by an AIDS death, but many cannot talk about it to friends or family; many people still believe they can get AIDS through casual contact; caring for an AIDS patient will *not* give you AIDS; blaming homosexuals for the AIDS epidemic is counterproductive and in the end blames the victim for dying; we must talk with our *children*—five- and six-year-olds even—about what AIDS is and how people get it and don't get it. Education is the key, she told us, to understanding and battling this disease. From the pulpit, she talked about "care teams" who "adopted" an AIDS victim and helped him or her with daily living, providing compassionate care, transportation, and companionship. She talked about the loneliness of dying alone with AIDS; she talked about the stigma attached to the disease and how sad and isolated both victims and families feel; she talked about families at this local church who had already been touched by the death of an AIDS patient.

I watched a man in the choir as he took off his glasses, wiped both eyes, then stared out the window, seemingly far away from the sanctuary and the woman's voice telling a sad story. I watched a woman's shoulders hunched over as she wept—was it a son? a daughter? I could only guess.

The pastor returned to the pulpit, asked for silent prayer for the AIDS ministry and all those afflicted by the disease, in whatever way they were touched by it. She prayed for compassion.

The pastor began to read the scripture lessons, her face framed from where I sat by the purple advent candles, one glowed with a flame across her cheek. She began.

November 29, 1993

It was cold and bitter. Thanksgiving had been white, slick, and dangerous. The following Monday was still bleak and frozen, a taste of the months ahead. We gathered at the front table near the frosty window of the Peking restaurant again, cupping our tea in our hands to gain warmth, conscious of the cold air standing there in front of the bay window, which faced the downtown Episcopal church. I did not see the resident winos today, perhaps the wind chill on the stone steps was too much for them.

As we gathered, first at the church, then as we crossed the street to the restaurant, the talk was all about the service on AIDS ministry. First one, then another, asked her how it went. How did she feel about it? Had there been any "fall out" or any comments at all? She was basking in what she felt to be her success; and I was there to confirm that the service had, indeed, been powerful. They asked her questions, talking over one another: Did the RAIN director give the "sermon"? When did she speak, before or after the pastor? Did anyone say anything to her after the service? Since Sunday? She answered each question, punctuating each with an exclamation about just how very glad she was it was over! Now, she could get on with Advent and the work that needed to be done—like with the AIDS ministry. But it had been imperative, she said, to first educate, to tell them about RAIN, then get them to admit in their hearts that they knew people with AIDS or knew people who had died of it, to confront their questions and, especially, their *fears* about giving care to an AIDS patient, and to stop condemning people for "causing" the AIDS epidemic. Her church, like so many others, she said, would like to pretend that AIDS hasn't touched them and won't; that their kids do not have to hear about AIDS or be educated against it; that it won't affect them. But she has, she told us, determined that none of this can be true and that she must lead the way toward education and action. She wants them to join the care teams, to take on the responsibilities of "care friends," to meet the challenge that AIDS presents to everyone in this day and age, to protect and hopefully save their own children. She spoke passionately, convincingly, and the words of her sermons echoed in my ears as I heard her tell her sisters there in the Peking restaurant how she had talked to her congregation about a topic many of them, she was certain, did not want to hear about, particularly from the pulpit. She admitted she talked about sexual intercourse and homosexuality and sexuality and condoms on the first Sunday of Advent. Since the congregation was present, they had to hear. But did they have to listen? She feared some were deaf to her message. Thus far, she said, she had heard no negative comments. No one had reprimanded her personally or indicated shock or concern about the topic or approach. Several people, maybe six, had actually told her it was good, or important, or provocative. Most were probably too stunned, she laughed nervously. We all cupped our hot tea and laughed, knowing neither the topic nor the response to her service was a laughing matter. We shared her convictions and her fears. We applauded her courage. The others wanted details, to try it themselves? I wondered to myself. Some had already, I knew, conducted an AIDS awareness service in their own churches; some seemed to be considering it. All were eager to hear about her experience and provide positive feedback to her for what she'd done. They seemed, in fact, in awe of her bravery. She basked in their praise and support.

Had she really feared someone would just get up and walk out, someone asked? No, not really, she told us. But it had occurred to her that someone might just blurt out a comment or do something really unexpected. This brought on a hilarious round of story-swapping about people who had stood up right in the middle of a service, even in the middle of a sermon, and yelled out something to the preacher. One woman told about a parishioner, many years ago in a church where she had been associate pastor, who would stand in the middle of the sermon and begin to rail about the sins of "drink."

"Was she drunk?" the others laughed. "What did you do?"

"I just let her finish, then I would proceed. It was hysterical." We all began to laugh. The others waited for another story.

"In my church," another woman told us, "there is one elderly lady who will, occasionally, at rather unexpected moments in the service, just blurt out a question. For the offering one Sunday one of the women elders had read a quote from the Buddha and had been nervous about doing that, had even asked the pastor for 'permission.' And, sure enough, immediately after the reading, this elderly parishioner had raised her voice with a question. The elder froze in her tracks. We were quite certain this woman would question the appropriateness of reading from Buddhist scriptures in the Sunday morning worship service. What she really wanted to know, however, was how to designate a contribution specifically for flood victims." Our narrator threw back her head, her face flushed with the sheer enjoyment of telling and remembering that story.

The waitress brought out what must have been the sixth pot of hot tea. We thanked her. The conversation quickly turned to what everyone had done with the First Sunday of Advent. Several said they had been influenced by last week's conversation to use most of the suggestions from the week before, about the leper who comes back, the only one who "gets it" and comes back to say thank-you and in that moment connects with God in relationship. They discussed, too, the suggestion of the theme of a "light" in the darkness, the "wait and watch" for Jesus theme extended a bit to looking for the light (for hope) in the midst of the darkness. They had discussed lighting the Advent candle at the end of the sermon rather than at the beginning, to signal the beginning, the advent of Advent. They thanked each other for all these ideas and told each other which ideas they had actually used. The Chinese waitress smiled shyly, peering over one woman's shoulder, as our fearless reader began to share the lectionary readings for the following Sunday.

December 18, 1993

We were all at the home of one of the women for the traditional "women ministers' Christmas party." I was so happy to see the faces of some of the ministers and the nuns I did not get to see on a more regular basis. These parties were always a time for hilarity and sharing. We played absolutely silly games that took us in and out of the small rooms in this house, even upstairs and down. Everything was exaggeratedly funny. We hugged, talked, and listened to each other. I always felt absolutely welcome, warm, included, a participant at these Christmas parties, fortunate to have been invited, blessed by the friendships of these strong and beautiful women.

Our hostess told a story which began something like—"Oh, I've got a wedding story for you" [we'd been talking about a photographer who had been a pain at a church during a recent wedding]—She laughed as she brought more bowls of food to the table.

"I was the associate pastor downtown, and Gilbert got very, very, very sick. He was in bed, had laryngitis, couldn't talk, and he was scheduled to do this wedding, see. So, he had his wife call me and tell me that I was just going to have to do this wedding. So I called the bride and told her the news as nicely as I knew how and what does she do? She begins to just bawl on the phone.

"She's in tears: 'My dress is the wrong size,' she says, 'and we have to take it up; the bridesmaids' dresses are the wrong color; and, now, you tell me we have to have a *woman* perform the ceremony. Oh, I think I'm going to just die!'

"Well, I was quite put off," our hostess says and everyone in the room seems to nod at once in agreement, "so I just got on the phone and called another male minister and he did it. But it sure wasn't very pleasant, and, most of all, she didn't seem to have a clue that what she'd just said to me was really rude."

The group at the table were as disgusted as their narrator, sharing her frustration with people who have no perception how that conversation would make a woman feel—when a rather quiet minister in our midst burst into the chatter with an exclamation, "Well, just let me get you somebody with a penis!" The table erupted in surprised and unabashed laughter. She had obviously said it to get a laugh, but they were all agreeing with her, too, that this was, in fact, the heart of the problem. "Right!" their voices echoed as our laughter died down.

April 4, 1994

On Monday, the clergywomen met for the lectionary lunch at a new restaurant, the latest addition to the downtown lunch scene. We sat on high bar stools around a too-small table and ate salads and bread and drank strong, freshly roasted coffee.

One by one, they came, hugs all around as each appeared. Lots of laughter and banter as we kept making more spaces on the awkward high stools. The new mom finally arrived with her new baby. We all shared her joy and awe at this late arrival. She had tried for so long to have this baby. For months we had all waited with bated breath, almost afraid to acknowledge her pregnancy, fearing this one, too, would not make it as the others had not. She was beaming as she struggled with the doors and the carriage. It was an odd sight. I watched other people as they watched this priest in her clerical collar push the baby carriage into the restaurant and receive hugs from us all. This was not a common sight, to be sure. Was the baby *hers*?

We straggled in, got in line to order our lunches, talking the whole time, unable to concentrate on the abundant menu before us—too many choices. Finally, we dragged two tables together to accommodate the full group. I held the baby and ate my salad with my other hand so his mother, the priest, could eat a meal in peace. After three of my own, this was easy for me.

"So!" a man said to them all as he passed by the tables, recognizing them as clergywomen, and knowing that collectively they had probably presided over or attended more than thirty church services in the past week, "So, there *is* life after Easter?"

They all laughed, "Why, yes, that's what it's all about, 'life after Easter.'"

"Which reminds me," the woman next to me prodded the group into action, "we all have to preach next Sunday. What *are* we going to do?"

"Well, hand me your book," our reader nodded toward the lectionary. "Let's take a look."

She read the verses. She almost always reads the verses, it occurred to me. There, in the new yuppie lunch establishment with ties to St. Louis, she read the scripture verses for next Sunday's service. I noticed people glancing our way. Not a common sight for them, I thought to myself.

"I like these verses," our reader commented. "They go really well with what I did on Easter Sunday, you know. I focused on, 'Do we celebrate Christ is risen, or Christ is alive in our lives?' But it's not about creeds and beliefs and things like that but about experiences in your life. The gospel here focuses on persons giving up their property, their possessions, and all being equal. That seems to fit with what I was telling them last week."

"What did you do?" She turned to the pastor who had spoken earlier.

"Me? Well, of course," she began to laugh, "I preached 'He is Risen!'"

"Noooo, well, that's original," we all pitched in, laughing.

"Actually," she continued, "I had a lot of fun yesterday. I think I startled everyone. I came in very stern and businesslike and I demanded of them, 'Why did you come here today? Why did you come? Did you come to pay your respects to a dead man?' And then, of course, I also talked about how God is alive here and now."

We were all startled when the new mom added, "I started to cry right in the middle of my sermon."

"Why?" we all wanted to know. "At what part did you actually begin to cry?"

"Oh, it really wasn't like buckets or anything," she chuckled. "It was just that looking down in front of me and seeing my Dad, my sister, my husband, and my *baby*, it really got to me. I just had to stop several times because I was just too choked up. They were about to baptize the baby. It was really neat. He was in my husband's baptism gown and my mother's cap, which is considerably older. But I was talking about how much of our lives we live in darkness and we really don't know what will happen, it's just darkness, but with the risen Christ we can live in the light."

April 14, 1994

We had not even sat down at our favorite booth in the dark restaurant when one woman began talking about her exasperating week.

"I nearly just quit being hospital chaplain last week. It's really getting to be too much. And it's hard to keep going. But then I realized just how short-handed they really are and I just couldn't walk out on them.

"But it was like a bad movie, like a slap-stick really. I get ready and go over to Regional Hospital and I get there and I cannot find my Bible and my notes. I look everywhere. Luckily, I'm a little early, so I drive back home to get them and I'm looking all over the house for them but I can't find them anywhere. So I get disgusted, get back in my car, and there they are on the front seat, under my purse. Been there all along. I'm really irritated. So I get over there and there's only one person in the chapel—"

"But isn't your sermon telecast to all the rooms?"

"Oh, sure, but the television monitor isn't working. Get this. The television monitor is all snowy, no picture at all. So they get a technician in there, but no good. So, I go ahead to my audience of one, just hoping that in the rooms the monitors are working better than the one in the chapel. It was horrible. So then I drive over to the Veterans Hospital and realize I haven't got the key for the hymnbook closet because I generally don't have to bring the little attaché case from Regional over to the Veterans. Anyway, no key. So they say, 'Do you want us to bring the technician?' And I'm like, by now you can imagine, I'm saying, 'Sure, bring the technician. Maybe he can open the door.'

"So this guy comes in and says, 'Well, there's this whole wall of keys, maybe you can try some of them.' So I try a bunch of them, but, of course, none of them fit. By now, I'm a mess. So he says, 'Well, I could take off the door for you. Do you want me to take off the door?' "

By now she is laughing so hard she can barely continue to talk and we, of course, are all in stitches.

"And I say, 'Well, how long would that take?' 'No more than five minutes,' he says.

" 'O.K.' I tell him, 'so take off the door.' So he takes about five minutes and does, he takes the door off the closet. So we get out all the hymnals and no one comes to the service. Not one person comes. All that and no one comes. That's when I just about threw in the towel."

April 28, 1994

It was time to share last week's sermons again.

"Well, I preached about witnessing," someone began the conversation. "I know, that's such an old topic. Kind of timeworn. But I talked about how it really didn't have anything to do with ordination or some official kind of designation one needed to witness. I told the story about how when I was first an elder and a deacon and one of my jobs was to do hospital calls, like two days a week, and the priest did the other two days. And because that was absolutely the last thing I *ever* wanted to do, somehow I would somehow forget, or let other things get in the way, whatever. And, when I got in there, it was not just 'chit-chat,' it was more like 'chatter-chatter' because I was so nervous and felt so uncomfortable that I would just come in and talk about the weather and somebody I just saw and what my friends were doing and on and on and on. Then, I'd look at my watch and, 'Oh, boy, look how late it is. I'm out of here. See you soon.' And in a flash I was out of there."

We're all laughing by now as she mimics her quick retreat, glancing quickly at her watch, and in a high squeaky voice, "Oh, dear, check that time. Gotta go. Splitsville." The others nod; we're all laughing.

"So there was this one older woman; I think she's still living. And she'd been in and out of the hospital just forever it seemed. And I'm in there, doing my normal five-second visit, ready to bolt. And, real calm, she says, 'How about a prayer?'"

"Hmmmmm," the others respond knowingly, and repeat, "how about a prayer?"

"Gulp. I gulped several times, I think. Muttering something about, 'Oh, of course, you want a prayer.' 'Well, then, shall we hold hands?' 'Yes, let's hold hands. And, let's see. I guess we could pray.'

"It was horrible. Simply horrible. But, I told my congregation, that woman was a witness to me about what my job should be like. She witnessed to *me* without the sanction of ordination. She was great, very straightforward. Told me just what I ought to be doing by saying, 'How about a little prayer, dearie?'"

"Yes, of course," the others answered.

"You know, I can really relate to that story," another woman spoke. "I always feel like I'm invading the most private area, their hospital room. It's so intimate. I feel so pushy. But you're right, they always ask for prayer. Always. I guess they see that as our role. And I generally hold their hands, too, and if there are other family members there I always ask that they all hold hands and we stand around the bed like that, holding hands, and pray."

"I do that, too. And sometimes, with some older people, it's really a shocker. We're standing there, holding hands, and I'm getting all ready— and from the bed comes, 'Dear God . . .' and I look up and lo and behold, they're praying. What a relief!"

We're all laughing now with her. "I didn't have to pray after all. Do you ever ask them what they'd like for you to pray for? You ever do that?"

"That's a tough one. You can't pray for God to take away her cancer, see, that's really tough. I'd never word it quite that way. Sometimes when I'm finished, I ask them or any of the family members if they would like to add anything; then I don't have to do that exactly. If they want to, then, that's o.k. by me, but I would never pray for God to heal them, that's really tough."

*   *   *

I have presented in this chapter only a small sampling of my recon-structed journal entries covering the various times and places this group of women met. Even this small sampling, however, indicates, I think, just how often and how regular the women do meet in a variety of informal contexts. These different spaces and places provide, however, a rich back-drop for their individual ministries. Collectively, collaboratively, through dialogue, discussion, laughter, sharing, and support, the women work together toward the creation of their individual sermons and their ongoing ministries of care and connection. Are their sermons similar because they meet and talk about them? Yes. Is this the only reason their sermons are similar? No. The way they approach their task, the experiences they bring to their discussions, the beliefs they hold dear, the attitudes they have honed over time and space while feeling marginalized and often ignored, all this is brought to bear on their collaborative efforts and, ultimately, upon their created sermons.

In all the contexts in which they meet, the women share their concerns, successes, problems, fears, and hopes—both personal and professional. Discussion of their churches often leads to talk about their sermons, but even if sermons are not spoken of directly, the talk at the lunches, the con-cerns expressed, the beliefs shared, provide a pool of shared experiences from which to draw. Such talk in safe spaces legitimizes the women's indi-vidual and collective experiences and authorizes the use of this material for their ministries and their sermon making. Women talking together about the work that connects each of them spiritually integrates their lives and work in such a way that none of them feels actually "alone" when they leave the table and return to their individual churches. They are not, in fact, alone. The supportive, collective act of sharing and connection through experience bonds them to each other. Collectively they become more powerful, stronger, and better able to face their lives and their min-istries. When I leave, I, too, know that I carry with me the warmth and strength of each of the women I encountered there.

The lunches, the lectionary discussions, the Christmas parties, the vari-ous impromptu meetings throughout the week, all serve to build this col-lective reality. It would be a mistake to say each of these women writes and delivers a sermon separately every Sunday morning, alone and isolated. Instead, as she stands in the pulpit, she must feel all around her the presence of the other women who stand, like her, in their own pulpits. Her voice is their voice. In their separate pulpits all over the city and the countryside, their voices mingle, becoming, not the same, but unified in spirit and design and in commitment to justice, to love, and to finding God.

A Grateful Heart

Carol Millspaugh
Locust Grove United Methodist Church
Columbia, Missouri
November 21, 1993

"On the way to Jerusalem Jesus was
    going through the region
between Samaria and Galilee.
As he entered a village,
ten lepers approached him.
Keeping their distance, they called out,
    saying,
'Jesus, Master, have mercy on us!'
When he saw them, he said to them,
'Go and show yourselves to the priests.'
And as they went, they were made clean.
Then one of them,
when he saw that he was healed, turned
    back,
praising God with a loud voice.
He prostrated himself at Jesus' feet and
    thanked him.
And he was a Samaritan.
Then Jesus asked, 'Were not ten made
    clean?
But the other nine, where are they?
Was none of them found to return and
    give praise to God except this
    foreigner?'
Then he said to him,

'Get up and go on your way;
your faith has made you well.'" [Luke 17:
    11–19, NRSV]

An amazing and wonderful truth
about Scripture
is that it is your story
and my story.
We find ourselves in these stories
written so long ago,
and we find God has a Word for us
in these stories.

The story of the ten lepers in Luke
is our story—
Many times
we have been in this group.
We,
like the lepers,
have been in need of God's healing.
We have needed relief
from physical illness
and distress—
an illness has brought us
to the brink of despair

and we have called out,
"Oh Lord, save us!"
We,
like the lepers,
have needed relief
from not only physical illness,
but we have known what it is
to feel isolated and alone,
to feel cut off from our loved ones,
to feel that no one understands or cares,
and we have cried out,
"Oh Lord, save us!" —
if only in the silent cry
of our own hearts,
which no earthly ear can hear.
We have traveled that road
with those lepers,
that road
where everyone around us
seems to be busily on the road
to somewhere —
but our road seems to be going
nowhere,
for we have lost hope
of finding our way.
Until one day,
we catch a glimpse of hope —
we see Jesus coming along that road —
he is nearby
and we call out to him,
in the midst of our pain
or social isolation
or loss of meaning
or whatever illness of spirit affects us.
We cry out,
"Oh Lord, save us!"

There are ten of us,
ten of us in the story.

Jesus answers our call.
He is not put off by our illness
of body or spirit.
He does not ignore us,
as others do.
He is not so scared of our pain,
as others are,
that he leaves us there
and walks on by.
He does not suffer from compassion
    fatigue,
as so many do.
He stops.
He gives us his attention.
He ministers to us,
and we are touched,
touched by his grace.
We are healed,
restored to community
where once relationships had been
    broken.
We are given health,
where we had been sick.
We are given hope,
where we had been despairing.
We are given new life,
where we thought death
was our destination.
He has healed us!
And we,
like the ten,
have gone on our way rejoicing!
Most often,
we have been the nine lepers,
those who received God's gift of healing,
who rejoiced in the gift,
but did not really come to know
and connect
with the Giver.

We have received God's gifts—
healing,
restored relationships,
all the blessings of life,
the goodness of life.
We have received these gifts
and gone on our way,
our needs having been met.
We have then focused
on what we need next,
not looking back,
not going back,
to the Giver of the gifts.
Most often
we are the nine lepers
who receive God's gifts and go on.
But sometimes,
sometimes,
we are the one leper—
the one who receives God's healing
and blessing
and love
and goodness,
who rejoices in the gift so much
that we are led beyond the gift
to the Giver.
The one leper,
the Samaritan
who was healed,
went back,
returned to Jesus,
kneeling there in the road
at Jesus' feet
and thanked Jesus
for his healing.
Sometimes
we are that one leper,
who receives God's goodness
and is grateful.

All ten lepers
received God's blessing.
God's generosity extends to all God's
    children,
to all the world.
All of us here
have
and do
receive God's goodness and gifts
in our lives.
It is a minority of us,
in this story,
one out of ten,
who gets past the focus on the gifts
and connects with the Giver,
the one who has given us the gifts.
One of the ten lepers
received more than a healing—
One entered into a connectedness,
a relationship,
with Jesus Christ.
One entered a new dimension
of living.
It was available to all ten,
but only one found it.
Why?
Because of gratitude.
One heart was grateful—
rather than take the gift
and leave with it.
One embraced the gift,
turned around,
and went back—
back to the One
whose love had healed him.

Thanksgiving—
Gratitude
was the pathway

into new life—
the road
which led not only to receiving God's
  gifts,
but connecting with the Giver of those
  gifts.
One leper,
through giving thanks,
received more than God's gift of healing
that day.
One received God's own presence
in the person of Jesus Christ.

A grateful heart
led one into a closer relationship
with God;
a thankful spirit led one to rejoice
in the Giver behind the gifts.

This Thanksgiving,
may the story of the one leper,
the one who returned to give thanks,
be our story as well.
Amen.

Christ's Healing Touch

CAROL MILLSPAUGH
Locust Grove United Methodist Church
Columbia, Missouri
November 28, 1993

I invite you to turn with me
in your pew Bibles
to our Scripture lessons.
You'll see that the first one
is on page 1057,
from First John, Chapter Four, verses 18
  to 21. [NRSV]
"There is no fear in love,
but perfect love casts out fear;
for fear has to do with punishment,
and whoever fears has not reached
  perfection in love.
We love because God first loved us.
Those who say,
'I love God,'
and hate their brothers or sisters,
are liars;
for those who do not love a brother or
  sister
whom they have seen,
cannot love God whom they have not
  seen.
The commandment we have from God is
  this:
those who love God

must love their brothers and sisters also."
And the second lesson we find in Mark's
  Gospel,
Chapter 1, verse 40. [NRSV]
"And a leper came to Jesus beseeching
  him
and kneeling, said to him,
'If you will, you can make me clean.'
Moved with pity,
he reached out his hand
and touched him,
And said to him,
'I will. Be clean.'
And immediately the leprosy left him,
and he was made clean.
And he sternly charged him
and sent him away at once,
saying to him,
'See that you say nothing to anyone;
but go, show yourself to the priest,
and offer for your cleansing what Moses
  commanded,
as a testimony to them.'
But he began to go out
and began to proclaim it freely,

and to spread the word,
so that Jesus could no longer go into a
    town openly,
but stayed out in the country;
and people came to him from every
    quarter."

Several years ago
our family had the wonderful experience
of living in Hawaii
while my husband was a pastor
in a local church there.
We lived on the island of Oahu
and we had the opportunity once
to go to another island by the name of
    Molokai.
Molokai for many years had been a leper
    colony;
and I remember that trip very clearly.
In my mind's eye I can picture that island
as we drew close to it—
the shore line was beautiful
with waves breaking on the rocky cliffs;
the palm trees were blowing in the
    wind—
the sun was shining.
It was just a beautiful, beautiful day
as we came up to this island.
And then the guide began to tell us the
    story
of what had happened
right there in the place where we were.
She said that boats used to pull up there
just offshore of the island
and these boats would have passengers
not tourists like we were
but instead passengers who were sick
who had come from all the different
    islands in Hawaii—

not come by choice
but come because the police had come
    to get them.
These people had leprosy.
She told us that the boat would anchor
    there offshore
and wouldn't land,
but instead would
make the people get off the boat—
push them off if necessary
into the water.
And if the people with leprosy were able
    to swim,
they would swim to the shore,
and if they weren't able to swim
they would drown.
And when they got to the shore,
if they were able,
they would climb up these rocky cliffs
get a hold somehow on the rocks
and get onto the shore.
But they weren't out of danger yet,
because once they got to the shore
they faced a different kind of danger,
and that was the lepers who had already
    come to that island.
Of course some were more healthy than
    others,
and so the weak were at the mercy of the
    strong;
women were at the mercy of men,
who didn't go by any laws;
children were defenseless,
if their parents weren't with them
and usually the children were there
    alone.
The disease of leprosy
was a terrible physical ailment
but it was also a terrible

social sickness,
because those who had it were cut off
doomed to live out their lives
in this terrible leper colony,
until something changed,
until some good news happened to them.
And that good news was Father
    Damian—
who you've probably heard of—
he was a Catholic priest;
and he came there to that island,
and he instituted the rule of law
and he brought compassion
and order,
and the leper colony was transformed
from a place of misery and despair and
    suffering
to a place of compassion and wholeness
    and caring.
Leprosy in Jesus' day—
like in this day in early Hawaii—
was a physical illness,
but it had terrible social repercussions.
In the New Testament no disease was
    regarded
with as much terror and pity
as was leprosy,
because there, too, the person was not
    only sick,
but was banished from society,
had to live far from other people,
and then if the person came near other
    people,
he or she had to cry out "Unclean,
    unclean,"
so that everyone would stay away.
Lepers also were thought to have
    committed
some terrible sin,

and they were shunned like the plague.
It was someone like this—
a leper—
who approached Jesus
in our scripture lesson from Mark.
Mark says a leper came to Jesus
    beseeching him
and kneeling down,
and said to Jesus,
"If you will
you can make me clean."
How did Jesus react?
Did he say,
"You're breaking the law—"
which the leper was—
"by coming near to me!
Go away!"
Or did he say that
by his sinful life
the leper was sick by his own fault?
Or did he just avoid the situation
and not want to know about it
and walk away?

Listen to what Mark says Jesus did:
"Moved with compassion,
Jesus stretched out his hand
and touched him
and said to him,
'Thou will be healed,'
and immediately this man was healed."

AIDS is,
in fact,
the twentieth century's
leprosy.
AIDS,
like leprosy,
not only kills people,

but too often leaves them socially
isolated
and stigmatized.
AIDS is a really hard thing to think
about—
it's hard to preach about.
We don't want to deal with AIDS.
Too often we would just rather not have
to know about it,
because HIV and AIDS
can confront us with issues that
we're not comfortable with—
like sexuality,
disease,
discrimination,
and death.

Why are we talking about AIDS in church
anyway?
What does this have to do with the
gospel?
It has everything to do with the gospel,
because you and I serve our Lord,
who reached out to the whole world,
especially those who are hurting
especially those who do not have love
and acceptance.
Jesus offered them new life.
You and I cannot define ourselves as
Christian,
on the one hand,
and on the other hand set up walls and
barriers
against other people
who Jesus loved as much as he loved us.
We're talking about AIDS in church today,
because if Jesus were walking
in our town
in 1993,

he would be ministering to those people
with AIDS
just like he ministered to lepers,
and he would ask us
to join him.
Our United Methodist conference
has asked all of our churches
to raise the subject of AIDS awareness,
and education
and ministry
in our churches.
And I'm glad that our church already
has people involved in care teams
here in Columbia,
and I hope more of us will be involved
not only in care teams
but in conversations
and prayer
and in the many ways that we can be in
ministry.

In thinking about this uncomfortable
and difficult subject
of dealing with AIDS,
it strikes me that part of the problem
is that you and I
also need healing.

Obviously,
we would want people with AIDS
to be healed in their illness.
But you and I need healing
of a different sort.
We need to be healed of our fear.
Those who shunned lepers
and thought that they were terrible
sinners
in Jesus' day,

those people were no more evil or mean
or cruel
than you and I are,
but they were afraid.
They were afraid that they would get
sick.
They were afraid of the unknown.
And it was their fear
that made them hostile and defensive.
We easily react that same way.
We're afraid of the unknown.
We're uncomfortable around subjects
like AIDS
or sexually transmitted diseases.
We're afraid,
but what we fail to see is that
our fears
and our judgments
put us in danger.
We are in danger,
and that danger is in not following Christ.
We are in danger, then,
of being part of the problem,
not part of the solution.
Did you catch the part where it says
that Jesus stretched out his hand?
He stretched out his hand
to heal this man.
You and I need to stretch also,
to stretch our hearts
and our faith
You and I need to reach
past the fear
past the natural discomfort
into compassion and action.

Education is crucial.
It is important that you and I know

what the Center for Disease Control has
told us.
They have assured us
that AIDS is not transmitted
by casual contact
by hugging
shaking hands
being near a person with AIDS.
In fact,
AIDS is a very difficult disease to catch.
We catch it through sexual intercourse
through shared IV needles
through contaminated blood
or through being born to a mother
who has AIDS.
And those are the only ways
we can catch it.
You and I need to be healed
of our fears,
so that we can follow our Lord
and stretch out our hands
across the brokenness
and the chasms
that this illness causes.

Jesus reached out
to those who were shunned in his
society,
the lepers,
promiscuous people,
the mentally ill,
the physically deformed.
Nowhere did Jesus put conditions on his
outreach.
He simply accepted and loved people
and he invited them into wholeness.
And that's what you and I are called
to do.

This is not easy.
It is really hard
to reach out to someone we don't
    understand
or whose behavior we don't approve of.
It calls on us to stretch ourselves
stretch our faith
and it is not easy.
But why are you and I part of this great
    experiment,
that's called the church,
anyway?
Not because it's easy,
but because we have heard Jesus call to
    follow him
and we have committed ourselves to do
    that.
The issue is not homosexuality,
drug abuse,
sexual promiscuity.
These are not the issues.
The issue for us
is whether the church,
you and I,
are willing to follow Jesus
and let him be Lord even in this area
of life.
Are we willing to follow him and reach out
    to others
with a healing touch?
Are we willing to see in another person
not a person to be condemned,
but someone to be loved
as a brother or sister?
Are we willing to use our words
not to hurt
or put down
but to heal and to care?

AIDS has already touched our church—
it is touching our church.
Many who are touched by it
feel uncomfortable bringing up the
    subject
with each other.
In our conversations with each other,
are you and I helping or hurting?
Are we supporting or condemning?
Are we a place where people can feel
    welcome,
where everyone can feel God's
    acceptance?
Because that's what we are called to do.
This is the first Sunday of Advent
where we await God's coming anew
into our lives,
and we profess that God's light
still shines
in the darkness.
Your bulletin, I think, explains it very well.
This picture of a candle
is surrounded by darkness,
but it proclaims that God
and God's love
are the hope of the world
and the light of the world.
Advent, in fact, proclaims
that a new day is coming.
It isn't here yet,
but it's coming;
and there is light
in any present darkness.
You and I
are invited to be part of that light
as we reach out and stretch
into the world.
Jesus broke the law

when he touched an unclean leper,
but that law itself
violated God's compassion.
Jesus stretched out his hand
and touched that man.
And Jesus has continued on his way
down through the centuries
reaching out
and over
the barriers
and the chasms that we create,
defying human obstacles,
like slavery,
sexism,
exploitation
segregation,
reaching out to touch
and to heal.
And you and I
are asked to be Jesus' healing touch
    today
that our fear may give way
to faithful actions.
You and I are called to be that healing
    touch of Christ.
Why?
Because we are his church;
we belong to God
not to ourselves.
And we have said "yes"
when Jesus has asked us,
"Will you follow me?"
There is no substitute

for outstretched hands
and outstretched lives.
God's love is the hope of the world.
And this Advent
God calls us to be part of that light
until, as Revelations says,
a new day will dawn
the shadows will disappear
and every tear will be wiped away.

On the island of Molokai,
the lepers were pushed off that boat
and they often drowned.
You and I were not there on Molokai,
but we are here in Columbia
and God has given us arms—
arms to hold
and to reach out
and to catch others,
so they may not have to struggle alone.

May God heal our arms
so we can open them wider
and wider
and wider.
May God continue to heal us
that we may, in fact,
be Christ's healing touch
today.
Let us pray for our own healing
and the healing of the world,
as we join in our next hymn.

Chapter 3
"Reading" Women's Sermons

Reciprocal Ethnography at Work

I enjoy going to hear someone put ideas and words and experiences together—it's like an art form. And that's what I try to practice. . . . I want to perfect the art form of sharing who I am and what I believe in in a real succinct and dramatic way. In a sense it is a performance.

—Clare

I want to respond to the idea of the sermon as an art form. I think it is an art form—a creative art form.

—Kim

Well, I think what this analogy and what was just said fit exactly—I think there's your book. What would it be like to compare it with artists who were on the fringe who began painting, expressing, offering new images of reality? They would have done something very different.

—Gertrude

In this highly literate and media-blitzed world, it is curious to find *ars praedicandi*, or the art of preaching, alive and well, thriving in the pulpits of every conceivable religious denomination that *has* a pulpit tradition. Deeply grounded in the tradition of traveling monks and itinerant preachers,[1] the sermon is an ancient artistic oral form. The classical study of rhetoric includes the study of the *ars praedicandi*, which emerged in the Middle Ages as the religious aspect of rhetorical studies. The preaching tradition has, of course, not only survived as the focal point of many religious services, but it has also entered the public arena via the media—especially in highly lucrative radio and television evangelism and in the audio tape industry.[2] In these contexts, the sermon does not always enjoy a great deal of respect and credibility, and several movies and recent popular books have focused on the cheap thrills and chicanery that continue to be the trademarks of the glitzy evangelist and his entourage of stage performers.[3] Negative publicity notwithstanding, however, in ordinary, and not-so-ordinary, churches and cathedrals throughout the world, the sermon persists as the mainstay of the typical worship service. Congregation members may look to the sermon for edification and guidance; they may sleep through it; they may disregard it, forgetting it even as they leave the church. No matter how seriously the sermon is perceived by the parishioners, it remains a significant and valorized duty of the pastors of the churches. Preachers, who wrestle with the sermon all week, ponder it, pray about it, search through sermon help-books for tips and guidance, write it out, revise it, and deliver it, take it very seriously, indeed. The women in this book who preach not only take their task to heart but also believe deeply that the sermons they deliver to their home congregations can and do affect their religion and their church community. But for these women, there is no returning to a collection of timeworn, standard sermon texts that explicate the scriptures and serve only to reassure the congregation of God's transcendent and awesome love and power. Each week offers a new challenge. The scriptures, whether taken from a lectionary or not, present themselves to the women bare, open for connection, relevance, and meaning. They read them early in the week, several times, together and alone. They wait and "listen" for the passages that will emerge as the ones they will need to weave a sermon around. Throughout the week, as each woman works toward Sunday's delivery, the sermon may slip and slide, refusing her attention or balking at an interpretation, refusing to be pinned down, asking her for more of herself, always more, to create a successful, meaningful sermon. What on Tuesday seemed reasonable and acceptable by Saturday night may have to be tossed into the trash. How to begin anew at 11:00 p.m.? They can and do. They never give up until, hopefully, the text "feels" right. Only then can they share it with their congregations.

In contemporary denominations, especially in this country, every woman or man who is ordained to preach is expected to have taken courses in homiletics or preaching in seminary and/or through a correspondence courses, seminars, or workshops. Generally, preaching courses include not only reading texts about how to preach but also a practicum: the neophyte is expected to write and deliver sermons from the pulpit, generally to an audience of peers. Very early in my work, however, the women in this study remarked to me that they had often resisted the more traditional, classical homiletic courses offered at their various seminaries. In many of the homiletic texts, they said, the young preacher discovers variations of the oft-repeated "tree of preaching," which graphically depicts the basic, paradigmatic three-part sermon. The word homily comes from *homilia*, or discourse in an assembly, which, according to Thomas Oden, consists of "practical discourse with a view to spiritual edification."[4] Traditional homiletic scholarship approaches the topic from at least two aspects: either as practicioner's art, or, on a more philisophical note, as discourse on the theological aspects of homiletics, or preaching. Many of the women learned to avoid the courses that approached preaching in this manner, or took them only when they were forced to do so. They rarely used the traditionally taught methods of sermon making and delivery, largely because they did not find the "three-part sermon with anecdotal/illustrative support" to be a sermon framework they felt comfortable using in their own sermon creations. Several of the women insisted that they wanted to preach differently from the way the homiletic teachers taught and differently from the expectations set by their preaching courses. I recall their agitation with me when I remarked upon the way they used stories "for illustration" in their sermons. They insisted that their stories served as the actual frame, the foundation of their sermons, not as "mere" illustration of a point. The stories *were* the point. The researcher in me wanted to probe that question. I wondered if, perhaps, they just *thought* they preached differently. I wondered if my research would reveal their sermons to be actually quite in line with a standard homiletic design and method of presentation. I wondered if I would be able to characterize women's sermons in any systematic and reasonable manner, especially in such a way that would address questions of "how do women preach?"

As a folklorist, I view the oral sermon as an artistic art form. Sermons are verbal/artistic texts orally "performed" in the pulpit by the artists who create them and who present them to their critical audience, the church congregation.[5] Folklore studies offer us a variety of ways to examine such oral texts. Several years ago, sermon texts would have been analyzed closely in terms of their structure, their formulaic qualities, their organization, their use of traditional language, the authorial voice, the repeated refrains, and other poetic stylistics, such as assonance and alliteration. This type of standard textual analysis of orally performed texts stems from textual studies in ballad and epic. Folklore studies in the early years of this century would also have guided us to study these orally performed texts in terms of the social and cultural context(s) in which they are created and thrive. Studies of sermons delivered by African-American preachers have used both of these approaches. For example, Bruce Rosenberg's classic work, *The Art of the American Folk Preacher*, is a prime example of a textual study with contextual information about the importance of sermons in the African American community. William Bascom, an anthropologist writing about folklore, cautions us to consider not only the cultural significance of an orally performed verbal/artistic text but also the social context of the performance—Who is in attendance? Who is the storyteller-performer? What does the delivery look and sound like?[6] More recent approaches in folklore emphasize a performance-centered approach that closely parallels a rhetorical analysis of performed texts.[7] Thus the folkorist analyzes these texts within their performed context *as* oral performances, with close attention to how the text is delivered in a particular context, keying tone, language, voice, and interactions with audience.

Krista Ratcliffe, a rhetorician and former colleague, whose understanding of rhetoric has greatly assisted my thinking about women's sermons, offers us a way to discern rhetorical strategies employed by women that may serve to subvert or invert the dominant rhetorical tradtion. That tradition, developed and utilized by male rhetoricians, may be rejected by women who speak in a female voice that does not reflect the traditional male model in terms of language, presentation, and discourse constructs.[8] Ratcliffe talks about how women speak from the cracks or fissures, creating a new voice and requiring an interaction with the listener that elicits a unprecedented response.

In my analysis of women's sermons, I draw on all these avenues of understanding and interpretation. In keeping with the image of the multistranded helix, I do not artificially separate the parts from the whole but use aspects of oral formulaic analysis, discuss performance, and examine how women in their pulpits, delivering their sermons, are speaking with new voices and evoking new responses.

When I began to formally analyze women's sermons, I found it extremely difficult to talk about performance—or style or content or structure—separately from creation and context. Just as I feel it is a mistake to analyze the text of the sermon separate from the contexts in which it is created and delivered, I think we cannot dissect and deconstruct these sermons in order to lay them open for close, neat inspection.[9]

As I worked with the sermons, I drafted a list of their "characteristics" and presented it to the women. Now I present to you that list and offer a portion of the clergywomen's responses to my observations. When I shared my list with the women, I acknowledged that it was a mélange of comments about the structure, rhetorical strategies, content and theme, point of view, and language. I hoped that my responses to their sermons would generate discussion among them about their sermons and about sermon making.

As I recall these conversations, I am struck again by the image of the multistranded helix; I suggest that the sermons represent one of the many strands in my reconception of the double helix as a model for this study. The strands of the multistranded helix, as I envision them, represent the clergywomen's lives, their stories, their experiences, their relationships, their connections—with each other and with the cosmos. One of the strands in this model is the sermons. Like the multistranded helix, which is capable of forever expanding and incorporating new strands, the various characteristics of the sermons themselves intertwine to form a braided "sermon strand." These characteristics are not finite, concrete, always identifiable aspects of women's sermons but fluid, expandable, ever-dynamic strands that work together to make the helix viable, vibrant, connected with the other aspects of women's lives. Meanwhile, each braid represents a different woman and is therefore at once similar to and different from all the others.

The helix model allows not only for an expanded notion of the collective of women preaching but for further exploration as a theological model. The weaving of scripture, relationship, family, and self-awareness together as the helix spirals around the center informs our understanding of how the sermons themselves explore the possibilities of the core, the center of the floating helix. As we invest this model with life, we might imagine the center as the different but collective perception(s) of God. The strands weave and spiral around that center, which draws them together yet enables their distinctive differences through expansion. The many strands, in turn, working in connection with the center, create the perfectly balanced movement, which we can imagine as all creation held together by the creative center. If we allow this expanding image to include the universe, then the model as a whole incorporates the essence of God at the center embraced by the curves of the helix. The strands are held in perfect balance by the forces in the center of the helix, even as the balanced strands in their perfect forms create the center. Neither can exist without the other. And because the mystery of the center allows for ever-expanding perceptions of God, the essence of the "core" must weave through and beyond the strands that frame it.

Characteristics of the Sermons

In very specific terms, I began to talk with the women about their sermons. I told them I felt a concerted effort on their part to make the scriptures relevant to modern audiences, not in an ahistorical way, but by *bringing the scriptures and people's lives into praxis* through storytelling. The clergywomen in this study are verbal artists. They know how to retell biblical stories to make them pertinent to the lives of the people in their congregations. They are willing to risk a great deal in these sermons; their methods are at times unorthodox; their presentations unique and provocative. Thus Carol Millspaugh tells her congregation: "The scriptures are your story and my story, the story of us and of God." She makes *us*, herself joined with her audience, the ten lepers (see pp. 72–76 for full sermon, "A Grateful Heart").

Maureen Dickmann has the creative ability to paint a picture of what various biblical scenes would have been like and making them "real" for her audience by allowing for the experiences to be remembered by her own congregation. On Pentecost Sunday, as the congregation sat beneath large red balloons intended to remind them of the upper room experience, Maureen invites them into experience: "The Holy Spirit awaits. You, too, can be set on fire." She gives detailed background on Pentecost and paints a picture of the streets of Jerusalem echoing with all the different voices as Jews gathered for the day of Pentecost. I could hear the voices in the streets, the rattling of goods, the people's voices. I was startled when different people in the sanctuary stood and quietly read passages in Estonian, Latin, German, French, and other languages not ordinarily heard on a Sunday morning in Columbia. Maureen then helped us to feel what the disciples would have experienced as they prayed and grieved the death of their beloved Jesus, since it had only been weeks since Christ's death and rising. Her storytelling transported us; we gathered with them and heard a great rushing of wind and listened incredulously to the strange languages as the tongues of fire rested on each one of them. We imagined the response in the streets as others observed their strange behavior with skepticism and thought they'd been drinking too much strong liquor. Maureen links the story with the lives of her audience, pointing to the multifaceted effect of this small event in Jerusalem on Christianity today by comparing it to a small stream in Israel that wends its way variously to the Jordan River, the Dead Sea, and then the Sea of Galilee.

Kim Ryan relates the story of Jonah, describing for us the surge of the sea, saltwater in our faces, and sea sickness, not merely to retell the story or to awaken us to the danger of a ship in a wild sea but to reveal what the biblical storyteller intended by telling the story of Jonah in the way that it was told, and particularly by ending with a question and offering no conclusions. God asks Jonah why he would not have God care for Jonah's enemies. Kim asks her congregation to have a very personal reaction to the notion that God does love *everyone*, even our enemies. "How will we respond?" she asks. "Like Jonah—in disbelief and anger?"

Peggy Jeffries, in her sermon on Samuel, informs Jesse that his son David is the favored of God. She invites us to "join with Sarah in laughing, you can almost hear the folks around the synagogue, around the temple, laughing as Samuel gets out the oil and begins to annoint the youngest of eight children. The youngest. The little one who goes out and plays with the sheep, who sings." Margaret Ann Crain talks about her understanding of "what kind of person Jesus was because that is why he still has something to say to me." Her sermon "Faith Goes at Its Own Pace" retells with dramatic emphasis what it was like for the disciples to see Jesus after his death. Margaret Ann's theatre background is evident in her presentation: "Who did you find yourself identifying with in our scripture for today?" she asks. "Did you identify with Thomas who had to touch the wounds and feel Jesus' side in order to believe? Do you need to see in order to believe?" Her sermons deal with the mystery of God within a modern, intellectual atmosphere. "How can we relate to the belief in the death and resurrection of Jesus Christ?" she asks. Religion for her is "living the questions." And so, she claims, there is at least one thing we can all agree upon: "something great happened, something that changed the entire course of history." She provides us with an explanation of why dramatic storytelling works from the pulpit: "I am content to take full responsibility for the creative imagination which is part of my response to the mysterious figure who passes so briefly through Palestine and leaves people unable to forget him."

In these women's sermons, I have noted a comfortable intimacy with the various texts, a weaving of scripture within the sermons that went beyond simply "using" the lectionary scriptures to "frame" the sermon. Although the biblical texts are often read at the beginning of the sermon, scripture is also often interjected at different points in the sermon; the verses are repeated again and again throughout the sermon, for emphasis, for clarity, for style. Even Gertrude Lindener-Stawski, a Unitarian minister, who does not read scripture at the beginning of the sermon, interposes many verses throughout her sermons. Furthermore, in their sermons, the speakers seem to be *re-thinking the messages in Biblical stories and in the process of preaching often disrupt the listeners' typical response to time-worn sermon analyses and expectations.* I wondered aloud whether there might be something particularly female about what is chosen as the crucial passage in the standard scriptures for the sermon texts. Not only that, I was willing to suggest that the angle taken on the text might be a particularly female angle.

For example, I recalled a sermon by Maureen Dickmann that dealt with the injunction about offenders in the church: "If that doesn't work, treat them as Gentiles and tax collectors" (see pp. 13–19 for full text of sermon, "Making Connections"). Maureen acknowledged that the passage *might* be perceived as a directive to actually treat them as offenders or outsiders, but in her sermon, she took a completely different approach. She pointed out, and we had to agree, Jesus *ate* with the Gentiles and tax collectors; "he sat with them, welcomed them, taught them, healed them." Oddly enough, she suggested to her congregation that day, perhaps Jesus was telling us "not to cut off the offenders, cast them away, but, instead, sit with them as Jesus had done." Perhaps her approach is not unique, but it is certainly a different way of perceiving things.

I returned to that Pentecost sermon in which Maureen suggested that "encountering the Holy Spirit is not always cataclysmic, sometimes it can be deceptively simple, a quiet voice," where she told her congregation that "the multitude of different and strange voices uttered on that first Pentecost is akin to the vast and varied reality that Christianity today has become." Again, a different way of perceiving things. The tongue-speaking becomes less the focus as acceptance of difference becomes more significant.

I remembered the sermon Kim Ryan preached on the Twenty-Third Psalm (see pp. 118–24 for full text of sermon, "Scraps from the Table").

Kim told her congregation that all week she had resisted using Psalm 23 because it was too familiar and timeworn, but then succumbed to the voice that told her she really needed to preach on that passage. However, when Kim uses the familiar text, she does not focus on the most recognized portion of the verses, "The Lord is my shepherd, I shall not want." She creates a message for her people "to slow down, not rev up for more good works or more and more Christian witnessing," not to sign the kids up for three more after-school activities. Rather than stressing the way God takes care of faithful followers, Kim turns her attention toward the calming effect of following the more simplistic life of the shepherd. She uses the text to suggest that it would be more beneficial to slow down and "spend more time with our families." Quietly, over and over, throughout her sermon, she gently prods her listeners: "Sat by any still waters lately? Seen any green pastures? Have you talked with your children? Who is your shepherd, anyway?" A different way of perceiving things.

I recalled Peggy Jeffries's retelling of the story of Samuel and David, infused with immediate energy, when Jesse introduces his eldest son with "the modern day version of popping his buttons." She repeats the verse, too, but each time in just a little different context: "My ways are not your ways." She allows this line to become the real focus of the sermon, suggesting that she and her congregation too often "concentrate on what is outside of a person." Instead, we should, she says, "See what's inside. Look at the heart, the soul, the spirit of the person." The youngest child, innocent, inexperienced, naive, would never have been the choice of the people, but he was the choice for God. She prays with her people for the power of discernment.

I remembered hearing Kim's surprising sermon entitled "Sometimes You Just Gotta Break the Rules," which was based on the story about Jesus healing a leper but focusing *not* on the "typical" aspects of the story (i.e., the man had been waiting by the healing waters but couldn't get in when the waters were stirred, and Jesus healed him with words only) but focused instead on the little-recognized fact that Jesus did this good deed *on the Sabbath*, suggesting that the infringement of the rules was one of the acts that "propelled him toward the cross"(see pp. xxviii–xxxv for full text of sermon). Furthermore, she points out, digging even further beneath the obvious surface of this story, "what really ticked everyone off" was that Jesus responded to his accusers by saying, "My father is working still and I am working." It was his "audacity," she told us, "in claiming this close connection with God the Father that actually made them angry enough to kill him." But there's more. "Jesus," she tells them, "invoked a close, personal connection with God as his own father. The closeness of that connection is the crux of the story," she says. She then takes her congregation into an exploration of "different images and notions of God—God as rock, God as shepherd, God as protector and mountain, God as mother, God as lover, and God as friend." "If," she tells her amazed audience, "we can conceive of God as all of these different aspects, we must be able to perceive God as vulnerable, as one who feels pain and is open to the hurt of hurting children. We must open to different images of God that work for us."

In short, I note the unorthodox nature of some of their sermons. For example, I could refer to Kim's sermon "Sometimes You Just Gotta Break the Rules," Gertrude Lindener-Stawski's "The Rule of the Heart: An Unorthodox Interpretation of Jesus," or Kim's "An Owner's Manual for the Bible" (see pp. 109–17 for full text of sermon), in which she outlines alternatives to reading the Bible as a literal historical document. Tamsen Whistler, a priest at a local Episcopal church (she recently moved to a parish near St. Louis), delivered a powerful sermon on the hemorrhaging woman, story she reinserted into the lectionary readings and used as her sermon text (see pp. xxiii–xxviii for full text of sermon, "A Woman's Faith"). In another sermon, Tamsen explained to her Episcopalian congregation that the Commandments are only guideposts, only the beginning—the message is really about right relationships and the power of *reconciliation*. In the sermon "Faith Goes at Its Own Pace," when Margaret Ann asks whether her listeners identified with Thomas or are able to believe without seeing, she validates *both* responses, because, she tells them, "faith grows at its own pace." She admits her own misgivings and questions in a modern world where blind faith becomes more difficult from one day to the next.

Not only are the sermons unorthodox in the way they question things, some of them suggest *that following the rules and regulations, the prescribed ways of doing things, is not necessarily the appropriate plan of action.* Jesus is often identified as one who ate with outcasts, healed the "inappropriate," and worked for his father on the "wrong" days—one who followed his heart more than he followed the rules. Kim tells her attentive congregation: "Sometimes you just gotta break the rules." Tamsen echoes those words: "The lessons today are about rules and choices and something which lies beyond those rules . . . God has left us in the power of our own inclinations." Sermons are often about the outsider, the outcast, the marginal, the youngest, the meek, the quiet one, the unlikely one getting chosen by God; sermons taking the unlikely point of view.

With these methods, and in others yet to be discussed, the clergywomen attempt to answer the question "Where is God?" rather than "Who is God?" The answers are intimate and again, perhaps, unorthodox. The sermons they preach locate God in places like the following:

- in connection: "How do we participate in God's healing action? We touch each other; we talk to each other" (Whistler, "A Woman's Faith," p. xxvi).
- in relationship: "'If I could go back, I would say that God lies be-

tween people and is to be found there.' . . . Nothing is more important than right relationship between persons. For we experience nothing less than the very presence of God in those relationships. It's all connected" (Dickmann, "Making Connections," p. 17).

- in the inter-connectedness of all things: In one sermon Margaret Ann demonstrates just how all of the inhabitants of the earth are connected and influence each other. Similarly, in a sermon entitled "Musings from a Hot Blackberry Patch," Gertrude Lindener-Stawski examines this intersecting of all life in the prickly bushes of the blackberry patch. (see pp. 26–28 for full text of sermon).

- in gratitude: Carol Millspaugh preaches about the ten lepers but focuses on the one leper who came back to thank the Giver. "God is there, evident in the gratitude." Hence "the leper who returned to thank the Giver received twofold blessings. He was healed, but he also was fortunate enough to encounter the Giver" (Millspaugh, "A Grateful Heart," p. 73).

- in the intuitive, the experienced; not in the factual, the cerebral: One of the preachers tells us God is evident in "something else that the believer knows to be true—a knowledge based on experience and faith." Another says: "Remember the Bible is not a science book. The question of science is . . . HOW. How does this work? How does this happen? The question of the Bible is WHY. Why does this work? Why does this happen? If we insist on wearing only our twenty-first century, modern, scientific glasses when we read the Bible, we will miss the deeper meaning of why" (Ryan, "An Owner's Manual for the Bible, p. 115).

- in dialogue: We are told that without the dialogue of the hemorrhaging woman and Jesus, or the dialogue between Jesus and the healed dead child and the child's parents, "the miracles have little meaning" (Whistler, "A Woman's Faith," p. xxvi).

- in the fluid characteristics of an image: "An image is an image, but by exploring it—seeing, hearing, touching, tasting, feeling it—we make it ours. It becomes a part of who we are." Kim Ryan explores all the various and different images of God that might work for different people. She points out that for an abused woman, the image of God as Father may not be effective or welcome, but images of God as Mother, God as Lover, God as Friend may offer new imagery that different people can respond to more comfortably (Ryan, "Sometimes You Just Gotta Break the Rules").

- in God's actions: "In the beginning was the word and the word was with God, and the word became flesh and dwelt among us. So we begin with God's actions." Margaret Ann compares God's actions with God's people's actions, saying that we all "crucify him [Jesus]," and we keep doing it "every day." Even in helping us through the dilemma of what do we do with our blundering selves, "God took the first step, by becoming human in the person of Jesus. . . . God continues to act first." Her sermon then is a list of actions we can take "because God took action first" (Crain, "What Should I Do," p. 201).

- in our own stories: In another sermon, Margaret Ann brings us back to the very beginning of this chapter and the importance of women's life experiences as the foundation for their stories and sermons. The stories of the Bible, Carol tells us, are our stories. Margaret Ann preaches about God's actions by telling her congregation to reflect on their own actions theologically, to ask "what effect the action has had on your understanding of yourself and your understanding of God?" Do this, she says, by telling your story: "Our stories are probably our most accessible resource for coming to know God" (Crain, "What Should I Do?" pp. 202, 203).

- in being vulnerable: On how we ought to respond to the book of Job, or how we deal with pain and the fear that God has deserted us, Kim's sermon on Job offers us a God who says, "I give life but I do not control it. Just like the loving mother who gives life but cannot control it." This preacher hears the words of a God unwilling to control people's lives. This unorthodox reading of Job deemphasizes the God who is always testing Job's loyalty and highlights the God who releases Job to the world. Thus, Kim's sermon allows for the possibility of a vulnerable God, a God who feels a mother's pain.

This suggestion of God's vulnerability arises frequently in the women's sermons. Kim Ryan's sermon compares God's parental feelings toward all humankind with her own feelings toward her first-born, but in *atypical* fashion. She does not emphasize here the parental feelings of protection and care giving, which certainly have been assigned to God before; rather, she focuses her sermon on the parent's vulnerability to pain—to suffering, to loving deeply and completely, to the helpless inability, ultimately, to protect or save the child.

I find women's sermons to be *rarely didactic*; that is, women do not tell their congregations, "This is what you should do." Kim's sermon "An Owner's Manual for the Bible" outlines "Eight Guidelines for Reading the Bible." Clearly, this sermon could have been didactic, but it is not. Kim begins, as usual, with a personal story about her own childhood and adolescent attempts to begin with the first page of the Bible and read it from cover to cover. She tells her congregation that she failed again and again. She encourages her congregation *not* to try to read the Bible straight through, as they'll lose interest. Let me summarize her main points:

(1) Begin with the high points.

(2) Use a Bible dictionary, because it has so much good and helpful information in it.

(3) Read more than one version of the Bible; note the critical differences!

(4) Read and study the Bible in a group.

(5) Take the Bible seriously, which may not mean taking it literally. To demand that the Bible can only be understood in its actual words means that we may even hold the Bible hostage. We may not be permitting the beautiful figurative, the symbolic language, to speak with its rich meaning.

(6) Remember the Bible is not a science book.

(7) Remember the Bible was not intended as a children's book.

(8) Learn to use the Bible as a tool to discover new understanding of God and self.

Her main point: "The Bible is a tool; it is not God. . . . It is about relationship. It is about a love relationship, about God trying to communicate God's love over and over and over again in new and different ways. And about people trying to learn how to respond to that love and to love God back in new and different ways." Like her sermon on different images of God, this sermon is radical and unorthodox, asking her congregation to stretch its collective mind: "The Bible isn't the final word. It is a beginning word. The final word is how we live our lives based on that foundation of love" (Ryan, "An Owner's Manual for the Bible," pp. 116–17).

Rhetorically, in these sermons, the women relate their beliefs "about where God is" to their style of preaching by *relinquishing typical pulpit hierarchical authority and claiming, instead, an authority based on equality and connection.* Except for their enthusiasm for the personal experience story, which of course endorses the use of a first-person singular narrative, the women typically use the collective "we" to talk about themselves and their audience as a collective of Christians. They tell their congregation: "We are like the hemorrhaging woman and the little girl because we are embodied beings" (Whistler, "A Woman's Faith, p. xxvi). And, they say:

There are ten of us (lepers),
ten of us in the story.
We are the lepers
We are despairing—

We see Jesus on the road—
We call out to him. (Millspaugh, "A
    Grateful Heart" p. 73)

In her sermon the following Sunday, Carol Millspaugh drew an analogy between lepers and people with AIDS as she continued to draw on her connection with her congregation (as examined in Chapter 2). Typical of this group of women, Carol turns the argument about who needs to be healed back to the congregation *and herself.* Whatever one might have expected from this sermon on AIDS and its connection with her own congregation members, the actuality was surprising and challenging. She told them:

We need healing.
We need to be healed of our fear.
We need to be healed of our judgments.
We are in danger of not following Christ.

We are in danger of being part of the
    problem.
We need to stretch out our hands.
We are called to reach out like Jesus.

She tells them emphatically:

The issue is not homosexuality,
drug abuse,
sexual promiscuity.

These are not the issues.
(Millspaugh, "Christ's Healing Touch,"
    p. 81)

As she lights the first Advent candle, then, she tells us it represents "God's love and hope and Christ's healing touch for *us.*" A new and radical kind of sermon. "How God loves people and how people try to love God back." A different way of perceiving things.

The *language used in these sermons is often poetic, powerful, sensuous, intimate, and evocative.* Gertrude's "Musings from a Hot Blackberry Patch" I recall with pleasure; we can nearly feel the blistering heat and pricks of the bushes she describes, and Maureen's Pentecost sermon, complete with red balloons bouncing on the ceiling to remind us of the "flames of fire." I recall Peggy's descriptions of how she felt closest to God when nursing her infant in the cold, dark hours of the night while the rest of the world slept; and I shall never forget the sermon where one preacher described how she made "real bread." You could almost taste and smell it. I was completely taken with Kim's story about her friend's "weaning party" and her own story about sitting in the dark in the hospital room contemplating the danger of caring for a newborn child; I was equally moved by Tamsen's image of the hemorrhaging woman and her touch of faith on Jesus' garment. This language is intimately connected to the content of these sermons. The images reflect the power of the visual, connecting the mental to the spiritual goals of the preachers and drawn from their own life experiences.

Above and beyond the significance of the characteristics outlined thus far in this chapter *lies the power of personal experience stories used by women in their sermons to frame their messages.* Without a doubt, the use of these personal accounts of women's experiences provides the best evidence for how these sermons are uniquely the creations of women. The significance of this observation cannot be underestimated. The historical use of *exempla,* or secular stories told for a (moral) purpose in a sermon, can be documented as far back as we have evidence of the orally performed sermon. However, to find women in the pulpit utilizing their own personal experience stories as rhetorical devices is surprising, given that women have claimed the pulpit in large numbers only fairly recently and given that their "right" to the pulpit has not been firmly established in many religious contexts. It might make perfectly good sense to find that women, like their male counterparts, often tell stories that have a life in the sermon gristmill, stories taken from books on the market for that express purpose, or apocryphal "preacher's stories" that have traveled from sermon to sermon, or jokes, or those rather generic stories that begin, "Jane and Tim had not been married very long when. . . ." Audiences accept these typical stories as rhetorical devices, not actually meant to be believed, told as exempla, stories that make a point, that punctuate the main points of the story— provocative stories that are more likely to linger in the listener's mind than the sermon itself.[10]

Women in our culture generally have been taught that, like children, they are to be seen and not heard. Most women of the "baby-boom" generation, our mother's generation, and our grandmother's generation live out their lives believing that their stories do not matter. We are not taught that our personal experiences are significant; we rarely think anyone might be interested in them. Although personally, or within an all-women's group, we may learn to prize our stories and those of our sisters, we have not found that very much of the public is interested in them. To find women in the pulpit using their private and personal stories as the frame, as the intersecting connections, as the core and essence of their sermons is surprising, indeed. For the first time I am hearing *women's stories and experiences from the pulpit.* From whence comes the courage, the audacity, the willingness to take such a risk? Because women have come to believe in their claim to the pulpit based not on their gender but on their humanity, their stories are recalled, honed, and performed for a mixed, public audience. In these settings, women's stories become stories enhanced, sanctified, endorsed, validated, confirmed, experienced, enjoyed, shared, and celebrated. And how are these private and personal stories embedded in the sermons of preaching women? They are not embedded at all. As the women had explained to me, stories often become the frame of the sermon, the foundation, the essence of the endeavor. Frequently, their sermons will *begin* with a personal story, sometimes *immediately* following the scripture reading, with little or no introduction. For example:

We lived next door to some pretty avid
deer hunters—

in Indiana. (Ryan, "Scraps from the
Table," p. 118)

Or:

It was about twenty-five years ago
that I sat in a congregation
and a minister called my name. (Ryan,

"An Owner's Manual for the Bible,"
p. 109)

Or:

Last Monday evening, one of our
deacons

told me the most amazing fish story
I'd ever heard.

Or:

My first experience with a plumb-line

took place about twenty years ago.

Or:

Several years ago our family had the
wonderful experience
of living in Hawaii

while my husband was a pastor.
(Millspaugh, "Christ's Healing
Touch," p. 77)

As the women weave their sermons, spiraling and curving, from scripture to experience, from experience to scripture, from relationship to God and back again, these personal stories become the frame for the sermons. After weaving into the story and away from it, like the strands of the helix, the preachers bring the sermon back to the images invoked in the stories they have shared. "Sermons are spirals," one preacher told us, and they are.

As I heard women's stories from the pulpit, it became apparent to me just how much *being female* affected their sermons. Using the first-person pronoun "I" in these sermons validated these women's experiences, but the preachers were also able to easily weave a connection with their audience by using the collective "we," at once embracing all the members of their audience. *Through their first-person stories, women's stories, the women were providing a new validation for the connection between women's lives and their personal, intimate relationship with the sacred.* However, a woman's stance *as a woman*, relating her experiences to her audience and relating her own experiences to her perception of God in her life, was not an exclusive stance. The stories of the women authenticate the immediacy of an immanent God prepared and willing to enter into relationship with them and with all other humans, in mutual and collective connection *in spite of differences.*

Let me provide an example. I recall a lively discussion we had several years ago about the group's dislike for a then popular song, "From a Distance," sung by Bette Midler. The discussion surprised me. The song, with its obviously religious overtones, had made it to the top of the charts. But the women were clear in voicing their objections: the song contradicted so much of what they were trying to convey in their sermons, in their lives, and in their ministry—that God is immediate, close, intimate, connected, that people develop a relationship with each other and with God and that the essence of God can be felt at the heart of that connection, in *right relationship* with other humans and with God. The lyrics of the song, in contrast, suggest "God is watching us from a distance, God is watching us." That transcendent image of God as distant, judging, inaccessible, and "watching" is an image they say they work hard to modify in the minds of their congregations. Like Celie in Alice Walker's novel *The Color Purple*, they believe the image of God as a white-haired old man in the sky *must* be replaced with images that are more accessible and immediate. Furthermore, Midler's song tells us that from God's point of view, "at a distance," the world looks all greens and blues, all distinctions are erased, people seem the same, war and peace are indistinguishable. What a terrible picture to paint, they declared. It sounds good, everything and everybody are basically the same, "from a distance." But the reality is that people are *not* the same, and their differences should be recognized and celebrated, not erased. Such a "rosy" picture ignores, as well, all the pain and suffering that is part of the reality of the earth: abuse, poverty, murder, rape, and war. If God's distance prevents God from recognizing differences and from becoming intimately involved with people's realities, then what kind of God is that for them to share with their congregations? Where's the "good news" in that song? They had a point.

Their personal stories are poignant, deeply private, and sometimes angry. Kim Ryan tells the story in her sermon "An Owner's Manual for the Bible" about receiving her first Bible in the third grade. She tells the congregation she remembers the minister "called my name and I went forward and he handed me *my* Bible. . . . I remember holding that brand new bible, crisp and fresh, opening the cover, and there was *my* name. Someone had written my name." (Ryan, "An Owner's Manual for the Bible," p. 109). Her story—*her name*—called out loud in church; her Bible. She conveys her innocent pride in her new possession; she invites her audience to remember their first Bible, their sense of pride and awe in receiving this sacred gift. And she aligns herself with her parishioners who may have vowed to read the Bible from cover to cover and failed. She admits she got only to chapter 3 in Genesis "and that is as far as I got." She renewed the same vow, she tells her congregation, a few years later when she was baptized. This time she got to chapter 26 of Numbers: "Does anybody remember chapter 26 of Numbers? There are about 4,000 'begats.' I quit. I couldn't do it."

Neither could most of the people in her audience, probably. They laughed knowingly. Telling this story about her own failure to read the Bible all the way through takes courage; it is not a story told to inflate her own image. On the contrary, it is intended to highlight her own shortcomings, to create a link, a space for understanding, between herself and her audience. Kim continues the story about her relationship with her Bible and recounts how, later, in seminary, she began to hear things about the Bible she had never heard before. And she admits not only to amazement, but also to *anger.* "I didn't know that!" she recalls thinking.

I didn't know that there were two creation stories in Genesis. I'd never read that part! . . . that one starts with God creating the sky and the earth and the animals and man and woman at the same time. And the other story, written by a different author, tells of God creating man and vegetation and animals and then woman. I didn't know that. (Ryan, "An Owner's Manual for the Bible," p. 110)

She explains her anger; she tells her congregation she had grown up in the church, had been in Sunday School almost every Sunday of her life, had been to church camp, *just like most of them.* Quietly, she whispers: "I was angry." Then, unexpectedly, her voice becomes strident: "Why did not somebody give me some guidelines and some instructions, an 'owner's manual' to help me understand this wonderful book—[softly now] the Bible?" She connects with her audience and shares her pride, her awe, and her anger. Her sermon challenges them not to make the same mistakes.

The stories told in these sermons are built on a reality based in women's experiences of connection and interrelatedness. Relationships, vulnerability, love, empathy, shared concerns, dialogue, and connection are the crucial themes that run throughout the sermons in every aspect—structure, language, storytelling, personal experience stories, and point of view. A textual analysis of the sermons, similar to what we might construct for a poem, a short story, an epic, or a novel, reveals more than a text dissected into oral formulas, poetic devices, the use of imagery, assonance and allieration. Our analyses also seeks to reconnect text and context, text and creator, text and audience, text and the world.

The Women's Response to My Analysis

On February 16, 1994, I met with the women in this study to talk more about preaching. I had been studying their sermons and trying to write this chapter of the book. I needed their help.

Gertrude began to respond to my questions:

It seems to me that in preaching we are talking about what you are really sure of, or want to be sure of. The question becomes how we know what we know and how do we share what we know?

I was intrigued:
"What *do* you know, and how do you share that?"

Kim answered.

That's a good question. What we think we're doing up there and how it is perceived may be two different things. We have one new congregation member who recently characterized the senior pastor's preaching as intellectual and mine as emotional. We both thought about this a bit, and my first response was, "Oh, so you don't think my sermons are intellectual?" And, of course, he responded with, "So, you don't think my sermons are emotional?" See, we both responded in that way; we both sort of took offense.

We talked for awhile about this stereotype of women bringing the emotional, the heartfelt, to preaching and the idea that, somehow, they are not "intellectual" as well.
Kim offered this:

I think women bring a willingness to talk about ourselves and our personal story.

This comment rang a bell for Clare, who agreed:

I use stories that I really connect with. And, actually, I know that my sermons are much more "intellectual" than my husband's. I recall a clergy friend saying, "My part in being here today is to be the most open, clear channel for the spirit of God to work through me that I can be, that's my responsibility for the next two hours. Your responsibility is to connect with me." So it is a dialogue, even if the congregation never says anything, in consciousness it's a dialogue. In my church 150 people are there needing and wanting different things, whatever their hearts are desiring—that's being addressed. And we're all one with God, so it's automatically a dialogue. We're not doing it *to* them—it's not me just delivering stuff to them. In consciousness, it's always a two-way flow. In my church, that 150 people changes dramatically from Sunday to Sunday, and I can feel that, even if I don't consciously say "so and so is missing and so and so is here this week." I feel that shift in my energy. There are days, and maybe the rest of you have experienced this, too, I'll have a whole talk written out and I won't give that talk. It will come out differently—so it is a dialogue.

At this point Kim laughed:

Oh, no, that never happens to me! I admire that. I stick pretty close to my written sermon.

Clare agreed:

I generally do, too, but there are times I just feel that something just takes over and I go off in another direction . . . and it feels good, it just flows, something has taken over and my talk becomes something very different than I had intended it to be. I attribute that to the energy of the consciousness of the people there and what they may need.

Peggy, who pastors two small churches and travels to both every Sunday morning, agreed with this notion of flexibility in dialogue with her audience:

That's why it's so difficult for the first weeks and months at a new place, because I don't know these people! I do the same thing. I go in with the same basic idea of where I'm going, but I have two different congregations. Two weeks ago the sermons were entirely different. They started out with the same basic idea for the first about four sentences, then they went [swisssh—gestures two different directions at once]. I went from manuscripts to outlines, to now about four words written out to cue me in what direction I might want to go. If I would go in with an outline, I would end up reading it. Or I would go off in another direction and would feel obligated to come back. Now I just think I'm going to go in here with some kind of faith and courage, because before I was making a mess of the whole thing when I would wander off.

(The reader is invited to read two sermons by Peggy Jeffries, "Bearing Fruit I" and "II," pp. 41–52, both preached on the same Sunday morning but delivered to two different congregations and preached differently to reflect the needs of the different audiences.)

Kim seemed to be thinking out loud:

Actually, our first service at 8:00 is dialogic. I introduce the topic and then they take it and get into small groups and talk about it. In that service, actually, there is a lot of give and take. And in that one I don't use an outline. Same topic. And I can always tell if it's connecting, because it either will really connect at that service or it won't. I've modified between the first service and the others. I'll even add, "Well, at the first service, we talked about this and this."

Maureen began to tell her story about the day she "played dead" on the floor in an attempt to experiment with different forms of "sermon making":

I've tried to break out of the traditional mode with my little plays—like last year when I did the Judgment Day.

She told the story we had all heard before, then offered another idea:

Someone in my church last week was suggesting something that is not exactly a dialogue, but is rather something like a "set up." To bring the subject of inclusive language front and center, to start talking about that, and then have someone in the audience sitting there shaking his head. And then I might say: "Well, Mark, I see you shaking your head there, do you disagree?" "Well, yes, as a matter of fact, I do . . ." Then you have a real dialogue.

I asked them whether they felt sermons were effective and necessary. They did.

Clare was the first:

I enjoy going to hear someone put ideas and words and experiences together—it's like an art form. And that's what I try to practice. It's like why go to a play? You don't get to get up and become part of it. But you get to experience the magic when something works well. And I get feedback when it works well and I know when it's happened. I also know when I give a talk and it didn't work well, or if I'm off track. Sometimes I feel like I was really close to sharing what I wanted to convey, but it didn't quite get there and I have to keep working at it. I want to perfect the art form of sharing who I am and what I believe in in a real succinct and dramatic way—in a sense it is a performance. Also, there *is* an underlying element of dialogue, because what is brought out is the audience's response.

Kim agreed:

I want to respond to it being an art form. I think it *is* an art form, a creative art form.

Peggy saw it as an opportunity to share, a time to connect the audience with the Gospels:

I find myself selecting those passages that are just outside the norm. I'll use the lectionary, but I'll select the Old Testament verses, for example, or look at it some Sunday and choose not to use the lectionary readings. I try to connect; I want to connect what's in the biblical witness to where we live today. I want to reintroduce them to the stories. Some of the stories are just phenomenal and surprising. And there is a kind of dialogue—sometimes I'll talk to them one Sunday about something and then the next Sunday I'll say, "Well, last Sunday we talked about such and such, what have you been thinking about that over the week, let's talk about that."

Kim was still musing:

I think we are articulating what they know and perhaps have not yet been able to articulate.

"How do they know it?" I wanted to know.
Her answer:

Same way we know it. Experience.

I persisted. She responded, all patience with me:

Well, I think more of them do than we give them credit.

Clare came back with:

I would agree with that. From my belief system, there is an inner wisdom. They may not know all the Bible stories—depending what denomination they grew up in—or the religious language, but there is an inner wisdom that every one of us needs to be reminded of and reminded of often. That's why, basically, if we looked at our talks[11] probably each one of us has a personal theme or certain subjects that would stretch throughout a lifetime that we could pick up, because there are things that we know that we need to keep remembering. I keep speaking because I need to still learn a lot of it and I speak it out. I think there is power in verbalizing something. When someone else says something, I often think, well, I knew that, but, gee, I needed to hear that from someone else today.

I reminded them of what a Margaret Ann used to say—that "preaching was living the questions." "How would Margaret Ann respond to what you just said?" I asked Clare.

Maureen was quick to get us back on track:

Well, I think you are translating our statements about "what we know" into *answers* and it's not necessarily answers—

Kim couldn't wait:

I agree, articulate the questions, explore and articulate the exploration of the answers to the questions. "What you know" doesn't have anything to do with objective fact—

Maureen interjected and continued:

—or knowledge acquired. Most people know there is something wrong with an image of God in which God would use a rapist and a murderer to call someone to heaven or take someone "home." I think people know that. Am I wrong? Do I know this just so strongly, no one else know it?

The others agreed. And Kim added:

There have been some real mental gymnastics people do to get into this kind of thinking. It was like when we were reading Sallie McFague and she was talking about rethinking the atonement and we say, 'I knew this!' [hits her hand with her other hand] It never felt right. It never fit. And she just says it, clearly and well. That's the kind of knowing that we are talking about. —[to me] You just know it!

Gertrude pointed out:

For Jewish scholars trying to understand, say, the Holocaust, the question is why does God allow this to happen? The question is always bigger than the answer.

And Maureen responded:

That reminds me of the Elie Weisel story about the little boy in the concentration camp who watches another little boy being hung. And someone behind him says, "So, where is your God now, where's your God now, where's your God now?" And finally, the little boy says, "Up there on the gallows." You can't have it both ways—that God is all-powerful and God is good.

They were back nearly where they had begun:

So, again, what we know are the questions.

I told them, "I have identified one characteristic of your sermons as addressing the question, 'Where is God'? more than you ask the question 'Who is God'? Or 'What is God'? Similarly, you often choose an unexpected portion of the scripture to preach on, giving it a new twist, a different angle. Could you talk about this?"

Gertrude responded immediately:

I am reminded of how in art the artist is always trying to get people to see things new, to see them fresh, to see them in a different way. You look at things and you always see what you expect to see. Artists go to all sorts of lengths to get you to look at it and see it differently. I see that in relation to this. We're saying, this is reality that we've looked at so often that we see the same thing, and we look at it with our usual filters, our usual schema. Now, we're saying open it all up and look at it again. Remember when we were working on your other book[12] and we were talking about this marvelous tapestry of reality [of their life stories] and all the interweaving and showing how wonderfully marvelous it was and not wanting to put it in boxes, to simplify it, but wanting to see it in all its complexity? I'm seeing this going on here in the sermon making as well.

"Would it be fair to say, 'women are doing this'?" I asked them all.

Well, I think what this analogy and what was just said fit exactly—I think there's your book. What would it be like to compare it with artists who were on the fringe who began painting, expressing, offering new images of reality? They would have done something very different.

The others agreed:

—The images were old; they were *trite*.
—People were no longer *seeing* with the old images.

"Then," I pushed them, "then you see things differently from the margins."

—Of course.
—Certainly.
—You bet.
—No kidding.
—Absolutely.

One woman seemed to be thinking out loud:

Well, we have all certainly grown up in a patriarchal society where there are certain ways, especially about women in the church, certain things are done, certain ways Scripture was interpreted. And there have always been even men who have stepped out of that and done things differently. But women, especially through the women's movement, say in the last forty years, have really had to push out and question everything, and as Tamsen [motions to the woman next to her on the sofa] was just saying, we have to think about the lens through which we see everything. And before we've seen everything through the patriarchal model and the women's movement has been about questioning words, questioning habits, questioning ways of being, so maybe we've been pushed to question more and to a larger degree.

This speech got a response from everyone; they all began talking at once, but Kim's voice could be heard saying:

Well, I think one of the defining characteristics of the patriarchy is dualism, which is the separation of body and mind, intellect and experience, men and women. And in this, women have been associated more with the body, with the physical, more with experience. That whole thing with the two pastors, one makes me think and the other makes me cry, fits in a sense with that. But what I think women are doing is, instead of trying to fit into this dualism that we have all tried to fit into, is to say, "It doesn't work, this dualism!" This all goes back to the interconnectedness of everything. It's not either or—and experience is important, so, okay, I'll make you cry, but that doesn't mean that I can't make you think as well. The key is that from the margins you do see things differently and what we see is valid and important.
—And the other thing that is happening is that anything you read now about the emerging worldview is this new worldview.
—Exactly.
—What is dying—the world, that is, the "bygone world," the world that is disappearing is patriarchal—
—dualistic—
—Dualistic, hierarchical, "power is dominance" kind of thinking—

I played devil's advocate: "And you think this world is dying out?" They responded:

—Oh, it's going to kick and scream.
—It is! But, you know, this whole uproar about the "Re-Imagining Conference" that the Methodists and Presbyterians have stirred up.[13] Why is it causing such a problem? Because they're a dying beast, and they see this reimagining that women are doing as claiming their own place and they are so scared, you know? [she throws up her hands in mock horror].

Clare, who had not attended the Re-Imagining Conference, had been listening and thinking:

I think all of this has something to do with dialogue—and I don't know if it's just women. A basic belief of mine is that human thought and understanding is always evolving. We're always pulling out of the "God-mind" new understanding, a wider scope, of who we are as spiritual beings, as human beings. I think the very act of writing talks and giving talks, and dialoguing with people, of all of ministry actually is part of drawing out that understanding. What I'm hearing about Sophia is a real need to claim back something that has been denied to us in all the patriarchy and that's why it's looked on as very threatening. But preaching in itself is an integral part of what is bringing forth in human consciousness new awareness, asking the questions. We don't know the answers. God is a mystery. But we keep asking the questions. I think our understanding continues to evolve, and I think that's a power. I do think there is a move away from hierarchy. I know there certainly is in Unity. But even in Unity, which tends to be very progressive, there has still tended to be a lot of male, top of the pyramid, all decisions made by men. The star, you know, gets up on Sunday morning. There's a real move away from that toward community building, where we are all more working together. Ultimately it's our togetherness that becomes more important than just one person making the decisions and doing it all. I see that all as an evolution that is happening. And every time I write a talk, I really feel I am helping draw forth from the great knowledge, from God's mind, whatever, yet I don't pretend to have all the answers, but the talks often ask the right questions and people respond to that.

I asked: "Where is God, if we look at the artfulness in a sermon?" Tamsen answered me:

Well, in artfulness—in the creation story. It starts with creativity and with that image of God.

Kim agreed:

We're not talking about 'art-ful' as our showing off in flowery language, but artful, a work of art, a balanced work of skill.

Gertrude was inspired:

If you stand in front of a painting and it moves something in you, it resonates, you may not have any words for it, and that's what a Sunday sermon or lesson can also touch— something at a different level. That's what I mean by a work of art.

Kim:

Like drama, or like my son looking at the Muir print and asking if it is a picture of God. It's all of that.

Peggy:

It's something beyond the rigidity of 'three points' in a talk, spit it out—chew it up for them and spit it out, and they'll get it. And what I hear us saying is that we draw something out of others by our stories, by our personal stories, but also by ideas, too; it's never just one or the other. Women bring both.

Our discussion reminded me of something Carol Millspaugh had said in another context about how a very well-known traveling male minister had interpreted the biblical scene of Jesus walking on the water and how differently *she* interpreted the same passage. Her reasons are telling and seem to be a fitting conclusion to a discussion of how women's lives and perceptions differently shape their sermons. Carol related to us:

He retold the story very dramatically, providing us with a vivid mind picture of the water and the boat being buffeted about and the disciples afraid, and then, there was Jesus. And the preacher said, "The point of this story is that Jesus came to them and Jesus was above them, he was above the storm. And then Peter got out of the boat and walked on the water and came to Jesus above the storm, up out of it." But I see it so differently. I think the point of that story is that Jesus joins them in the middle of the storm, in their struggle, there.[14]

The conversations I had with the women in this study on sermons and sermon making validate my analysis of women's sermons. What these clergy say about women's sermons as skillful art forms, filled with stories, images, and experiences that link their lives with the lives of their congregations confirms my own reading of the significance of their use of personal experience stories as a rhetorical device that conjures images of connection, interaction, and relationship—human to human and human to God. Women are calling for connection in a disconnected time. They articulate the questions, the sense of vulnerability, the insecurities that come from living in a disconnected time. They speak from the margins, they say, but they invite all who are listening to join them there on the edges.

I like this image of the women standing at the margins invoking a new era. And the floating multi-stranded helix reminds us that the edges are not the margins at all but are rather the essence of the model itself, vital to the integrity of the image, working in tandem with the core and with the other strands, weaving and converging—parallel differences and similarities, dancing in harmony.

Notes

1. See Elaine J. Lawless, "Narrative in the Pulpit: Persistent Use of *Exempla* in Vernacular Religious Contexts."
2. See William Clements, "The Rhetoric of the Radio Ministry."
3. See, e.g., Carol Flake, *Redemptorama: Culture, Politics, and the New Evangelicalism.*
4. Thomas C. Oden, *Ministry Through Word and Sacrament.*
5. Folklorists who have studied the oral, formulaic, and stylistic characteristics of sermons, in both African-American and Anglo-American traditions, include Gerald Davis, Jeff Todd Titon, Elaine J. Lawless, William Clements, and Catherine Peck.
6. William Bascom, "The Four Functions of Folklore," in Alan Dundes, ed., *The Study of Folklore.*

7. See Richard Bauman, *Verbal Art as Performance.*

8. Krista Ratcliffe, *Anglo-American Feminist Challenges to the Rhetorical Traditions: Virginia Woolf, Mary Daly, and Adrienne Rich.*

9. Clifford Geertz's holistic approach also guides my methods here. See his "Thick Description: Toward an Interpretive Theory of Culture."

10. For an overview of the historical and contemporary uses of *exempla,* see Lawless, "Narrative in the Pulpit."

11. Clare, as a member of the Unity Movement, always refers to sermons as "talks."

12. She is referring to my previous book, *Holy Women, Wholly Women.*

13. See Chapter Five for a discussion of the Re-Imagining Conference.

14. Dialogue session, March 2, 1994.

An Owner's Manual for the Bible

Kɪᴍ Rʏᴀɴ
Broadway Christian Church-Disciples of Christ
Columbia, Missouri
September 16, 1990

"The law of the Lord is perfect, reviving
    the soul;
the decrees of the Lord are sure, making
    wise the simple;
the precepts of the Lord are right,
    rejoicing the heart;
the commandment of the Lord is clear,
    enlightening the eyes;
the fear of the Lord is pure, enduring
    forever;
the ordinances of the Lord are true and
    righteous altogether.
More to be desired are they than gold,
    even much fine gold;
sweeter also than honey,
and drippings of the honeycomb." [Psalm
    19: 7–10, NRSV]

You may have noticed
that in the service following this one,
at 11:00,
we are giving Bibles to our third graders.
Sixteen third graders
will receive their Bibles.

Today we celebrate.
It was about twenty-five years ago
that I sat in a congregation
and a minister called my name
and I went forward
and he handed me *my* Bible.
And I remember going back
and sitting down in that pew—
I don't recollect a whole lot
about the rest of that service,
but I remember holding that brand new
Bible,
crisp and fresh,
opening the cover
and there was *my name*.
Someone had written
my name
in a very, very pretty handwriting—
much like Debbie does for us here
in the Bibles we give.
And I remember
sitting there and holding that Bible
and promising myself,
and promising God,

that I was going to start in Genesis
and I was going to read it all the way to
    Revelation.
And I went home that afternoon
and I started reading
and I got to chapter 3 in Genesis
and that is as far as I got.

Well, a few years later,
I was baptized
and that seemed like a good time to
    renew that promise
that I had made,
so I promised again,
I'm going to start at Genesis
and read until I get to Revelation.
And I started in Genesis
and I made it to chapter 26 of Numbers
does anybody remember chapter 26 of
    Numbers?
There are about 4,000 "begats."
I quit.
I couldn't do it.

It was a number of years later
that I found myself
sitting in a seminary classroom,
listening to a teacher
tell about the Bible.
And I began to hear things
that I had never heard before
and I was amazed.
And as I sat there,
with my mouth open, [nearly a whisper]
I could not help but think
"I didn't know that!"
I didn't know that there were two creation
    stories
in Genesis.

I'd never read that part!
I didn't know
that there were
different
creation stories
in Genesis,
that one
starts with God creating the sky and the
    earth
and the animals
and man and woman
at the same time.
And the other story,
written by a different author,
tells of God creating man
and vegetation
and animals
and then woman.
I didn't know that. [very softly]

And I didn't know
that the four Gospels
in the New Testament
didn't all tell exactly the same story.
It was a surprise to me
that the Gospels of Matthew, Mark, Luke,
    and John
were not photographs of Jesus' life,
but instead
were like four artists looking at the same
    model
and painting
and creating their
picture
of that person.
They brought their own style
to that portrait
and they had certain characteristics

that they chose to emphasize
and tell about.
Well, I didn't know that. [very softly]

And after I got over my
surprise
about how much I didn't know,
I felt angry.
Why hadn't someone
told me?
Why didn't somebody
tell me about this incredible book,
the Bible
and the richness
and the treasures
that were inside.

I had grown up in the church;
I had been in Sunday school almost
    every Sunday of my life!
I had been to church camp.
I was angry. [very softly]
Why did not somebody [quite loud]
give me some guidelines
and some instructions,
an "owner's manual"
to help me understand
this wonderful book—
the Bible? [very softly]

You know owner's manuals can be pretty
    important—
not the ones that go out of the box and
    into the drawer.
We have a drawer just for those,
you know,
you take them out,
they go right in
and you never look at them.

No, the ones that you really need
can be very, very helpful.
Not too long ago,
my dad came for a visit to our house
and before he had arrived
he and Grandma had decided
that grandson Gage needed a swing set.
So Gage and Grandpa
hand-in-hand headed to the Sears
    catalog order department,
because, mind you,
no ordinary swing set would do.
It had to be super duper deluxe model.
Ordered the swing set.
Grandpa went home.

Six weeks later the swing set arrived
in a box
about this tall. [gestures far above her
    head]
One Sunday afternoon Bill and I decide,
o.k., we'll put that swing set together.
We opened up the box and we started
    taking out a piece
and we'd take out more pieces
and we'd take out bags that have bags of
    pieces inside.
And we laid them all out in the back yard,
and for about ten minutes
we'd look and we'd maneuver
and we'd fiddle
and it didn't take us long
to figure out that we were missing the
    most important piece—
the manual—
the instructions.
Well, sure enough
it was at the bottom of the box.
So, we pulled it out

and it made it so much easier.
It only took us seven hours
to put that swing set together!
Seven hours! [in a hoarse whisper, for
    emphasis; congregation laughs]
But I am here to tell you
that if we had not had that set of
    instructions,
we would still be in the backyard with four
    million pieces
all over the yard.
They made a difference.

It makes a difference.
When we give our third graders their
    Bibles this morning,
we're giving them more than a gift.
We are giving ourselves
a big responsibility.

What kind of guidelines will we offer
    them?
What kind of accompanying
"owner's manual"
will we give to them?

How will we teach them about this Bible?

How will we
help them
make this Bible a part of their lives
so that it will be as the psalmist declared,
"something that revives their soul,
that brings joy in their lives,
that gives them light,
something that will be more precious to
    them than gold.
How will we do that?

I have been thinking a lot about that this
    week
and I have come up with eight guidelines,
for the third graders and for their
    parents—
in particular.
But they are also for anyone
who is looking for a way for the Bible
to have a more essential,
a meaningful place in their lives.
You will find on one of the inserts
on one side, it has a place,
labeled one-through-eight,
where if you chose to,
you can write down these suggestions
and these guidelines as I go along.
And if you chose to,
I would encourage you to put them in
    your Bible
and to keep them there
as some instructions,
as some suggestions.

Number one.
Begin with the high points.
Don't do as I did,
don't start out in Genesis
and make your way,
all the way to Revelation.
Begin with some of those high places.
Begin with those two creation stories
in Genesis.
Begin with the Ten Commandments
that came to people who were searching
    for a home
and for a life
in a new place.
Begin with Psalms

that speak out
of a God who is personal
and a God who is real.
Begin with the parables of Jesus.
They appear simple
but they are very complex.
Begin with the Scripture readings
that we name and we read in worship
on Sunday morning.

If we start out at the beginning
trying to go from Genesis to Revelation,
there is a good chance that we are going
  to get discouraged,
that we're going to get bogged down
and we may never go on to discover
the treasures that the Bible holds.
Begin with the high points.

Number two.
If you get lost, use a Bible dictionary,
or a Bible commentary.
A Bible dictionary,
or a Bible commentary
are wonderful things
that can tell all kinds of information
about the Bible.
It may help you understand a word
or it can tell who wrote that particular
  book,
when it was written,
why it was written,
to whom it was written—
it does make a difference.
Bridging the gap of the differences
of that day and our day can be made
  easier
when we have some insight into the
  background

of the sixty-six different books
that are all a part of the Bible.
If you need a suggestion for a good Bible
  dictionary,
try studying the Bible
with the Bible dictionary in hand—
it makes a big difference.
Try it.

Number three.
Read different versions or translations of
  the Bible.
There are many.
There is the Good News Bible,
the American Standard,
the King James,
I hear there is a new King James version
  coming out.
There is a new Revised Standard
  Version;
that's the version that we are giving our
  third graders today
because it brings the newest,
the best work of scholarship that they
  know—
all together.
But the benefit of reading
different versions
is other versions can offer a slightly
  different perspective
or understanding of a word.
And especially if we're reading familiar
  verses
if we read it in a different version,
it may be just enough different to catch
  us off-guard
and say something new to us.
Quick commercial:

The Christian literature display in the
  fellowship hall
has new copies of that New Standard
  Revised Version,
take time to look at it.

Number four.
Read and study in a group.
Reading the Bible privately can be
  inspirational,
there is no question of that,
but reading
and discussing
the Bible
in a group
can stretch
and challenge
or confirm
our understandings.
Most of the Bible was written to groups—
not to individuals,
for individual direction.
The prophets wrote to a nation,
the psalmists to a worshipping
  congregation,
the gospels and most of the letters of
  Paul
were written to early Christian
  communities for a reason,
it was written for a group
and if we read it in a group,
we may find a deeper meaning
a deeper understanding,
as individuals, certainly,
but also as a community of people
who gather together and live our faith
  together.

Number five.

Take the Bible seriously.
Take the messages of the Bible
seriously
and the words
and the pages.
In recent years—
and in not so recent years—
Christians have held other Christians
hostage
with one question:
Do you take the Bible literally?
If you say no,
then you may stand accused of not
  taking the Bible seriously—
or of not really being a Christian.
If you say yes,
there may come a time
when you feel the conflict
when reason can't ignore the reality—
there are two different creation stories.
There are four versions
of the resurrection of Jesus Christ
that are not identical.
It makes a difference
how we understand that word
literal.
The dictionary defines literal
as being based on actual words,
not figurative or symbolic
words.
To demand
that the Bible can only be understood
in its actual words
means that we may even hold the Bible
  hostage.
We may not be permitting
the beautiful, figurative,
the symbolic language
to speak with its rich meaning.

Taking the Bible literally
does not necessarily mean that we take
   it seriously.
Taking the Bible seriously
does not necessarily mean we must take
   it literally.
Take the Bible seriously.

Which brings me to Number six.
Remember
the Bible is not a science book.
It was not written as a science book.
The question of science is HOW.
How does this work?
How does this happen?
The question of the Bible
is WHY.
Why does this work?
Why does this happen?
Why was I created?
Why did Jesus come?
If we insist on wearing only our
   twenty-first century,
modern, scientific glasses
when we read the Bible,
we will miss the deeper meaning of why.

Number seven.
Remember the Bible is more than a
   children's book.
If we try to make it a children's book,
then we are tempted to leave it behind
when we are no longer children.
Serious reading of the Bible reveals
that there are some very serious adult
   stories there.
There are some R-rated stories there!
Or at least PG-13—

that will make the third graders go home
   and read the Bible,
I am sure.
The Bible was written for adults.
If you missed it as children,
don't worry,
this church has two Sunday school
   classes
that are Bible study classes;
there is an adult evening Sunday group
that meets to study the Bible,
and our Christian education department
is right now looking into a broadscale
adult Bible series
to help us grow in our understanding
of the Bible for us as adults.

Number eight.
Learn to use the Bible as a tool
to understanding God
and self.
Learn to use the Bible as a tool
to understanding God and self.
The Bible is a tool;
it is not God.
In fact the Bible has a word
for those things
that we try to make God that aren't
   God—
it's called idolatry,
and if we idolize the Bible,
we run the risk of putting it above the
   ongoing,
the present work of God
that is in the world
and is in each one of us.
We run the risk of making God static—
bound between bindings and pages.
A real witness of Scripture,

the real witness of the Bible
is that God is alive.
God is present
God is working
in our lives.
It was true then,
and it tells us that it is true,
now.
As a tool,
it is important to know how to use it.

There is a story told about the man
who decides to purchase a new saw
to help clear away some of the property
    that he owned.
Of course in Columbia right now,
he could be in big trouble for doing that,
but as the story goes,
the salesman showed him the latest
    chainsaw
and promised him that it could cut three
    to four cords a day.
The man took it home and the first time
    he took it out,
and it barely cut one cord.
So the next day he got up an hour earlier
    and he worked really hard
but he just had just a little over one cord.
And the next day,
he got up even earlier and he worked
    even harder
and the most he got was a cord and a
    half.
Well, this was ridiculous.
He took the chainsaw back to the store
and told the salesman it wasn't
    producing as he'd been promised.
The salesman was puzzled, said,

"I can't understand what's the problem."
He pulled the cord, the chainsaw started,
the man sprung back and said, "WHAT in
    the world is that noise?"
[loudly; the congregation laughs]

Knowing how to use the tool
is just as important as having it.
Part of discovering the richness
the beauty
the meaning
of the Scriptures
is learning how to pull the cord
so those words
and those verses
and those stories
can come alive.

Those eight guidelines:
Begin at the high points,
if you get lost—
before you get lost—
use a Bible dictionary.
Read more than one version.
Read and study in a group.
Take the Bible seriously.
Remember it is not a science book.
Remember it is more than a children's
    book.
And learn to use it
as a tool
to discover.

But most important,
the Bible is about relationship.
It is about a love relationship,
about God trying to communicate God's
    love

over and over and over again
in new and different ways.
And about people trying to learn
how to respond to that love
and to love God back
in new and different ways.
It is about God
working with the wild assortment of folks,
sometimes insignificant,
sometimes very surprising kinds of
  people,
attempting to do the most exciting
and the most wonderful
kinds of things.
And if we learn about this,
it can remind us
that it is possible

for that same thing to happen here
and now.

And one final thing:
If you do read the Bible from Genesis to
  Revelation
don't think you have come to the end.
The story of God loving
and God being loved
goes on and on and on.
The Bible isn't the final word.
It is a beginning word.
The final word
is how we live our lives
based on that foundation
of love.
Amen.

Scraps from the Table

KIM RYAN
Broadway Christian Church-Disciples of Christ
Columbia, Missouri
November 21, 1993

Our Scripture reading for today
is a Psalm of Thanksgiving,
the Twenty-Third Psalm:
"The Lord is my shepherd, I shall not
    want.
He makes me lie down in green
    pastures;
he leads me beside still waters;
he restores my soul.
He leads me in the paths of
    righteousness for his name's sake.
Even though I walk through the valley of
    the shadow of death,
I fear no evil.
For thou art with me.
Thy rod and thy staff they comfort me.
Thou preparest a table before me
in the presence of my enemies.
Thou anointest my head with oil.
My cup overfloweth.
Surely goodness and mercy shall follow
    me all the days of my life,

and I shall dwell in the house of the Lord
for ever and ever." [Psalm 23, King
    James]
Amen.

We lived next door to some pretty avid
    deer hunters—
in Indiana.
Mike was really, really into it
and in fact that's why his wife took it up,
because during deer season
she really didn't ever see him.
So, she took up the bow and arrow,
and she went with him.
They were both pretty appalled
when Bill and I told them that neither one
    of us
had ever tasted deer meat.
They assured us that when,
not if,
when,
they got their deer,

they would bring some of it for us to eat.
One night when Bill and I were both
    about to walk out the door,
there was a knock,
and there at our back door
was their daughter, Candice,
holding a plate that was just heaped with
    meat and gravy.
And Candice said,
"My mom told me to bring this over to
    you because . . ."
And I said,
"I know Candice—"
See, I was in a hurry,
I was going to a meeting—
I said, "I know what that's for.
Thank you very much, tell your folks we
    said thanks a lot."
She sticks it in the door,
I shoved it into the refrigerator,
because we were heading off to our
    meetings.
Bill and I rushed off.
We got back from the meeting,
and we hadn't had time to eat dinner.
So we got that plate out,
and we heated it up and we ate it.
And we thought, hummm,
not bad,
for our first deer meat.
[pause]
A day went by,
and there's a knock on the back door.
And there stands Melanie,
holding a plate,
and it had two thick,
venison steaks on it.
And I said,
"Melanie, what's this?"

"Well, you know we told you we'd bring
    you over some deer meat,
and so I brought this by for you."
And I said, "Oh, you didn't need to do
    that,
just the other day you sent over that plate
with all the meat and gravy,
and we warmed it up,
and had it for dinner after our meeting
    that night."
[pause]
Well! The color was just draining right out
    of her face—
[people are beginning to laugh here]
and her eyes
were getting bigger and bigger—
[more laughter as Kim's eyes, too, get
    bigger and bigger]
And she said, "Those, those were scraps
    for your dog . . ."
[tremendous laughter from the
    congregation at this point; Kim's mouth
    is open in horror, recalling
    that moment]
I haven't eaten deer meat since!
[laughter]
There's a moral to this story.
If you get into too much of a hurry,
you may find yourself eating table scraps,
dog food,
instead of steak.
[pause]
This past week I was at a conference in
    Minnesota,
and I was sitting next to a man at my
    table,
who was telling me about his family.
He's married,
has four children.

His son is a high school senior,
and especially active in football,
plays the saxophone,
and is also on an academic, competitive
    team.
He also has a daughter in high school.
She's also in a specially selected choir,
and she plays two instruments,
the flute and the cello,
and she has to go forty miles to get to
    those cello lessons,
two times a week,
and she is also in gymnastics.
And I thought,
as I talked with him,
you know I know some families like
    yours.
In the church where I go,
I know some families like that.
And I worry sometimes that the church—
that we just sort of contribute to that
    busy-ness,
and people are exhausted from the
    hustle and bustle
of that experience.
And he said, "Oh yeah, I'd forgotten,
they're all four in youth group at church
    on Wednesday night."
And we laughed.
And then he said,
"You know, it just makes me tired telling
    you all this."
And we laughed.
And I said, "Well, I'm so tired listening
    to it
that I'm going to go back to my room and
    take a nap."
And we laughed.
And then Craig said,

"It's destroying us."
And I said, "Excuse me?"
He said, "It's destroying us.
We maybe see each other thirty minutes
    a day,
maybe.
It's killing us."
And we agreed,
we must do something about it.
But we didn't know what,
and we weren't sure how—

And the next day
I came back to my life
and my schedule
and to the things that I was doing.
And one of the things that I had to do
was look ahead
to the Scriptures
for today,
anticipating this sermon,
and looking for just which one would
    give me
information and the inspiration,
that we would want to be a part of our
    service.
And there were four scriptural texts:
Ezekiel, Matthew, one in First
    Corinthians and Psalm 23.
And as I glanced over them
I knew right away
which one of them
was *not* going to be the source of
    information—
It was far
too familiar.
I'd memorized it in second grade.
It's probably the one part of Scripture
that most of us could say we recognize—

Psalm 23:
"The Lord is my shepherd."
Not that one!
No!
I wanted something more intriguing.
I wanted something *provocative!*
Something *challenging!*
And as I kept going through
those other three possibilities,
Psalm 23 quietly tiptoed up behind me
and tapped me on the shoulder
and whispered in my ear,
"Got any green pastures?"
"Got any still waters?"
And I said,
"Go away.
I'm too busy for this
I don't have time to listen to this
I've got a sermon to write
I got a calendar to keep
I got to get Gage to gymnastics
and to the rock club
and maybe to that
introduction to boy scouts meeting
    they've got going;
I've got some important meetings that
    I've got to go to;
And I've got to tell Bill about his
    important meetings
before I go to my important meetings;
I've got suitcases to pack
for our trip to Baltimore for Thanksgiving
and Advent's next Sunday—
Where are those Advent calendars?—
And I've only got about half of my
    Christmas cards done—
now those of you who know me
know that I haven't sent Christmas cards
    in about four years—

[all this is related fast and in a breathless
    manner]
Meanwhile, what's going on?
Psalm 23 says again,
"Got any still waters?
Got any green pastures—
on your list?"

"Who is your shepherd, child?"

And suddenly those old,
familiar,
words of poetry
became quite challenging
and provocative.

I hear my friends say,
"I'm so sorry to call you,
I know you are so very busy.
I promise I won't take much of your time;
I'll really be quick."
Now obviously I do not appear
to be following the shepherd
of still waters.

And I heard my twenty-one-month-old
    say
as I headed out the door,
again,
"Don't leave, Mama."

A friend of mine from St. Louis
came to see us last week
and I hadn't seen her for a while
and she told me something that I hadn't
    known—
that her sister had cancer
and the whole family had been dealing
    with that

and it had been real hard.
But it had, she said, given the family
a new perspective
on what was important—
what's really important.
It has kind of come into focus for them,
family, and friends,
and slowing down,
and enjoying one another.
And she said,
"Why is it that it takes your sister getting
    cancer
to show us how to enjoy the simple
    pleasures of life?"

Like still waters—
like green pastures—
And I have to admit
that I
don't take the time
for those still waters
and those green pastures.
With my friend,
I ask,
What are we going to do?

And it's a question for each of us
who find ourselves dissatisfied
with the scraps from the table.
What are you going to do?

I see Mary only two times a year,
but I can count on Mary to be up
on the latest of parenting skills—
she just reads that stuff
all the time—
So I can count on her to know
the newest approach to managing
    children's behavior

and parents' behavior—
now she says it's called
    neurolinguistics—
you know about that?
You may know about that—
I didn't.
Neurolinguistics.
But she gave me an example
of how it works:
Two children are fighting
over a toy
and the mom comes in and says
"What are you doing?
All you do is fight!
You can't get along,
fight, fight, fight, fight.
You can't play together." [loud and
    emphatic]
And she sends one child out of the room.

Now, what has happened
in the brain of those children
is that they have heard those words
and they're thinking,
"Gee, I thought we were fighting over a
    toy."
But Mom says we can't get along.
Mom says all we do is fight.

Her words go into the brain
and into the behavior
and sets up a pattern—
Neurolinguistics.
It makes sense.
So just think
if neurolinguistics
can create negative behaviors
and patterns,

can it create positive behaviors
and patterns?
I'll have to ask Mary about that
the next time I see her.
We didn't talk about that—
but I wonder—
I wonder
if we told ourselves
something
over and over again,
could it change
what we do
and how we live our lives?

What if—
what if—
with this holiday season—
if we approached it
by saying,
by telling ourselves,
"The Lord is my shepherd,
I shall not want."
When we plan our personal calendars
and fill up those little squares—
those little lines
that we find there—
what if we said to ourselves,
"The Lord is my shepherd."

Before we sat down
to plan and organize our life together
as a church,
what if—
we looked at one another,
and we reminded ourselves,

"The Lord is our shepherd,
we shall not want.
We are made to lie down
in green pastures
and we are led beside
still waters."

And what difference would it make,
if, before we planned the social activities
for our children,
we said,
"The Lord is our shepherd."
What if
Psalm 23
were a way of life
instead of a send-off into death?

Ask yourself,
What are you going to do?

"The Lord is my shepherd,
I shall not want." [in a whisper]

"The Lord is my shepherd—"

"We are made to lie down
in green pastures—"
"We are led beside
still waters—" [in a whisper]

Who *is* your shepherd?

What *are* we going to do?
Amen.

Chapter 4
Her Stories in Bold Form

Narrative in Women's Sermons

I think women bring a willingness to talk about ourselves and our personal story.
—Kim

I use stories that I really connect with.

—Clare

And what I hear us saying is that we draw something out of others by our stories, by our personal stories, but also by ideas, too; it's never just one or the other. Women bring both.

—Peggy

This chapter focuses on one sermon, entitled "Letting Go and Letting Grow," delivered by Kim Ryan on May 8, 1994, at the Broadway Christian Church-Disciples of Christ, in Columbia, Missouri (see pp. 140–46 for full text). On a typical Sunday morning when she preaches, Kim will deliver three sermons: 8:30, 9:30, and 11:00, usually to 85–150 people at each service. Kim is a rather young but experienced preacher, who, as the associate minister, preaches once or twice a month. I have come to appreciate her sermons as artful, complex, and sophisticated especially in their use of narrative; she has an impressive ability to weave a sermon together in terms of structure and interconnected components. Kim is a petite white woman with very light blonde hair about shoulder length. She seems dwarfed by her black robes; her gestures are dramatized by the large, oversized sleeves.

Kim uses a traditional format to frame her sermons; that is, she reads the scriptures she has chosen for that particular service (usually from the New Revised Standard Version), then she almost always begins her sermon with a narrative, always told with her particularly captivating narrative style. The stories Kim tells are generally personal experience stories, and thus her pulpit discourse most often begins with the pronoun "I." Her narrative style is dramatic; she uses pauses to great advantage; she employs hand and facial gestures that enhance her story; and she is adept at dramatic dialogue. She is a master storyteller and keeps the audience riveted. Her listeners know Kim's stories to be entertaining, but, much more than that, they expect the stories to transcend their entertainment value.

Kim is fully conscious about her use of narrative to frame her sermons. Telling stories comes naturally to her anyway, and she notes her own daring in bringing her personal story to the pulpit when she tells our group, "I think women bring a willingness to talk about ourselves and their personal stories."

At this point I am going to give the introduction to the first story in Kim's May 8 sermon. She usually pauses after reading the Scriptures; this pause serves to segue from one element (scriptures) to the other (sermon/story). The words lead directly into the story that will frame the entire sermon; the reader may wish to read the sermon through before looking at the analysis which follows here.

I have a good friend named Michelle—   and there's nothing
    [pause]   that she can tell me that
I hope you have a friend like Michelle,   would shock me—
because I can tell her anything,   or so I thought.

Even as a reading audience, we are able to perceive that Kim has entered a storytelling mode. She is a truly talented narrator, filling her stories with dialogue, gestures, and lively facial expressions. She has at her disposal all the dramatic strategies necessary to hold her audience—she uses dramatic pause and stage whispers for effect. Although her sermons are mostly written out, she knows all the attributes of a good oral presentation. She often uses repetition, formulaic patterning, assonance, and assimilation. She naturally uses imagery, metaphorical language, and dialogue. She often uses colloquial language in her dialogue to verify its authenticity: "My mom and Gage and I are going to be coming through Dallas." She helps us hear the characters in her story: "But then she called me back, about three days after that, and she said to me—I can still hear the excitement in her voice— 'Oh, I'm so glad you're gonna be here,—I've worked it all out and the morning before you leave we're going to have a weaning party.'" Her breathless, rapid presentation now matches the excitement she remembers in her friend's voice. All the more effective, then, is her own hilarious mistake in hearing this as "weinie party." Her audience would have laughed no matter what! But by now they are intrigued. With Kim, they are beginning to wonder what her friend has in store for her. Guessing the problem, her friend spells it, as Kim does, w-e-a-n-i-n-g, a weaning party, and she begins to explain that the mother in this story does not want to stop nursing her growing child. The party is actually suggested by a woman rabbi who explains the value of a ritual for this transition from breastfeeding, acknowledging the significance of this weaning of child and mother. As the sermon unfolds, the significance of the shared rituals is highlighted again only once, but our examination of the sermon will reveal just how important this aspect is as Kim explores issues of diversity, difference, and inclusion.

Women telling stories. Is this a difficult concept for us to imagine? When do women tell stories? In what contexts? To what audiences? Are women known and admired for being raconteurs? Folklore studies of the past century or so have indicated to us that women are, indeed, recognized as verbal artists.[1] Often they are balladeers, religious song singers, proverb users—but *storytellers*? Certainly the Grimm Brothers located housekeepers and nannies who knew German märchen, and Linda Dégh has documented the role of Hungarian women who know and tell the stories of her research community. But, in general, we have been informed that more often than not women are *not* the "village storytellers" or tribal keepers of the history or the boisterous storytellers captivating the family clan at festive gatherings. Women have been, more often, like folklorist Karen Baldwin's grandmother, the more quiet partner in a storytelling duo—the man claims the foreground, while the woman takes the background space.[2]

We learn that women are more likely to tell stories and jokes behind the kitchen door, like Rayne Green's bawdy family womenfolk in Texas or female joke tellers in women's groups,[3] or in all-female rap groups like Susan Kalčik's experience;[4] or they tell stories of supernatural experiences to other women and willing listeners, as Gillian Bennett has documented.[5] But the picture of the female storyteller out there, front and center, is a little more difficult to conceive. Most often we hear in the scholarship how male researchers, particularly anthropologists, have failed to get the women's stories because they have not had access to them, or did not realize those contexts existed, or, more blatantly, assumed the more public male contexts were the culturally significant ones and failed to talk with or listen to the women.[6]

Women researching folklore have recently challenged us to reconsider these misconceptions about women's spheres and have, in their own field research, sought out female contexts and attempted to write ethnographies about women's worlds and the art thriving there—both material and verbal. Often, as Joan Radner and Susan Lanser warn, the materials of women's lore are difficult to "read" because women have long been aware of their cultures' perceptions of them and thus actually "code" some of their experiences in order to protect the material and themselves.[7] The researcher's task, then, becomes even more difficult: to decode the women's lore and make it accessible. Of course, once we do de-code, we must also ask the question with Judith Stacey, "Can there be a feminist ethnography?"[8] Or, in the very act of exploring women's worlds and making our work public, are we exposing the women we are studying and perhaps making them, once again, vulnerable?

Women's sermons offer a public kind of research context. Sermons are, indeed, public speech acts, delivered to critical audiences of both males and females.[9] And in this context, we do find women telling stories.

But, interestingly, I am exploring women's storytelling within a context that has historically banned women from its public, authoritative spheres—the religious pulpit. It is perhaps most interesting to me that once women have gained access to the pulpit in various denominations in this country and around the world, they have claimed it as their own and use that context as a place to tell their stories—stories that connect the religious message with the stories of their own lives.

The concept of women reclaiming their collective "her-story" by "telling our stories" has emerged powerfully in a variety of contexts. Since the 1980s, feminist anthropologists, folklorists, literary scholars, sociologists, creative writers, theologians, and scholars in the communications fields and in education have been advocating—to a greater or lesser degree—the desirability, even the imperative, that women reclaim their own stories in order to "write" women back into history and into the picture of humanity at large. Women's stories have not been told publicly nor heard. The effort to reinstate women's voices and lives is a monumental one but one that is inspiring and fully credible.

Perhaps, then, it should come as no surprise that women who gain access to a public forum, one which demands them to be "verbal artists," would claim this forum to "tell their stories." Conversely, perhaps we are surprised to hear women "telling their stories" in a context where they are already, in some cases, on thin ice. Many mainline congregation members are still quite surprised to see a woman in the pulpit. Some are hostile, some merely tolerant. Perhaps everyone is cognizant that the pulpit is not accessible to all women everywhere. The Pope refuses even to talk about the possibility of ordination for women; Baptists "allow" women to become ordained but actively work against their employment as pastors of churches; seminaries are full of women who may never be ordained or find a church that will hire them—and then, more than likely, it will be as an "associate" or "assistant" or they will take on "charges" of two, three, or even more, small rural churches, a heavy work load with little or no salary. It might make sense, then, to think that women who *do* gain access to the pulpit might well be cautious and rely on their homiletic training in seminary, preaching sermons as expected by their preaching professors, sticking closely to the traditional expectations of church congregations, trying to make certain they do not draw attention to themselves *as women* since their presence in the pulpit, in the robes, with full clerical authority and power, already poses difficulties for many in their audience. This scenario is, in fact, what I found to be true with Pentecostal women preachers, as I discuss in my book *Handmaidens of the Lord.*[10] Pentecostal women preachers are aware of their precarious position in the pulpit, and their sermons reflect their discomfort. Their disclaimers as to their personal desire to be in the pulpit, as well as the way in which they present themselves and preach sermons that distance them from the material through many different strategies, assure their audience that they make no claims on the power and authority that should come with their position.

Women preaching in the denominations represented in this book, however, proudly accept their positions as pastors and preachers, claiming the rights and privileges of the pulpit. The sermons the women in my study preach draw on their experiences *as women,* contributing an aspect to preaching hitherto seldom articulated in the Christian world. The new paradigm of which I speak in Chapter 5 begins with the words of the women's sermons. In the pulpit, as at the altar or communion table, we find semiotic and linguistic markers that shift our cognitive sensibilities. We find women's faces above the robes, draped in stoles or chasubles of vivid colors that bear the most ancient Christian symbols.[11] We watch female hands rise in enormous sleeves to greet the people, to invoke God, to bless and offer sacraments. We hear softer voices. And we hear women's voices tell us *their stories.* They make no excuses for this. They do not try to tell men's stories. They do not try to mimic men's sermon styles, narratives, jokes, mannerisms, or dramatic presentations. They stand as women and tell women's stories; they weave sermons that are clearly *women's sermons,* in content, in structure, in presentation, and in style.

What does that mean—*women's sermons?* And how can I defend such a statement? Am I being "essentialist" when I make such a claim? Not at all. The sermons themselves are my best evidence. For example, take Kim's weaning story. No man I have ever known would have told that story—not even the most sensitive father, the best parent. It simply *is not a man's story.* And there is more. Return with me to the beginning of the sermon. Kim begins this *sermon* with a very personal comment: "I have a good friend named Michelle." Women's networks, women's friendships, the importance of friendship, the power of such a relationship with another woman: all are evident in that first line. And her next line is equally surprising: "I hope you have a friend like Michelle, because I can tell her anything, and there's nothing that she can tell me that would shock me—or so I thought." This is a woman's definition of friendship: "I can tell her anything and there is nothing that she can tell me that would shock me." We learn in the next few lines that Kim planned to travel with her mother and her small son to Dallas, which is a very long way from mid-Missouri, yet she can still speak of her friendship with Michelle in these intimate terms. She knows she can tell her good friend *anything* and she believes she knows this woman in Dallas so well that there is nothing Michelle could say that could shock her. The way she tells the story, her audience realizes that these two women are such good friends that Kim can simply pick up the phone and tell her friend out of the blue that she and her mother and son will be traveling through Michelle's city and can say openly, without hesitation, "and we want to spend the night at your house." She does not ask if it will be all right; there is no formal protocol here, no pretense, no waiting for Michelle to think of the idea; Kim is perfectly comfortable saying they want to stay there. I believe these first lines of this woman's sermon are critically important clues to her audience about how women speak and what they choose to speak about. Kim has, in the first ten to twelve lines of her sermon, established herself: (1) as a woman, (2) as a woman with a close friendship with a woman who lives far away; (3) as recognizing the importance of close friendships for human survival; (4) as knowledgeable about just how close women's friendships can be; (5) as able to include her audience in this examination of friendship, bringing them closer with the line "I hope you have a friend like Michelle"; and (6) as a woman who knows how to define true friendship, for women, as "I can tell her anything, and there's nothing she can tell me that would shock me." Kim has foregrounded women's friendships as a key element in the framing of this sermon.

Her next line in this introduction to her narrative, the tacked on "or so I thought" is a narrative device. She is not actually suggesting to us that Michelle has betrayed their friendship by managing to shock her; the "or so I thought" introduces her actual narrative—the story about Michelle's "weaning party." Kim's "shock" is part of her narrative style. Her confusion at Michelle's words is a device to make her audience laugh. It also aligns them with her—they probably heard the words incorrectly the first time Kim said them also—a "weinie party?" she muses, innocently, willing to play the confused listener here with her audience. And even when Michelle spells the word "w-e-a-n-i-n-g," Kim allows herself to continue to be skeptical, for *she assumes her audience are skeptical.* It was interesting for me during this sermon to watch some of the congregation audience members as Kim preached on the private, intimate, physical, sensual, topic of weaning a child from breastfeeding. One man in the choir, for example, shifted a great deal during the sermon, diverting his eyes toward the floor in an obvious demonstration of discomfort at the subject matter of Kim's presentation.

Breastfeeding, weaning, mothers, nurturing, enjoyment, intimacy between infants and mothers, sadness, the community of women are all aspects in this sermon, which I can call without hesitation a *woman's sermon.* Several other characteristics of these first few lines are also important. Kim is traveling alone with her mother and son; she calls her friend and the friend tells her she can stay at her house without any mention of her spouse or partner; the weaning party itself is a women's gathering where only women's voices are heard. My guess is that most, if not all, of the women in Kim's audience were reacting and responding to this sermon in a way that they never had responded to a sermon before. I did. I cried when Kim described the gathering of women, aged ninety-two to twenty, who joined together with Michelle in a ritual of sharing their own stories to ease the pain of a woman losing the intimacy, the connection, of a nursing infant; I heard evidence that women around me were quietly weeping as well. This is a powerful woman's story of milk and bodily pleasure, of connection and growth, of pain and separation, and of women together sharing stories and sharing the experience of mothering and feeding babies with their breasts and cradling their offspring with their arms and bodies, of women ritualizing an experience only women can *know*.[12]

At the beginning of this sermon, Kim reads but does not comment on the lesson. She does not set the historical stage; she does not explain or interpret the Bible passages. There is no exegesis here. She does not, in fact, seem to be overtly connecting her words, her story, with the Bible passages, but to think that she does not intend to link her words with the reading would be a mistake. In fact, her audience, who hears her at least once a month, trusts that she will weave this sermon back toward the Scriptures. They, and I, know from experience that this personal story will fold back into the biblical story—as indeed it does. Kim includes Hannah in the weaning party as a participant. She tells us that there are not just seven women present at the weaning party, there are actually eight, for Hannah has been invited to be there, too. Without an obvious seam, Kim has woven Hannah's weaning story into her own and into the stories of the women at the weaning party. In this sermon, Kim has relied on women's experiences and the sharing of women's stories to interpret and explain the essence of a biblical story, which more often has been explicated with a focus on the young son Samuel, not on the pain of the mother forced to part with him early. The story demonstrates the power of the mother willing to "lend" her son to God. She suffers for losing him early and emphasizes her devotion by returning each year with a new and longer coat, knowing that her release is the only requirement for her son's growth and independence. To acknowledge the critical praxis of story/experience/connection/scripture/message/meaning in this sermon is to understand just how women preach and how complex Kim's creations actually are.

As a storytelling device, Kim develops the frame of a story within a story.[13] She has woven together her friend's and Hannah's weaning stories *by including Hannah in the retelling of Michelle's ritual.* As listeners, we find ourselves, too, at the ritual, seated with seven women, ages ninety-two to twenty, sharing stories about motherhood and parenting. In the context of this storytelling event, we hear another narrative, we "hear" and understand, with Kim, Hannah's story:

And I heard	in a way that I have never understood it
and I listened	before.
and I understood Hannah's story	

Now, there is exegesis. Hannah is not *actually* at Michelle's weaning party. She does not *actually* tell her story there. Originally, the rabbi told the story of Hannah's weaning of her son, and her story was recalled collectively by the women at the ritual. Kim's retelling of the weaning story has provided a window, a space, for bringing us back to the Scriptures, to Hannah's story and to exegesis, interpretation, and explanation of the biblical passage about

Hannah who kept baby Samuel with her	to the temple hall
until he was weaned,	and she lent him to God
and then she took this child of her deep longing	and for all of humankind.

Kim has brought us back to the scriptures. But rather than explain Hannah's relationship with her child and their relationship with God immediately after this, Kim first narrates a moving story about a friend of hers who has a weaning ritual because she is reluctant to let go of her suckling child. She juxtaposes the contemporary ritual with the ancient one. She invokes Hannah's story as one of several stories told there by "seven women ages ninety-two to twenty," but "actually there were eight of us there . . . , because Hannah was invited to be there as well." We are captivated by these stories within a story. We are there with Michelle and Kim, the seven friends, and Hannah, sharing stories.

Thus far in Kim's sermon, her themes or messages have already been revealed through vivid images. We find ourselves and our close friends sitting with Kim, her friend, and Hannah, sharing stories. But Kim has hardly begun. This first narrative sets the stage for more layers of complexity and multiple meaning/message(s).

In her exegesis of Hannah's story, Kim alludes to some of the aspects of the story that will eventually be folded into the intricate structure of her sermon. She emphasizes that the Bible says

Hannah took this child of her deep longing	to the temple hall and she lent him to God.

Kim will return to this notion of the mother "lending" her son to God. She also talks about how Hannah sews a new coat for her son each year and brings it to him when she visits "because she knew he was growing." She will also return to this theme in her sermon. She is, in fact, sowing the seeds here for the most prominent theme of the sermon—a theme that has not yet even emerged. It will, rather, unfold slowly and will be constructed carefully with the themes already revealed: friendship, relationship, parenting, ritual, the power of storytelling, growth, and change.

In her narrative, Kim leaves Hannah's story with the comment: "Well, none of us can tell a weaning story quite like Hannah," and weaves *another* personal experience story into her recounting of the storytelling ritual at Michelle's weaning party. Here is the story that Kim tells us she shared with the other women at the ritual:

And I remembered and told about Bill   [laughter from the congregation]
 and me   standing there on the porch,
standing on the front porch of our house arms around each other,
and watching as our first grader ran to but knowing,
 catch the bus,   knowing,
for the first time,   that that was part of
that backpack just a-flapping.   letting him go,
That was a great scene: and letting him grow.
Gage thrilled, Bill and me crying,

We have now, for the first time, actually heard the words that constitute the title of Kim's sermon, "Letting Go and Letting Grow." She then relates this story back to the weaning party:

And it didn't take us long   that most of parenting is about just that,
at the weaning party   letting go
to understand   and letting grow.

It is here, then, that she relates this segment of her storytelling to the dedication of infants in the morning service—a significant and empowering kind of connection. She reminds her congregation that

We have our own rituals here at church, when parents and children stand
just like the one that we got to be a part   before us
 of today.   and they make a commitment
I love this season,   to raise their children
this part of the year   in the Christian community.
and this part of the service,

Traditional homiletic texts instruct preachers to "insert" stories and anecdotes in appropriate places within the conventional "three-part" sermon, for emphasis, explanation, illustration, or entertainment. Innumerable books available to the sermon writer provide stories and anecdotes appropriate for this use. The women I talked with claim that they do not "insert" stories into their sermons; rather, *the stories are the actual frames of the sermons and they preach what they know*. Together, they have reinforced the notion that experience is an authentic avenue for acquiring knowledge of God, even though they fully recognized that historically this concept has been questioned. In their sermons, women tell stories mostly from their own experience or they use stories they "connect with," but these stories are not "inserted" into a sermon outline in the way the homiletic instructors were suggesting, not at all. The stories become the frame for the sermons. Experience, theirs and others', is hermeneutical; experience constitutes how they know what they know—religiously, spiritually, and theologically.

*   *   *

In this book, I have suggested the imagery of a multi-stranded helix to help us understand the interweavings of factors in women's ministries and sermons. In this close reading of one woman's sermon, I look to the helix again to help us unfold and discern the various strands that wind and double back through the structural and storytelling aspects of the sermons. Kim's sermon is an especially noteworthy example of how the strands weave around one another, folding back again, spiraling, encircling, supporting, balancing, connecting the narrative components, the biblical passages, the speaking woman herself, and her audience.

The sermon begins with Kim's mention of a good and close friend. She carefully weaves her definition of what a good friend is with an invitation for her audience to recall their own close and dear friends and to remind them and herself about the importance of close, intimate connection with other humans. Already we can see the slowly moving double helix, we see strands of connection, friendship, speaker and audience. Seamlessly, Kim then weaves strands of breastfeeding, nurturing, mothering, connection between child and mother, pleasure and pain, as strands brought into the helix, woven together by the voices of the women sharing stories in a ritual meant to join them in experience and in words. And we find the multi-stranded helix growing as strands of age are added, women "ages ninety-two to twenty." We realize that, if we listen carefully, we can also hear the voices of the infants we know are there as well—Michelle's baby who has pulled away, Kim's child who is traveling with her, and other children we can only glimpse briefly as their strands are woven in with the voices of the women speaking. Then Hannah, too, adds her story. The voice of the biblical mother who is forced to wean her son too soon joins the voices of the other women in the room in Michelle's house in Dallas but connects as well and as perfectly with the silent voices of women in the audience who know both the pleasure and the pain.

Our perception of these interweavings of the many strands of this sermon is expanded even further if we attempt to bring the entire service into our image of the multistranded helix. This entire service has been developed and orchestrated by Kim Ryan, the preacher. It is a special service to "dedicate" infants, which in this denomination affirms their inclusion into the community of the church and formalizes the responsibility of the church for the instruction and well-being of the child. It means to give them a blessing that brings them into the fold of the church family. This aspect of the service is poignant as Kim steps away from the pulpit, dressed in her robes, claiming the power, holding babies in her small arms, lifting them before God and into the care of the congregation—a dynamic new image, a disarming portrait of the priestly role, a woman holding a baby in a sacred embrace—in that act bringing the natural and the spiritual together in a perfect moment of connection.

When we place Kim's "weaning" story in the context of this "infant dedication" service, the strands of the service emerge as new aspects of our swirling, encircling image. We hear the choir sing, "Hail, Holy Mother," a song from the recent film "Sister Act," and know why Kim wanted that particular song for this event. We hear the verses from 1 Samuel and find that the Bible passages, too, take their place in our multi-stranded model, weaving in and back, folding and unfolding in a sacred dance with Kim's story of the women's stories told at the weaning party, with Hannah's story, and back to Kim's audience. They have been woven into the image already, brought there by Kim's invitation to know and experience friendship. They are brought around to the foreground again, though imperceptibly, when Kim tells us how Hannah crafts a new coat for her son each year. Many members of her congregation are parents, she knows, and she repeats the theme for her sermon, "letting go and letting grow," several times. She tells them that "parenting is a lot about weaning" and uses that observation to bring her audience into the metaphor of the church as a parent. By so doing she gently embraces all the members of her audience, even those who might not have felt included at the weaning party. She reminds her audience that, with her, they have participated in a ritual that morning, a ritual of parenting, akin to the gathering of women, one where the "community shares the responsibility of that child." In their ritual, she tells them, "that child belongs to us as well." And in that promise, the community promises the parents: "We promise to help you let go at appropriate times and in appropriate ways. And we promise to stand with you in the letting go and the letting grow of these children." She reminds them how this happens in informal conversations in the hallways, around the coffee pot, in private homes: "What we see and experience happening is the listening ear and the reassuring smile and the arm around the shoulder, and it's all a part of the weaning ritual."

What Kim has not stated in this sermon, up to this point, is that she is concerned about how her congregation is responding to the recent growth of their church. The membership has voted to build a new sanctuary and new classrooms. They are a growing church community, and she has been preaching inclusion and expansion. She has preached sermons on new ways of perceiving community and on how to embrace people of different races, backgrounds, cultures, and sexual orientation. She never retreats from the critical issues of the contemporary church; she pushes her congregation to think, to probe, to experiment, to grow, to seek and find God in unexpected places, and to love the imperfection inherent in all humans. She has understood, even shared, their hesitation about growth, about expanding their church family, of adding new members, embracing the unknown. It is also important to notice how Kim talks about her congregation's hesitation. *She takes it on as her own.* This, too, seems to be a woman's way of speaking. She never accuses them. She does not direct them how to think, or act, or feel. She takes on these conflicting realities as her own (because some of them *are* her own). But in another revolution of the helix, she relates her reactions in terms of *Hannah's voice* speaking to her. She conjures the image of Hannah holding the baby Samuel in her arms, begging him not to grow too fast.

I heard Hannah's heart speaking
in a particular way,
and in a totally different context,
but I heard her speaking
in my voice.
I think
it's because we are getting so much
 closer,
to our building expansion plans.
I'm starting to believe it's really going to
 happen,
and I hear a voice inside of me say,
"I don't want to give it up—
our comfortable church community."
I hear the voice inside of me say
"Just wait,

wait,
wait,
I really like it the way it is."
I heard that voice speaking.

I have heard myself turning to Hannah
 for encouragement,
Hannah deliberately sewing a larger
 coat,
for the boy that she could not keep
from growing.
And I have asked her,
"How did you do it?"
How did she set her fears aside
and bless his growth
and bless the changes in his life

and the changes in her life?
And the scripture witness of Hannah
convinces me that Hannah
could only let Samuel go
because she believed so strongly
that Samuel was not hers—
that Samuel was God's.
Oh, Samuel was hers to birth and hers to
    nurse,
but Samuel was not hers to own and
    control.
And the scriptural story of Hannah
has convinced me that Hannah
could let Samuel go
because she could read the signs of her
    time.

Her people and her community
were changing so drastically.
. . .
And so I hear in my heart
the voice of Hannah's wisdom
speaking to me.
And she whispers to me,
"Let the church go
and let the church grow.
You can birth it—
you can love it—
you can tend it—
and you can nurture it—
but it is God's church—
it is not yours to own
or to control."

It would be simplistic to state that the sole theme of this sermon is the expansion of the church community, but a view of the sermon as a whole provides evidence that this expansion was indeed the initial motivating theme. But what Kim has created here is a sermon that weaves that important and relevant reality of her church community together with all the other strands of the sermon into a complex multistranded message that in its totality far surpasses any one theme. Most important, for our purposes, we can recognize how she creates this narrative-driven presentation from the very core of women's experience, women's voices, and women's ways of knowing how community, through connection and ritual, shapes a people's perception of God's place in all human nurturing. Imagine once again the weaving, encircling motion of the multistranded helix: this woman's sermon revolves around the speaker herself, with each revolution embracing each of her congregation members, the biblical story, and the morning ritual of infant dedication and inclusion into the church family. Thus, we can conceptualize how the sermon, as represented by only some of the strands, seeks to engage the margins of the moving helix even as it defines its center. Imagine the helix growing as more strands are incorporated, and notice how the margins disappear as the center expands.

In the first pages of this book, I offered the living, revolving, multistranded helix as an image for exploring the many and varied facets of these women's lives, their ministry, their created sermons, and their theology. Here I have sought to illuminate the content and structure of Kim's sermon through the image of the multi-stranded helix. It is also possible to see how this sermon can suggest how the image places God in the center, at the essential core, of the named connections: women, parents, children, preacher, audience, sacred scripture, ritual and story, pleasure and pain, physicality and spirituality. Thermodynamically, a critical premise of this model is that without the multiple strands of the helix itself, the center would vanish; so, too, symbiotically, the central core holds the strands in tension one with the other. Crick and Watson first imagined a dynamic, living model. The women involved in this very serious, sacred business of connecting people with each other, through and with God, do not *imitate* the DNA model but elucidate that model, rendering it complete in their sermons by adding the idea of "God" as a participant. Watson and Crick were right—the pulsating, revolving, multi-stranded helix *is* "the stuff of life." But, taken to this extension, their image also offers a way to understand the living universe in its connection to and with God as perceived by the women preachers in this study. I find confirmation for this interpretation of the helix model in Kim's words:

I hear Hannah encouraging us
to redefine the church in tune with the
    changing times,
because I hear about those signs of the
    times
in places I go—
. . .
and what they say is that the American
    church
is in a time of
tremendous transition
and that what is needed
to take us into the future
are churches that are willing to be
    leaders,
churches that are willing to
stretch out,

widen the boundary,
and not draw the circle in tighter—
churches that have stretched those
    boundaries and say,
"Differences are good,
come on in,
we don't have to agree
on everything,
it's all right to be different"
Churches that are willing to be inclusive
instead of exclusive—
churches that are willing to create a
    place
where people can stand
in their differences
and in their disagreements,
in unity with Jesus Christ.

Kim ends this sermon by asking that they all find encouragement from mother Hannah to "lend to God the church we love." Kim offers here evidence of a different kind of sermon creation and delivery, a sermon based on women's ways of trusting what they know.[14] And what they know comes from their own experiences just as they articulated in our discussions about their sermons. Hence we have, in a very public form, the American pulpit, women speaking and telling their own stories within the traditional Christian story in order to frame a message of integration and connection.

Notes

1. Scholarship on women's folklore, which includes attention to women as verbal artists, can be best traced via several works that have appeared in the last fifteen years. See especially Claire Farrer, ed., *Women and Folklore: Images and Genders*, first published as a special issue of *Journal of American Folklore* 88, 347 (1975); Marta Weigle, "Women as Verbal Artists"; Rosan A. Jordan and Susan J. Kalčik, eds., *Women's Folklore, Women's Culture*; Susan Tower Hollis, Linda Pershing, and M. Jane Young, eds., *Feminist Theory and the Study of Folklore*; and Joan Newlon Radner, ed., *Feminist Messages: Coding in Women's Folk Culture*.

2. Karen Baldwin, " 'Woof!' A Word on Women's Roles in Family Storytelling," in Jordan and Kalčik, eds., *Women's Folklore, Women's Culture*. See also several articles in Elizabeth C. Fine and Jean Haskell Speer, eds., *Performance, Culture, and Identity*. especially Kristin M. Langellier and Eric E. Peterson, "Spinstorying: An Analysis of Women Storytelling," pp. 157–180, and Kristin B. Valentine and Eugene Valentine, "Performing Culture Through Narrative: A Galician Woman Storyteller."

3. Rayna Green, "Magnolias Grow in Dirt: The Bawdy Lore of Southern Women"; Carol Mitchell, "Some Differences in Male and Female Joke Telling," in Jordan and Kalčik, eds., *Women's Folklore, Women's Culture*.

4. Susan Kalčik, " '. . . like Ann's gynecologist or the time I was almost raped': Personal Narratives in Women's Rap Groups."

5. Gillian Bennett, " 'And I turned round to her and said . . .': A Preliminary Analysis of Shape and Structure in Women's Storytelling"; and Bennett, "Heavenly Protection and Family Unite: The Concept of the Revenant Among Elderly Urban Women."

6. For an insightful critique of how women's lives and spheres have fared in the work of male anthropologists, see Trinh T. Minh-hah, *Woman, Native, Other*.

7. This is the focus of Radner's book, *Feminist Messages: Coding in Women's Folk Culture*. See especially, Radner and Lanser's lead article in that work, "Strategies of Coding in Women's Cultures," pp. 1–30.

8. Judith Stacey, "Can There Be a Feminist Ethnography?"

9. See Richard Bauman's explanation of competence as judged by a critical audience in *Verbal Art as Performance*.

10. Elaine J. Lawless, *Handmaidens of the Lord: Women Preachers and Traditional Religion*.

11. For an extensive look at the semiotic messages inherent in a woman in the pulpit, see Elaine J. Lawless, "Writing the Body in the Pulpit: Female-Sexed Texts."

12. I make the same kind of arguments when I teach women's literature, asking my students to identify what about a text might make it a "female text." In comparison with Kim's sermon about breastfeeding, for example, I can suggest the words of St. Perpetua, in one of the earliest recorded women's mystical writings. Perpetua, in prison and about to be persecuted as a Christian believer, suckles her young son, then prays for her breasts to dry up so that her body will not cry for his tug. Similarly, her heavenly visions invoke a softened Jesus figure who milks the goats and shares large bowls of warm milk with Perpetua and the others who will soon

die. See "The Passion of Ss. Perpetua and Felicitas," in Elizabeth Alvilda Petroff, ed., *Medieval Women's Visionary Literature*, pp. 70–77.

13. This framing device of a story within a story can also be argued as a characteristic of women's writing in general, fictional and otherwise. Beginning with Mary Shelley's *Frankenstein*, we find women much less likely to adhere to the typical, and simplistic, Freytag plot model of rising action, climax, and falling action (understood as possibly a male model). Women's writings tend to a more complex weaving of different narratives, narrative voices, discourses, and even genres. The multiplicity of texts within a text is suggestive of the interior and exterior complexities of women's often interrupted and, hence, segmented, lives. The "logical" three-part sermon was developed by male theologians and clergy and more likely invokes a tripartite, "logical" sequence that replicates the intention of the Freytag plot model. Women's writings, on the other hand, more often invoke images closer to the circle, the spiral, the double helix.

14. Compare Mary Belenky et al., *Women's Ways of Knowing*.

Letting Go and Letting Grow

KIM RYAN
Broadway Christian Church-Disciples of Christ
Columbia, Missouri
May 8, 1994

"The man Elkanah and all his household
went up to offer to the Lord
the yearly sacrifice, and to pay his vow.
But Hannah did not go up, for she said to
her husband,
'As soon as the child is weaned, I will
bring him,
that he may appear in the presence of
the Lord, and remain there forever;
I will offer him as a nazirite for all time.'
Her husband Elkanah said to her, 'Do
what seems best to you,
wait until you have weaned him.'
When she had weaned him, she took him
up with her,
along with a three-year-old bull, an
ephah of flour, and a skin of wine.
She brought him to the house of the Lord
at Shiloh;
and the child was young.
Then they slaughtered the bull, and they
brought the child to Eli.
And she said, 'Oh, my lord!
As you live, my lord, I am the woman
who was standing here in your
presence,
praying to the Lord.
For this child I prayed;
and the Lord has granted me the petition
that I made to him.
Therefore, I have lent him to the Lord;
as long as he lives, he is given to the
Lord.'
She left him there for the Lord."
[1 Samuel 1:21–28, NRSV]

I have a good friend named Michelle—
[pause]
I hope you have a friend like Michelle,
because I can tell her anything,
and there's nothing
that she can tell me that
would shock me—
or so I thought.
I called Michelle a few months ago,
and we're such good friends
that I said to her,
"My mom and Gage and I are going to

be coming through Dallas
on our way to see my grandma
and we want to spend the night at your
  house."
She said, "Great! No problem."
But then she called me back,
about three days after that,
and she said to me—
I can still hear
the excitement in her voice—
"Oh, I'm so glad you're going to be
  here—
I've worked it all out
and the morning before you leave
we're going to have a weaning party."
  [long pause]
a 'weinie' party? [softly, as if pondering]
And I said,
"We're gonna have hot dogs
in the morning?"
And she said, "No, no!
We're going to have a weaning party."
And I said,
"Well, that's nice . . ." [with a lot of
  hesitation]
And then she spelled it—
"W-e-a-n-i-n-g—
a weaning party!" [long pause; her look
  was of eyebrows up, head cocked—
  congregation laughs at her pose]
Well!
I don't know if it was my lack of
  enthusiasm
or the silence on the other end of the
  phone,
but something convinced Michelle that
  she'd better start explaining. [pause]
It seemed that Amanda,
Michelle's ten-month-old,

had decided to stop nursing—
her second child,
her last baby,
and Mama Michelle wasn't ready,
she was really sad.
So a friend of hers,
a Jewish woman rabbi,
suggested that
they create a weaning party.
Michelle was thrilled with the idea,
and she was even more excited
because I was going to get to be there,
  too!
Hmmmm . . . [again, surprise on her face
  but hesitation; audience laughs]
Well, I didn't even tell my mom
until we were already on the road
and half way there—[more laughter from
  the congregation; they know Kim's
  mother]
But it was beautiful—
let me tell you.
It was wonderful:
seven women ages ninety-two to twenty,
sharing stories about motherhood
and about parenting,
listening to one another—[softly, with
  emphasis]
seven of Michelle's closest friends.
But actually there were eight of us there,
because in the ritual they created,
Hannah was invited to be there as well.
And I heard
and I listened
and I understood Hannah's story
in a way that I have never understood it
  before.
[softly] Hannah who kept baby Samuel
  with her

until he was weaned,
and then she took this child of her deep
    longing
to the temple hall
and she lent him to God
and for all of humankind.
That is what the Scripture says.
The Scripture doesn't say
she gave him to God;
the Scripture says
she "lent him to God."
But Hannah left Samuel there,
and every year,
once a year,
Hannah would go back to see Samuel
at the temple,
and in between
she would sew for him a coat.
Each year one a little longer
because she knew he was growing,
and she would take it with her
on her visits. [pause]
Well,
none of us can tell a weaning story
quite like Hannah,
but we laughed
and we cried
as we told our stories.
And I remembered
and told about Bill and me
standing on the front porch
of our house
and watching as our first grader
ran to catch the bus,
for the first time,
that backpack just a-flapping.
That was a great scene:
Gage thrilled,
Bill and me crying, [laughter from the

congregation; they know Bill, too]
standing there on the porch,
arms around each other,
but knowing,
knowing,
that that was a part of
letting him go,
and letting him grow.
And it didn't take us long
at the weaning party
to understand
that most of parenting is about just that,
letting go,
and letting grow.
Parenting is a lot about weaning.
Unfortunately, the church just doesn't
    have a ritual
for that bittersweet reality,
maybe we should.
Some of you have family rituals,
and we have our own rituals here at
    church,
just like the one that we got to be a part
    of today.
[She had just conducted a dedication
    service welcoming several babies into
    the church community that morning]
I love this season,
this part of the year,
and this part of the service,
when parents and children stand
    before us
and they make a commitment
to raise their children
in the Christian community.
They witness today what a difference
    that makes,
and how the community shares
the responsibility of that child—

that child belongs to us as well.
And I think there is something unstated,
in our ritual,
something that says,
"We promise
to help you
let go
at appropriate times
and in appropriate ways.
And we promise to stand with you
in the letting go
and the letting grow of these children."
For us, it doesn't happen in organized
    parties.
For us it happens
in the hallway,
and in the classrooms,
and around the coffee pot
and the doughnuts.
Haven't you heard it?
"My two-year-old is so bossy and so
    independent."
"My six-year-old has gotten so sassy and
    uncooperative."
"My nine-year-old is going on sixteen."
"My sixteen-year-old just got her driver's
    license!"
"My seventeen-year-old is graduating
    from high school—yikes!"
"My eighteen-year-old just got an
    apartment."
"My twenty-four-year-old just moved back
    home . . ." [knowing laughter from
    congregation]
—That one doesn't quite fit, does it?
    [more laughter]
Well, what we see and experience
    happening
is the listening ear

and the reassuring smile
and the arm around the shoulder,
and it's all a part
of our weaning ritual.
It's all a part of our being able to say
to one another—
"It's okay.
Being a parent—
It's okay—
let'em grow,
we are with you.
But it's not just true of parenting;
it's true of life.
It's true of us,
and it is one of the wonderful things
about being in the church and in a
    community,
because like no place else I've seen or
    I've been—
here,
we offer
and we receive
encouragement for the living of our day,
for our own growth into well being,
as well as our children's in our midst.
It's part of life.
And I think we need that kind of
    encouragement,
because otherwise,
we might not be able to do it.
We might not be able
to let go
and to let grow.
Since the weaning party,
Hannah has been a rather quiet and
    persistent companion of mine.
I have felt her presence with me
as we have gone through the last few
    weeks,

and I have imagined Hannah.
I have seen her in my mind
holding baby Samuel in her arms,
looking at him,
and her heart breaking.
Could you just stop growing?
Stay little a little longer.
And I heard Hannah's heart in my chest
when Bill said
after looking at our two-year-old,
"Isn't he great and cute
in his little pajamas,
I wish we could keep him this way
    forever."
And I suggested we wait
until we potty train him! [Laughter]
And then,
while I was thinking about it—
I heard Hannah's heart speaking,
in a particular way
and in a totally different context,
but I heard her speaking
in my voice.
I think
it's because we're getting so much
    closer,
to our building expansion plans.
I'm starting to believe it's really going to
    happen,
and I hear a voice inside of me say,
"I don't want to give it up—
our comfortable church community."
I hear the voice inside of me say,
"Just wait,
wait,
wait,
I really like it the way it is."
I heard that voice speaking.

I have found myself turning to Hannah for
    encouragement.
Hannah deliberately sewing a larger
    coat,
for the boy that she could not keep
from growing.
And I have asked her,
"How did you do it?"
How did she set her fears aside
and bless his growth
and bless the changes in his life
and the changes in her life?
And the scripture witness of Hannah
convinces me that Hannah
could only let Samuel go
because she believed so strongly
that Samuel was not hers—
that Samuel was God's.
Oh, Samuel was hers to birth and hers to
    nurse,
but Samuel was not hers to own and to
    control.
And the scriptural story of Hannah
has convinced me that Hannah
could let Samuel go,
because she could read the signs of her
    time.
Her people and her community
were changing so drastically.
It was a time of great transition for them.
They were going from small groups of
    tribes
to getting used to thinking of themselves
    as part of a whole,
a united kingdom,
and what was needed was a whole new
    identity,
with a whole new kind of leader.

And I believe Hannah sacrificed her own
desires
in the hopes
and a prayer,
that possibly her child,
God's child,
could be an instrument for the change
that was coming,
could be a leader
for a new day.
And that's exactly who Samuel was—
the scriptures tell us,
he did just that!
And so I hear
in my heart the voice of Hannah's
wisdom
speaking to me.
And she whispers to me,
"Let the church go,
let the church grow.
You can birth it—
you can love it—
you can tend it—
and you can nurture it—
but it is God's church—
it is not yours to own
or to control."
And I—
I hear Hannah encouraging us
to redefine the church in tune with the
changing times,
because I hear about those signs of the
times
in places I go—
ministers I hear talking about what's
happening,
and our own general minister is present
in the midst of the discussions,

and what they say is that the American
church
is in a time of
tremendous transition,
and that what is needed
to take us into the future
are churches that are willing to be
leaders,
churches that are willing to
stretch out,
widen the boundary
and to not draw the circle in tighter—
churches that have stretched those
boundaries
and say,
"Differences are good,
come on in,
we don't have to agree
on everything,
it's all right
to be different."
Churches that are willing to be inclusive
instead of exclusive—
churches that are willing to create a
place
where people can stand
in their differences
and in their disagreements
in unity with Jesus Christ.
And what I'm hearing
is that
we're going to need churches
that will provide meaningful worship
and churches that can offer significant
small groups
like People of the Covenant,
and like ABIL,
that help us experience spiritual
transformation

and spiritual stretching.
And what I know—
what I know—
is that Broadway
is that kind of church [strong emphasis
    here]
and can be
one of the leading churches
for today
and for tomorrow.
What I know
is that Broadway
is held in high esteem
and is regarded in our denomination
as one of the best,
most dynamic congregations.
And what I know
is that Broadway can be
an instrument for change
to usher in a new day—
if—
if—
we are willing.
like Hannah,
to sacrifice
what we hold in our arms today,
and let it go.
Like Hannah,
I am wanting a deeper meaning
of sacrificial giving.
[pause]
One more thing—
have you seen the posters
that our children have made
about sacrificial giving?

Some of them are here, [gestures around
    the room]
a large number of them
are down the hallway—
you've got to see them,
you've got to learn from them,
but I can tell you about my favorite one,
it's by Katie Adams—
and it's right by the water fountain
in the hallway—
and Katie has said,
"What can I sacrifice for the church?
Jesus gave his whole body,
all you have to give is an arm and a leg!"
Isn't that wonderful?
It is hard to sacrifice.
It does hurt.
Sometimes it does feel like
an arm and a leg,
to let go of this church,
as we know it now,
this church that we love,
this place that feels so comfortable—
to let go
and let it grow.
May we find encouragement with one
    another
for the living of our lives,
and may we find encouragement
from Mother Hannah
to lend to God
the church we love,
and to offer to God our church
for the present and the future time.
    Amen.

The Good News According to Ziggy

KIM RYAN
Broadway Christian Church-Disciples of Christ
Columbia, Missouri
September 19, 1993

The Scripture selection suggested for the
church this day
is from the book of Exodus.
We find ourselves part-way
through that story,
the story about how Moses was called to
help
the Israelite people be free from the
bondage
and the slavery of Egypt.
Those people left.
They left their homes
and found themselves on a journey
in the wilderness.
The place where our Scripture begins,
Moses has gone up on the mountain
and left the people far below.

"When the people saw that Moses
delayed
to come down from the mountain,
they gathered themselves together, to
Aaron
and they said to him,
'Up! Make God for us.

God who shall go before us.
We have heard this Moses,
this man who brought
us up out of the land of Egypt,
We do not know what has become of
him.'
And Aaron said to them,
'Take off your rings of gold
which are in the ears of your wives,
your sons, and your daughters,
and bring them to me.'
So all the people took off their rings of
gold
which were in their ears
and brought them to Aaron.
And he received the gold of their hand
and fashioned it with a brazen tool
and made a molten calf.
And then said,
'Behold your God, O Israel,
who brought you up from the land of
Egypt.'
The people made an altar before it,
And Aaron issued a proclamation which
read,

'Tomorrow shall be a feast to the lord.'
And they rose up early on the morrow
and offered burnt offerings
and brought peace offerings
and the people sat down to eat
and drink
and rose up to play.
And the Lord said to Moses,
'Go down!.
For your people, whom you brought up
    out of the land of Egypt
have corrupted themselves;
they have turned aside quickly
from the way which I commanded them;
they have made for themselves a molten
    calf,
and have worshipped it
and sacrificed to it, and said,
'these are your gods, oh Israel,
who brought you up out of the land of
    Egypt.'
The Lord said to Moses,
'I have seen this people,
and, behold, it is a stiff-necked people.
Now, therefore, let me alone,
so that my wrath may burn hot against
    them
and I may consume them;
and of you I will make a great nation.'
But Moses besought the Lord his God
    and said,
'Oh, Lord, why does thy wrath burn hot
    against thy people
whom thou hast brought forth
out of the land of Egypt
with great power and a mighty hand?
Why should the Egyptians say,
with evil intent,
that their God brought them forth

to slay them in the mountains
and consume them from the face of the
    earth?
Turn from thy fierce wrath
and repent of this evil against thy people.
Remember Abraham and Sarah,
and Isaac and Israel,
Thy servants,
to whom thou did swear by thine own self
and did say to them,
'I will multiply thy descendents
as the stars of heaven
and all this land that see here
I will give to your descendents
and they shall inherit it forever.
And the Lord repented of the evil
which he had thought to do to his
    people." [Exodus 32:1–14]
This is the word from the history of our
    people
to the people of today,
for our purpose and for our future.
May God bless us.

A group of women.
They'd come together in Marion, Indiana.
And when I got there—
I had never met these women before—
and when I got there,
I realized that they really were
a rather common, ordinary
group of women—
ones that I might see at the grocery
    store,
or in my neighborhood,
or they could be seen driving down the
    street,
a lady I sat next to in church—
but this group of women

was not really a common group of
women,
they shared a similar problem—
and their problem is not a common one,
although probably
it is more common than what I would like
to think.
For you see
these were women who had come
together,
who had been abused,
physically,
by their partners,
by the people they loved.
And they had invited me
to come and spend that evening with
them
because I was connected with
a hotline for abused women at a nearby
town,
and because I was a minister.
And in the course of their group getting
together
they had begun to discuss
some kind of spiritual questions,
and so they invited me to come
and talk with them.
And you can probably guess
what some of their questions were all
about—
they asked questions about forgiveness
and how to give it to others,
and how to give it to themselves.
And they asked questions about
strength—
where to find it,
where to get enough of it,
to get them through the day.
And they asked questions

about how God factored in their lives,
and where God was—
One woman said,
"Well, you know, my husband told me
that
as the head of the household,
he represented God,
and he was only carrying out God's
punishment for me,
when he beat me."
"I used to believe that,"
she said,
"but I'm not so sure anymore.
What do you think?"

Well, you can probably guess what I
think! [with a tough look on her face]
[some laughter, or chuckles, from the
congregation]
And I realized,
as we spent the next hour and a half
together,
that a part of what their questions were
about—
were trying to understand—
What's God like?
What is God really like?
And how could they trust God?
And I wondered how they might describe
God.
What were some of the descriptions
that they were operating out of?
A vengeful God?
A patient God?
Yes, those were there.
A powerful God?
A controlling God?
Probably.
But they were beginning to question

those descriptions
and understandings.
And there are times
for each one of us,
maybe not as dramatic
or as life-threatening
as it was for those women,
but there are times
when each of us
begins to ask,
what if God is not like my assumptions?

What if God is different
from what I've been told?

So we begin to think about
and explore
that kind of question.

I recently saw this very question
addressed in a source
of highest scholarship,
one of most profound inquiry—
Ziggy!
[laughter]
You may be surprised,
but listen to what Ziggy
is doing
with this question.

Ziggy's walking along and Ziggy says,
to a little weed with a bug on it,
"Look at that little insect.
If I choose to exercise
my all-powerful,
my Godlike control,
I could squash this little life out."
And then Ziggy said,
"On the other hand,

it might be more Godlike and
all-powerful,
if I choose not to squash
this life out.
Yeah,
I like that better.
Fly away little bug
have a nice life."
And then Ziggy looks out at you and me
and says,
"Hmm,
now I really feel all-powerful and
Godlike."
I wish I had had this cartoon
when I met with those women.
I wonder if we had talked about it,
could they have begun to see God
in a different way
than what their experience had taught
them.
Their experience had taught them:
God will squash your little life out,
or someone that you love will do it in
God's name.
Would it—
would it have made a difference to
them—
could they have even heard
the possibility that God's power
is in giving life,
encouraging life?

Fly away,
have a new life.

Probably the most important—
a more important question—
for us today is
can we hear?

Can we hear the possibility
of God being different from our
  assumptions?

Did you hear in the Scripture
for today—
did you hear
that description of God?
Did you notice what that said about God?
Now I have to admit,
when I read that story,
my attention tends to be drawn to the
  people
and what they're doing.
I have this reaction:
why is it—
shame on them—
they should have known better—
how dare they make that calf—
and worship it.
And then on the other hand,
I find myself trying to make excuses for
  them.
Well, I mean, after all,
they had to leave their home
they had to go down to Israel.
They were following a man,
who said he represented God,
who makes promises and then leaves
  them.
This guy disappears,
and they're stuck out in the middle of
  nowhere.
They're tired—
they're impatient—
and waiting.
They want action.
So they call on Aaron,
the second in command:

do something,
make something happen.
And I read that
and I begin to see myself
and see those folks as kind of a reflection
of me,
when I start feeling scared
or impatient
or uncertain and I start looking for a way
  out
and I start looking for help—
where's the power?
Where's something to help me out?
Is it in the golden dollars?
Is it in my dreams
of bigger and better?
Can I find it in something as simple
as holding onto the thrill
of my favorite football team victory?
[laughter]
Well, what I know is that
there have been a few golden calves
that've taken shape in my life,
created out of my perceived treasures
and valuables.
What about you?
Do you understand these folks
coming to us from Exodus?

And so it takes some effort
to pull my attention away from them
and from myself,
and look at God
in that Scripture selection,
and look at how God is described
in that story.
God is a God of feeling—
a God who experiences the pain of
  betrayal,

and who is hurt,
who takes that all too common leap
into anger.
You know the feeling. [whisper]
And this is a God
of relationships,
of give and take
God's not in a vacuum saying,
my way's the only way,
my thought's the only thought
to think.
God's in a dialogue
with Moses,
a relationship
of mutuality,
and intimacy.
And then,
that most surprising part of all—
did you hear it?
God repents.

Well now, I've heard about people
    repenting,
but have you ever heard about God
    repenting?
God turning around?
God choosing a different direction?
God listening to Moses,
and God changes God's mind?
It's there!
And here we are with some rather
    intriguing
descriptions of God:
a God who feels pain and anger,
a God involved in a relationship of
    closeness,
of intimacy,
and a God
who opens up

to the possibility of change.
How could this be?
Who could cause God to change God's
    mind?
In the midst of their relationship,
Moses reminds God:
"Remember who you are.
Remember you are the God of life.
You brought us
from destruction to life
You brought us
from oppression
to freedom.
You brought us
from violence into safety.
Remember,
You promised life
to Abraham and Sarah
and Isaac and Ishmael.
And the Lord remembered
and repented
of what he had thought to destroy—
and I'm reminded of Ziggy—
it might be more Godlike
and all-powerful,
If I choose not
to squash their little lives.

I think about those women in Indiana
and the sad reality
that there are women
and children
and men
just like them
in probably every community in this
    country.
And I try not to despair.
And what I hope and I pray for them
is that they find a way to discover

that God is not to be understood
or interpreted by the abusive hand
or through the voices of anger and pain.
I hope that they can come to describe
and experience God
and to love life.
I pray for them a God of safety
and not violence—
a God of freedom
and not oppression—
a God of encouragement
and not destruction.
And I hope they know
that God is to be understood
and felt
in the hotline number
that can be called,
and internally
in the voice and the person
at the other end of that phone,
in the place where there's a safe bed
and protection in one another
and in themselves,
as they offer support
and encouragement
to each other.

How we understand
and how we describe God
is very, very important,
and for God's sake—
and for our own—
it is especially important
if we understand ourselves
to be created in the image of God.
If God can be understood as
a God who feels pain and anger,
then we can trust
that God feels our pain

and our anger,
and we can give ourselves permission
to feel pain and anger,
for ourselves,
and for someone else.
And if God is a God
who allowed for a relationship of
    dialogue,
not monologue—
not my way's the only way—
then we can search for
relationships of dialogue
relationships of closeness
and intimacy and mutuality,
and we can enter into those relationships
with one another
and with God.
And if God can choose
to change course
and to turn away from destruction
toward the preference for life,
so can we,
so can we.
And in doing so,
we can really feel powerful
and Godlike.

That Ziggy cartoon reminded me of
    something
that I thought I had forgotten,
but when I looked at the picture,
a memory resurfaced,
an image from
ten or fifteen years ago.
And I remember a little boy about
seven years old—
his name was Toby
and he had come to the camp for
    disabled little children

and I worked there that summer.
You need to know that
Toby's disability,
I don't remember now what was the
   cause,
but he had to wear braces
that were somehow connected
and they kept his feet apart,
and that he could walk,
even like that,
he could manage to walk.
 And that afternoon
I saw Tony a little ways down a path
all bent over
and he was reaching down
and staring at the ground,
and I got closer,
and I could see
that Tony had found
a butterfly on the ground.
It must have had a broken wing,
and he kept picking it up,
and he'd say,
"Fly!
Fly butterfly!"

And I remember that
and realized
that there was an image
of God
in that scene,
but an image
of God
as a God who knows the pain,
and out of the knowing
encourages life
and flight.
An image of a God
who can in all power
and in all love
help us to fly. [whisper]

I think Ziggy's right,
and I think
the story from Exodus
about a feeling,
intimate,
life-choosing God
is right on!
Amen.

Chapter 5
A Dialogic Paradigm

What Women Bring to Christian Religion

Preaching, in itself, is an integral part of what is springing forth in human consciousness—a new awareness, asking the questions. We don't know the answers. God is a
mystery. But we keep asking the questions and I think our understanding continues to
evolve, and I think there is power in that.

—Margaret Ann

The messages I discern in the sermons of the women in this study are like-
minded invitations toward community, connection, solidarity, reimagining,
inclusion, and affirmed diversity for all humans. This new dimension is
closely associated with the emergence of larger numbers of women in the
pulpits of Christian churches everywhere. Although I am quite aware of the
pitfalls of any suggestion that women are "inherently" one way or another
or that they are "essentially" prone to collaboration and community, I am
prepared to argue that women's lives and experiences, their roles within
the sociopolitical and domestic spheres of their worlds, their interactions
with one another, and their private and collective explorations of who God
is and how God is revealed, make them conscious of the importance of
such concepts as community, connectedness, collaboration, inclusiveness,
diversity, empathy, and love in ways that critically inform their lives and
their ministries. They would, in fact, claim these concepts to be essential
for survival. In this chapter, I name the present religious shift the "dialogic
paradigm," which represents new possibilities beyond what Loren Mead
calls the "Christendom paradigm."[1] I relate the ministries and sermons of
the women in my study specifically to a controversial conference and then
evoke a larger picture of the face of Christianity today as reflected in and
by the presence of women in ministry in general and in the pulpit in particular.

The Re-Imagining Conference

In November 1993, several women in my research group attended a four-day ecumenical Christian conference held in Minneapolis. When they first heard about this conference, they suggested that we all go. As it turned out, I was not able to attend, but several of the others in our group did. The Re-Imagining Conference was attended by over 2,000 women and 67 men from 49 U.S. states and 27 countries. The conference was organized to mark the midpoint of the World Council of Churches Ecumenical Decade of the Churches in Solidarity with Women (1988–1998); the format of the conference was designed to celebrate contributions women have made to the Christian church through leadership as laywomen, pastors, and theologians. As it turned out, however, this event, intended to mark the Decade in Solidarity with Women, has instead become the benchmark for how churches have drawn the line in terms of supporting (some) women's ways of knowing, experiencing, and "imagining" God.

At this conference, women (and a few men) gathered to share Christian ministries, theologies, rituals, and concerns about the present and future reality of the Christian faith. Chinese theologians and ministers shared the podium with African-American and African ministers; Korean women spoke; and openly lesbian women led prayers and rituals. The divine was addressed in a wide variety of ways, including with the name of Sophia, or Wisdom, a practice that goes back to the Hebrew Scripture. A milk-and-honey ritual was designed to represent the earliest Christian eucharistic rituals and to make all participants feel welcome at "the table" by reclaiming some ancient biblical symbols. Conference organizers and most participants were surprised and pleased with the numbers who attended, with how crowded all the rooms and auditoriums were. They were amazed at how powerful and "empowering" some of the services were, how inclusive and embracing the conference was, how experimental, how inspiring, how diverse, how collaborative, how thought provoking, how respectful of diversity, and how inclusive the activities of the four days were. The women in this study also spoke of how often they felt it was all "too much" at once, an overload of possibilities, beliefs, rituals, and speakers. The women I know who went are extremely glad that they did. What they brought home with them was a wide range of possibilities for their own spiritual growth and some thoughts for how to claim the spirit of the conference for their own congregations at home.

But not everyone agrees with these perceptions of the conference. Denominational newsletters have been filled with pages either decrying the conference or supporting its efforts; major metropolitan newspapers have covered the conference with headlines such as "Reacting to Re-Imagining: Women's conference sending shock waves through Protestant denominations" (*Atlanta Journal,* May 21, 1994); the highly conservative American Family Association published a separate report for April 1994, "The Re-Imagining Conference: A Report—Information on a pagan conference sponsored by mainline denominations," blasting the conference for what they considered to be heretical rituals and warning denominations to find ways to reprimand those who participated. Most of these reports focused on the sensual text of the milk-and-honey ritual and on several statements made by keynote speakers—all taken out of context and presented as "evidence" of the non-Christian tendencies of the conference. The debate continues three years later.

The backlash against the conference, its speakers, and the participants has been vocal, angry, and in some cases has caused women involved with the organization of the conference to lose the support of their denominations and even to lose their positions as pastors or administrators. Those who decry the conference are shocked because they are learning that the conference cannot be easily dismissed as the brainchild of a number of warped, deviant, pagan worshippers, nor have they been successful in taking a paternalistic attitude toward ordinary women and ministers who attended. Those who organized the conference, and those who attended as willing participants, do not see the conference as an abberration, a fluke, nor did they return from it filled with so-called "pagan" inclinations. For most, it was a conference over-filled with possibilities, respectful and tolerant of some of the many and varied positive directions they see Christianity moving. The conference also marked the first time many women had seen the female experience of the divine freely embraced.

Negative coverage of the Re-Imagining Conference sought to mobilize a conservative show of strength to protest the use of church funds and the participation of church officials in a conference that was accused as including pagan rituals, worshipping of 'the female goddess Sophia,' celebrating lesbianism, and rejecting the atonement of Jesus Christ. However, Catherine Keller, in an article about the conference published in *Christian Century* entitled "Inventing the Goddess: A Study in Ecclesiastical Backlash," enthusiastically endorses the conference, explaining that the liturgies, workshops, talks, sermons, rituals at the conference affirmed the diversity of female experience and "celebrated the sacredness of women's lives as reflecting the image of God in which we are all created."[2] Keller claims the heresy hunters themselves created "the goddess Sophia" and the supposed worshipping of her at the conference. She traces biblical references to Sophia, concluding that "This Sophia, not a goddess but simply a biblical female metaphor for the holy . . . . offered a luminous—if rather modest—point of connection between traditional biblical language and the feminist evolution of faith. She [Sophia] does not replace but rather refreshes traditional talk of God and Christ."[3]

Keller suggests that the controversy over the Re-Imagining Conference is "another chapter in this century's battle of the evangelical right vs. the liberal pluralists."[4] I appreciate much of what Keller has written about the conference, but I would go even further than she has. I propose that the Re-Imagining Conference represents the first collective glimpse of a paradigm shift in modern Christianity—a view of the dialogic paradigm at work: women together, exploring the possibilities for diverse ways to re-imagine what they know about God, to reimagine concepts of the deity, of spirituality, of connectedness, collaborative knowing, learning, and questioning.

The emergence of this new paradigm creates suspicion and fear. Reminiscent of the witch trials in both Europe and the Americas, critics of the conference, bishops, and high church officials are poring over pieces of the ecumenical conference material to examine it for orthodoxy.[5] Liturgies are being distorted by "ripping image after image out of context, yoking together the most sensuous metaphors in order to create an aura of pornography."[6] The criticism is blatant: "to picture the divine through *female pronouns, experiences, and bodies* is heretical and obscene" (emphasis mine); self-appointed disciplinarians of the church are "charging apostasy, heresy, and demanding purges," and calling for "church discipline."[7] We ask with Keller, "what sort of language is this?" It is, she acknowledges, the language of *fear.* "In this time of transition to the next millennium, we are all a bit scared. We are afraid that change will not be for the better."[8] She notes that the criticism is coming largely from those who already see a change in their own church membership, attendance, and things religious. She claims that since pastors themselves are not being pastored through "the sacrifice of traditional modes and symbols of masculine power,"[9] they turn to scapegoating as a way of coping. Keller admits that the power of women can appear overwhelming to those, men and women alike, who currently hold church authority and are on the defensive. Indeed, as women gain both power *and* authority, men who feel that their own power is diminished by having to share authority are tempted to stress the "her" of "heresy," but Keller finds strength in the chaos: "The strength of the backlash is testimony to the power of our accomplishments. Our diversity gives us an unprecedented healing force—especially as we mature in solidarity with like-minded men."[10]

The conference has gained widespread publicity, especially after its denunciation by the Presbyterian publication the *Presbyterian Layman* and its key reporter, Susan Cyre, who debated Rita Nakashima Brock on Ted Koppel's *Nightline* program (May 24, "Is God Necessarily Male, and What If She Isn't?"). Subsequent reports have flourished in denominational publications, some pro, some con, and in the public media as well—on the *MacNeil Lehrer Newshour* and on National Public Radio, for instance. The backlash has been most harsh from the conservative members of the Christian community, protestors who have been successful in influencing others. For example, the Reverend Mary Ann Lundy, the highest-ranking national Presbyterian woman and director of women's concerns, lost her job because she obtained funds to help support the conference and the denomination withdrew its support after hearing "what happened there"; another woman, United Methodist bishop Susan Morrison, has been charged with heresy as part of the backlash.

Meanwhile, Rita Nakashima Brock, a theologian, describes the conference in positive terms as a place where "women and men re-envisioned Christian faith through theology, art and liturgy in ways that affirmed the full humanity of women created in God's image."[11] What actually *happened* at the conference, Brock claims, was "singing, dancing, praying, drawing and thinking together . . . [learning] how diverse Christian theology becomes when women take experiences of the Holy Spirit in our lives seriously."[12] What Brock says she learned from the conference is "how elastic, big, and alive the gospel is."[13] But certainly not everyone sees it this way. Critics claim that rituals were distorted, that goddess worship was encouraged, and that homosexuals were encouraged to believe they were welcome in the proceedings. What I explore in this chapter is how this conference, intended as an ecumenical statement of solidarity with women in the church, may actually be far more than that. The conference represents one aspect of the emergence of a new Christian paradigm; one of dialogue, not only between parties who agree with one another but between parties who have agreed to disagree yet stand together in their differences and proclaim they are all Christians. What happened at the Re-imagining Conference was perhaps not what the denominations thought was going to happen, perhaps it became even more significant than the coordinators had ever dreamed. The backlash and the emotional response to the conference go far beyond negative reactions to particular acts done in Christian space; the intense responses arise from the fear that takes us by surprise when we are confronted with the very real possibilities for change and catch a glimpse of the future. We are all awed. In this moment, some members of the Christian community run and hide, screaming all the way. Others walk boldly forward, embracing the new with trembling arms.

The Future Church Is Here and She Comes with a New Vision

In his 1991 book, *The Once and Future Church*, Loren Mead posits that since the life of Jesus, two major paradigms have captured the religious world. The first he names the "apostolic paradigm," which dictated for good Christians a way to live an evangelistic life based on the mission work of

Jesus Christ: the intimate religious community formed the basis for fervent work among outsiders who were hostile to "the word." Mead sees the collapse of this paradigm, which was relatively short lived, with the conversion of Constantine and the wedding of church and state, creating a world where dedication to the church was synonymous with dedication to the state, a paradigm Mead identifies as the "Christendom paradigm." In this worldview, the object of mission was understood to be the heathen lands yet to be dominated and converted by the empire. Everyone in the kingdom belonged to a designated parish, which worked to connect local persons with the dictating hierarchy.

Mead proposes, in his small but important book, that this long-standing paradigm has begun to crumble in recent times and that a new paradigm is emerging—one that has not yet been identified. Mead argues that some of the characteristics of the Christendom paradigm have remained somewhat secure, even though the rhetoric would suggest otherwise. Our Constitution may mandate separation of church and state, he argues, but Christians nevertheless remain more comfortable when neither church nor state is challenged, and they still perceive missions as appropriately somewhere "over there," among supposed "pagans and primitives." Individual congregations, however, begin to identify their "turf" as distinct from that of other congregations as they draw their identifications more narrowly than before, and the drive for unity disappears as diversity and difference become all too clear. Yet hindsight reveals that uniformity is the typical mode, and difference becomes only a tool for differentiation between groups, not a characteristic *within* groups. Difference is rarely the praxis for the kind of dialogue and discussion that might lead to change and revolution.

Several aspects of Mead's essay are pertinent to our consideration of the Re-Imagining Conference of 1993. Most important, perhaps, is how the women attending and participating in the conference were, and are, re-imagining what "standing in unity" might mean—that is, standing together *in their diversity.*

Mead seems genuinely concerned about the different possible forms this new paradigm might take. He insists that the shift has already begun to occur, that there is nothing we can do about it, that it is God's will, and Jesus never said it would be easy. He claims Christians have been "nurtured in this fractionating Christendom paradigm and living within institutions shaped by it, we have begun to awaken to the early stages of a new one. *Neither the new age nor the new paradigm has arrived, so we are pulled by the new and constrained by the old without the privilege even of knowing fully what the new will be like. But as the new has begun to reveal itself, it has made us profoundly uncomfortable.*"[14] According to Mead, the crisis for Christians is that the outlines of the new paradigm are not yet clear: "The new paradigm may call for more diversity than we are used to or may feel comfortable with."[15] In fact, while Mead insists that the new church cannot be seen yet, he says he works toward it because it is inevitable: "A new church is being born," he tells us, but "it may not be the church we expect or want."[16] Mead's rhetoric reflects the reluctance of many Christians to actually embrace change and diversity. The rhetoric implies that it offers "hospitality" but can also seduce the membership into a *laissez-faire* attitude of "anything goes."[17] Clearly, diversity and how the congregations are going to stand unified in their diversity is a dilemma for all Christian groups to ponder.

In reading Mead's widely acclaimed book, I found it surprising and not a little disconcerting that he implies the "new paradigm" is emerging but that "we" don't yet know what it looks like and may not be particularly pleased with its shape and form when we *can* see it. I would like to suggest that his neatly constructed, three-part paradigm is too simplistic (as all such outlines really are destined to be) in that it ignores some of the efforts that have been made all along by believers working *from the margins*, taking different stances within the traditional Christian discourse. Work from the margins is always the work of change, of revolution, of rethinking, and of reimagining.

In particular, I am surprised that Loren Mead does not acknowledge or explore how women are, and have been all along, radically changing the face of Christianity, or how the image or reality of a woman in the pulpit automatically creates a significant cognitive and imagistic shift. In chapter 3 of his book, "Cracks in the System," Mead recognizes that "systems that seem stable and secure often have internal tensions and pressures that lead to dramatic, surprising changes."[18] He admits that "Changes of paradigm are, by definition, matters of perception, feeling, world view, consciousness; they are not external changes like the leveling of a mountain."[19] Christendom has never felt "stable and secure" for many female Christians. Early Christian women's writings point to the pain of their own exclusion from the priesthood and from religious power and to their reliance on spirituality for sustenance in oppressive religious and cultural arenas. For women who have been praying for an opening-up of the Christendom paradigm, this shift will not be viewed as frightening, but as challenging, exhilarating, appropriate, and *about time*.

I would like to suggest that the new paradigm Mead prophesied has emerged, is currently visible, and is taking shape as a direct reflection of women participating in the work of ministry, holding posts as clergy, preaching in the pulpits, and doing theology together with their sisters, lay and ordained, and with men who are listening and willing to participate in this important revolutionary work. The Re-Imagining Conference did not so much herald the new paradigm as acknowledge its already manifested form. A shift has already occurred, and the prognosis for the survival of Christian thought and influence is quite good. The new participatory, influential presence of women in religion, particularly in the pulpit, offers glimpses of the new paradigm and what it is becoming; community, relationship, shared authority, and connectedness are becoming charters for theology, liturgy, and living the Christian life.

The Emergence of the Dialogic Paradigm

How new, how radical, is the theology, the thinking, and the approaches of the women at the Re-Imagining Conference? How well does it represent what women are doing within the Christian world at large? How *ought* the institutional leaders respond to the conference? I think the Re-Imagining Conference represents, in many ways, the language, the frustrations, the experiences of Christian women worldwide. Collectively, the activities at the conference represent no one aspect of the new paradigm of the new church, but together they do afford a glimpse of the concerns, the values, the beliefs, and the shift that has begun to take place in Christianity. This shift has occurred because women are speaking from pulpits across this land and beyond. Women, speaking from their own experiences in the margins, have cracked the old paradigm beyond repair. Emerging from the cracks and fissures are glimpses of the new, and what women worldwide are calling for is dialogue between the old order and the future order. The groundwork for this dialogue was laid long before the 1993 conference. Several key theologians and practitioners of Christian religion have served as midwives for the birth of this new dialogic paradigm of the new era. Some of them used language and approaches that led naturally to the openness and creativity evident at the Re-Imagining Conference.

Foremothers of the New Paradigm

In 1982, Sallie McFague wrote in *Metaphorical Theology: Models of God in Religious Language*,[20] "I have not found it possible as a contemporary Christian to support an incarnational christology or a canonical Scripture; nevertheless, I have found it possible to support a 'parabolic' christology and Scripture as the Christian 'classic.' "[21] Religious language, according to McFague, is a problem for women because we are unsure not only about how we talk about God, we are also unsure about God: "For most of us, it is not a question of being sure of God while being unsure of our language about God. Rather, we are unsure both at the experiential and the expressive levels." In speaking about God-talk or how humans conceptualize God, she argues that feminists generally agree that whoever names the world owns the world.[22] McFague stresses the appropriate use of God as a *person* because, she says, "as we were made *in the image of God* [Genesis 3: 27], so we now, with the model of Jesus, have further support for imagining God in *our* image, the image of persons. This means that *personal, relational images* are central in a metaphorical theology—images of God as father, mother, lover, friend, savior, ruler, governor, servant, companion, comrade, liberator, and so on. She quotes from Ursula LeGuin, who says "truth lies in the imagination." [23] The tasks of metaphorical theology, McFague tells us, are to understand the centrality of models in religion and the particular models in the Christian tradition; to criticize literalized, exclusive models; to chart the relationships among metaphors, models, and concepts; and to investigate possibilities for transformative, revolutionary models.[24] She continues: "The classic models of the Christian tradition have been and still are hierarchical, authoritarian ones which have been absolutized. Feminists have become conscious of the profound structural implications of this model as a form of ecclesiastical, social, political, economic, and personal oppression." [25] The model of "God the father" has "established a hegemony over the Western religious consciousness, which it is the task of metaphorical theology to break." According to McFague, the "outsiders" to the mainline Christian tradition—women, blacks, third world people—are questioning the hierarchical, authoritarian, patriarchal models of Western theology. In a hopeful spirit, she claims, "we will look at new religious images and models being suggested by women and we will do so in the spirit of openness to the future and to the unity that lies in the future." [26]

The fifteenth annual meeting of the Women's Interseminary Conference at Princeton Theological Seminary (April 1987) was conceived as an "ecumenical dialogue" among women of diverse backgrounds. The volume of collected essays emerging from that conference was published in 1988 as *Inheriting Our Mothers' Gardens: Feminist Theology in Third World Perspective.*[27] The Christian women contributing to this volume attest to "alternate religious and spiritual reality taught to them by their mothers and grandmothers, great aunts, and wise women, one based on their very real life experiences." After listing all the groups the various authors belong to, meet in, and continue to support, the authors of this collection comment: "We believe our network has to be a global one in which women of all colors, cultures, and continents share their stories of faith and struggle. Our stories here are an invitation to join us in this very local and yet worldwide network." [28] In the introduction they talk about women developing together "theologies in partnership." Many of the speakers and writers in this conference re-emerge as keynote speakers and preachers at the Re-Imagining Conference in 1993. Kwok Pui-lan, a Chinese Christian, writes about her mother, mother-in-law, and grandmothers in China, in her essay "Mothers and Daughters, Writers and Fighters"; her words could be claimed by women worldwide: "The stories of my mothers drive home to me a very precious lesson: as women living in a patriarchal cultural system, they are oppressed by men, but, never contented to be treated as victims, they have struggled against the forces that seek to limit them and circumscribe their power.[29] She acknowledges the power against women as evidenced in sexism, racism, and classism in her homeland and in Christian churches in her country. Women joined forces to fight for literacy, health care, and associations for women, and to fight against the crippling tradition of footbinding. "These activities allowed women to come together and talk about their problems and to find ways and means to tackle them. . . . [T]hey bear witness to a faith that empowers people [women] to break through silence and move to action."[30] Kwok Pui-lan rejects the arrogance of the claim that "outside the church, there is no salvation" and celebrates the possibilities for a kind of realistic syncretism of beliefs, advocating a "constant *dialogue* with [China's] rich cultural heritage," which is radically different from the Christian tradition.[31] Chinese folk religion never did exclude female perspective, imagery, or symbolism. Only Christianity did that!

Kwok Pui-lan's writing represents a lifelong love for the Christian faith but an honest appraisal of its failings for women. She advocates approaching theology through women's experiences: Women have been excluded from the mythology- and symbol-making processes. Women must reclaim their right to be involved. Doing our own theology(ies), she notes, requires "moving away from a unified theological discourse to a plurality of voices and a genuine catholicity." Her criterion for judging how theology gets done lies at the heart of our concern here. Theology must include human concern for freedom and justice, peace and reconciliation: "Unity does not mean homogeneity, and catholicity does not mean sameness."[32] In "doing theology," she claims, diversity is paramount: "Women's stories will be heard and our experiences valued in our theological imagination."

In the same volume, Chung Hyun Kyung's article, "Following Naked Dancing and Long Dreaming,"[33] recounts how both her mother and her birth mother managed to combine their Korean heritage with Christian teachings.[34] Similarly, Marta Benavides, in her essay "My Mother's Garden Is a New Creation," tells us, "My Mother's definition of spiritual was to care and act on behalf of life, to keep people alive."[35] "Religion," she says, "is not sacred; people and life are sacred. So I learned the banality of rituals and religion that don't respond to justice."[36] Letty Russell, in her concluding article, "From Garden to Table," calls for women to unite and share their stories, asserting a need to "discuss our theology around the kitchen table," acknowledging, of course, that theology courses that begin with ordinary stories of women as they gather around their kitchen table or cooking areas are not considered to be professional theological courses by those who do so-called "classical" theology. Yet Russell remains steadfast: "Approaching the table as partners requires that we begin where people are and stay connected to the reality of their lives." Here Russell advocates reimagining the kitchen table, as well as the communion table, as a round table, known in the African-American community as a *welcome table*: "We have to make provision to welcome all the gifts persons bring to the meal and design structures in communities where there is no head or foot, no corners where persons get lost."[37] The effort, she says, may take creativity and determination, and it may be painful to accomplish, but the new paradigm is a challenge to be tackled, gladly, not a malignancy to be feared.

Like the other authors in this volume and like the women in my study, Katie Geneva Cannon locates power in the efforts of women working collectively. "The oppression exercised by men in the church is still profound and capable of killing the spirit of women. The situation changes only as women band together, find their common voice, and begin the struggle to challenge the status quo."[38] She finds that "A network is . . . a source of inspiration and motivation. It is an empowering force."[39]

In 1992 Elizabeth A. Johnson published her provocative book *She Who Is: The Mystery of God in Feminist Theological Discourse*, in which she offers a way to think theologically, from a base of women's experience, about divine power: "We seek an understanding that does not divide power and compassionate love in a dualistic framework that identifies love with a resignation of power and the exercise of power with a denial of love. Rather, we seek to integrate these two, seeing love as the shape in which divine power appears." Significantly, Johnson locates the power of women's experience in their position in the margins: ". . . women who know the breakthrough of their own strength, usually under duress" are the ones whose experiences can teach us what this kind of empowering vigor, this vital form of power is like, based in the courage of (violated) women who reach out to establish connectedness, "deriving energy that they critically turn toward the well-being of others."[40]

Midway through the Ecumenical Decade of Churches in Solidarity with Women, Kathleen S. Hurty spoke at the Arizona Ecumenical Council's 1993 Donohoe Forum on "Collaborative Leadership in Chaotic Times." In two days of speaking, she argued that "the full acknowledgement of women's experience, women's ways of knowing, styles of leadership, and gifts to community have been ignored, demeaned, or considered peripheral."[41] Calling for an understanding of leadership that would include women's voices is long overdue, she claims, and proceeds to outline what "collaborative leadership" might look like. Hurty says her presentations are a "woven fabric of theological, social, and organizational reflection" delivered with plenty of time for "hefty mutual dialogue." Her three major themes are power and partnership, conflict and the collaborative community, and leadership and the language of love.

Hurty claims women look at and conceive of the uses of power differently. "If I believe that power is a finite resource—meaning if I have more, you therefore have less—I would be likely to choose a controlling 'power over' style of leadership. If, on the other hand, I believe that power is an expandable resource—that power can be shared and enlarged—I would be likely to choose an empowering, enabling 'power with' style of leadership."[42] She asserts that power in the public world and thus in the church has been historically defined predominantly out of male experience, "resulting in a fractured and partial understanding of the dynamics of power."[43] Alternatively, Hurty suggests that women have a collegial style that reflects cooperation, connectedness, diversity, subjectivity, attributes more in line with the original Latin "posse" for the word power, which means "to be able." Creating space where power is "enabled" for all participants as a possibility, an energy, an ability to act is an entirely different approach from seeking power which is understood as a noun—a quality or property, something to have, own, earn, or take. She claims women seek to develop a kind of "power with" divine reality, rather than a "power over,"—the hierarchical power long established by the patriarchy. Hurty's research identifies a "different voice" when women take on leadership roles in both educational and religious arenas—a voice that emphasizes connectedness, co-activity, shared and expandable power, and empowerment. The elements of co-active empowerment identified by Hurty include emotional energy, nurtured growth, *reciprocal talk*, pondered mutuality, collaborative change. Significantly, she claims "these are not particularly unusual attributes of human interaction, nor are they limited to women's use—*they have simply not been equated with power!*"[44]

In her second Donohoe lecture, also delivered six months before the Re-Imagining Conference, Hurty asserts that "when reflective struggles are grounded in daily experiences of living faithfully, then we are 'doing theology.'"[45] She calls for a "lovers' quarrel" with the churches, suggesting that quarreling is evidence of caring, evidence of a relationship that is dynamic and in which love is central. She calls for *dialogue* in a new way: "Taking seriously the Ecumenical Decade of the Churches in Solidarity with Women is one way of quarrelling with the status quo in the churches."[45] Indeed! She notes that Mary Ann Lundy and Forrest Stith call for the churches to "engage in women's struggles and create a sharing, healing, empowering ministry" in the preface to their 1991 publication *Women and Church: The Challenge of Ecumenical Solidarity in an Age of Alienation.* Hurty congratulates these authors for denouncing hierarchy and the oppression of women, and for freeing themselves from racism, sexism, and classism in modeling new forms of partnership. Hurty describes the challenge for those involved in the ecumenical decade in solidarity with women to explore, reflect on, and act together in full, collaborative, co-actively empowered partnership! How badly this challenge has been accepted is evidenced in the backlash against the Re-Imagining Conference where female power has been evoked only to be viewed with fear and loathing.

Re-Imagining as a Reflection of What Women Bring to Religion

What took place in Minneapolis was not a freak occurrence; nor was it very different from what is happening in many churches across the United States and elsewhere as women enter the pulpit and preach newly inspired messages of diversity and collaboration. To be sure, these and other new approaches to community and diversity are not embraced by all women, clergy or lay. Certainly many women claim indignantly that they never feel "oppressed" in their Christian churches and feel completely comfortable with the image of "God the Father." Others may never have heard of or read feminist theologians such as those discussed here. For some women, on the other hand, these approaches are "too little, too late," and they find it more and more difficult to remain connected to any form of institutional Christianity.

But enough women in the pews and now in the pulpits of mainstream churches are questioning the rigidity of how Christians "paint" God and interact with God and each other on a regular basis that their discomfort has caused them to shift their ways of thinking, seeking spirituality, doing theology, praying, worshipping, studying the Bible, and imaging how God works in their lives. For these women the Re-Imagining Conference delivered very little they would find entirely "new." But certainly they found it provocative, radical, experimental, exploratory, exciting, and connected.

If women are not preaching to support and preserve the major paradigms of the traditional, dominant Christian discourse(s), then what are they preaching? Are they preaching in such a way to disrupt the traditional Christian discourse(s)? Is their message radical, revolutionary, or reformatory? If their message is different, how does it interact/intersect with the traditional discourse(s)? How does it build on or disrupt the dominant discourse(s)? Where are the fissures in the current Christian paradigm that allow for the disruptive message women want to bring? What liberating possibilities emerge from a new religious discourse brought to the pulpit by women preaching? Resistance to and rejection of the "old discourse" brings with it the possibility for a new discourse. What would/can we call this new discourse? I suggest we name it dialogic discourse—the word "discourse" implies dialogue, a new, open kind of religious discourse based on communication and experience, one that reimagines both God and the human relationship with God as fragile, vulnerable, experimental, limited only by our own human limitations. According to the preachers in this book, this reimagining places the very essence of God at the praxis of vulnerability and relationship: *here* is where God is.[47]

In claiming that women's sermons are "dialogic," I want to explore some of the ways in which I see this dialogue taking place. Some of the avenues for exchange and dialogue that I have identified in the sermons and ministries of the women I know include:

- the woman's dialogue with herself, stemming out of and building on her own personal experiences;
- the woman's dialogue with God;
- the woman's dialogue with her closest family and loved ones;
- the woman's dialogue with other women ministers;
- the woman's dialogue with the congregation in which she works;
- the woman's dialogue with the Bible;
- the woman's dialogue with her society and culture; and
- the woman's dialogue with the denomination in which she is ordained.

These dialogues are not separate and isolated; they are, in fact, multi-leveled and interactive in different ways and at different times, invoking once more the multistranded helix, the guiding metaphor for this work. The spiritual and theological dialogue inherent in a sermon is often poly-phonic, needing to be "read" or "heard" within the context of that particular sermon being preached to a congregation on a particular Sunday morning. None of the women I know best would describe their role as preacher in terms of being merely a "mouthpiece for God." Such a de-scription would ignore and dismiss all the dialogues I have listed above and would minimize the importance of their role within the congregation, their participation in the world as individuals and as clergy, and would misrepresent their perceptions of God in dialogue, God as vulnerable, and God as/in relationship.

Women in the clergy create a space where *shared* power and authority and collaborative learning about things spiritual and religious can happen through free and unrestricted dialogue and respect for difference. Women in the ministry, in the pulpit, preaching, leading prayers, healing, confer-encing together are creating the framework for the new dialogic paradigm. The space that is being created is a welcoming space, not a restrictive one. All are invited to participate. Obviously, it is a space that makes many powerful leaders uncomfortable. The language is new, the liturgy is chang-ing, rituals are being transformed, power and authority are being shared, expanded, and exchanged on a regular basis. Traditional images of God are being challenged, new ones explored. Questions are acceptable. God is understood through experience rather than (only) through doctrine. And though it may certainly be true that some of the male clergy, long in power and comfortable with the status quo, may be discomfited, millions of women, minorities, and children will rejoice that the wall has crumbled. Already they are preaching the new paradigm. Who is listening?

Re-Imagining Comes Home

Because so much of what was appearing in print about the Re-Imagining Conference was based on the mistaken and sometimes irrational perceptions of people who had not attended, or who had attended only with the intention of "reporting back" the "horrors" they might witness, I decided to interview the women I knew who had attended. I thought it important to hear about the conference from *women who had attended*, something I felt had been terribly lacking in the recent coverage of the conference. Moreover, as an ethnographer, my work is always firmly grounded in field research.

In my methodological approach, which I define earlier in this book as "reciprocal ethnography," I seek a dialogue between myself and the participants in my study and attempt in the final product (the published text) to incorporate both their and my own voice(s) and honor dialogue and diversity within the ethnography itself. In the case of the work I have done on women's sermons, I have shared each chapter of this book with them, seeking their response, critique, and assistance. After working together for more than ten years, we have developed a rapport that allows for difference, disagreement, argumentation, support, and diversity. Therefore we felt entirely comfortable recording their discussion of the Re-Imagining Conference. On May 19, 1994, the clergywomen were all laughing and talking about how they had had no idea that the Re-Imagining Conference was going to be such a "big deal" when they attended, but now they were *really* glad they had gone, even though it had been a bit intense and even, at times, disconcerting. It was actually a badge of honor to have been there!

First, somewhat amused, but clearly recognizing the potential for invocation, they sang (complete with hand motions that indicated the north, south, east, west, the heart, and the world) the "Sophia" song/prayer they had learned at the conference: "Bless Sophia, / dream the vision, / share the wisdom, / dwelling deep within." Then the conversation began with one of the women telling the following story:

In January, I was at this district meeting that had a lot of lay people and clergy from all over our district, and the bishop, who is retired and fairly elderly, was preaching. And he started holding forth about this Re-Imagining Conference, which he certainly did not attend, and calling it "heresy," claiming that at the conference we tried to replace the second person of the trinity, I assume he meant Jesus—
—Yes, that would be Jesus [the others respond in jest]
—with a fertility goddess—
—what fertility goddess? [the others questioned loudly]

—Sophia!

—Sophia? I thought she was a biblical image—I didn't know. [laughter]

—And saying that those people at that conference picked an obscure term out of the Old Testament—he didn't say Hebrew Scripture, of course—which translates "wisdom" but the Greek name of it is Sophia—that's just a literary device and tried to make it into the second person of the trinity. And I sat there and I was so angry. Really, I could hardly breathe I was so angry, and I felt so utterly alienated, and so like I was being called all these names I didn't deserve. I almost stood up in the middle of that sermon, in the middle of that sanctuary, those people who don't even know who I am to say, "Excuse me, Bishop, you have to stop. This is not true!" Well, I didn't. And I'm sure it's a good thing I didn't because it would have been my death knell in that conference. As soon as it was over, though, I went up to him and politely introduced myself as a minister at such-and-such a church. And then I said, "And I would really appreciate it if you would stop speaking about the Re-Imagining Conference until you find out what happened, because it is very irresponsible to misrepresent it the way you did."

—You didn't!

—Good for you!

—"You know [she continued to tell the bishop], 'Father' is just a literary device, too." And he just blanched and turned away from me and started talking to somebody else—

—He didn't even respond!

—Totally cut off.

—Well, that says a lot, doesn't it?

One woman at the table was reading aloud some of the reports that were emerging about the conference in various denominational publications, but which seemed to focus on the Presbyterian and United Methodist responses:

"Bishop blasts the naming of Sophia in worship." "Recent efforts by some Christians to fuse worship of Sophia with Christianity nothing more than an effort to reconstitute the godhead."

—"Bishop told more than 1,000 Methodists gathered in South Carolina at a conference on evangelism that 'Sophia is a weird prostitution of the Eastern Orthodox idea of St. Sophia that must be eliminated NOW.'"

—"Bishop claims the emergence of such trends signals the need for 'a deep and sweeping change, a radical transformation across the United Methodist Church.' He calls for: 1) belief in the Bible as authoritative; 2) a recovery of intelligent and informed Christian understanding of eternal life; 3) a loving of all people, including homosexuals, and "coveting transformation for them.'"

—[from *Good News Magazine*] "This issue of Good News carries the most disturbing news story we have ever published, the report on the Re-Imagining Conference. Without question, this event was the most theologically aberrant I have ever read about, far removed from the Christian tradition."

—The Presbyterians are having a terrible time with this.

—Well, a friend of mine says they may split over this!

—People have been worried about the Methodists splitting over it, too.

—And this has been the catalyst.

—Yes, but it's more than just over this conference, but it's over the theological issues that it's raised.

—Well, there was some stuff we laughed about, but—

—Yeah, like lots of it.
—But, I just find it incredible. I am just stunned at this reaction.
—The lashing out must mean that they are really scared.
—Well, yes, we're touching a nerve.
—What are they so threatened by?
—Well, I think they are frightened by women.
—I think women is part of it. But I don't think it's just women. It's like they felt all the structures were being attacked—
—I was thinking about this driving over here, I think that conference was about spirituality and it was an exploration of spirituality from a number of different cultural contexts—
—And not in a controlled way—
—the lack of control is essential—
—And I think that's it—the lack of control, in religion, it's so threatened by the free-flowing spirituality—
—or like the "nectar between our thighs"—[they all laugh]
—Ah, that's the one that gets repeated time and again, "Look what these women are saying when they get together—"
—Well, even those of us who were there, some of us were saying, "Wow! this is getting to be a little much!" [they all laugh again]

Several aspects of this conversation are worth nothing. First, it is clear that the experience of the Re-Imagining Conference was completely different for the women who willingly attended as participants from what is being reported *about* the conference by persons who were not in attendance or those who were sent to "report back." It is also clear that the women who attended did not agree with everything that was said or done, nor did they necessarily share all of the belief systems represented at the conference or enthusiastically embrace all of the liturgical or ritualistic opportunities available at the conference. After all, it *was* an ecumenical gathering and literally a world of different Christian experiences were represented. The women at this table admit to their own discomfort with some aspects of the conference. I have seen them "perform" the Sophia invocation on several occasions, but I would be greatly surprised to find any of them introducing this into their regular church services. But I could perhaps see them sharing it with any number of people as representative of one of the more interesting, provocative, and moving aspects of the Re-Imagining Conference. Did the initiators of the invocation have anything more than this in mind? Perhaps. At the conference, participants learned the prayer song and performed it in the way they might have learned and attempted to sing a Native American prayer or a Korean chant.

The women who attended the conference talked openly about finding it to be "too much" at times—overwhelming, gluttonous, a smorgasbord of ideas and approaches to spirituality and Christianity. It is ridiculous, they claim, to think that any one person attending the conference would have shared all the beliefs represented. Again, it was an ecumenical conference.

They expected diversity and they found it, but they also discovered unity in the hearing of women's shared voices. What they praise about the conference was the openness to diversity, the willingness to create a space for sharing beliefs and ritual, for respecting different viewpoints and beliefs and *entering into dialogue about the differences.* The conference demonstrated the possibilities of *uncontrolled* encounter, for all persons present were free to share their beliefs and trust they would be respected. No one person or group or denomination was *in control.* For the attendees this fluidity did not create total chaos, but for outsiders or those who would not engage with the possibilities it offered, the lack of control, the willingness to listen and share, are very threatening. Who is in control? Who is designing how Christianity should look and be? Who is making the rules and enforcing them? No one is—and everyone is. And there's the rub.

At this point in the conversation, the clergywomen began to discuss my suggestion that the Re-Imagining Conference provides a glimpse of the new paradigm Mead speaks of in *The Once and Future Church.* They did not necessarily agree with me that Mead himself was fearful or nervous about the thought of the emerging new paradigm; rather, they thought he was merely looking forward to it and saying, "We'd better be ready for it." Their conversation went like this:

—Well, I don't think it is [the new paradigm]. I think it's rather on the way to a new paradigm. What was there [at the conference] that's significant was the freedom of it.
—It was so eclectic. There really wasn't any focus.
—But I think the lack of focus and the freedom and the lack of control are all ways of getting toward what might be understood as a "new paradigm," a new living spirituality.
—That's what people are longing for.
—Exactly.
—I don't think the new paradigm is going to look exactly like that conference in Minneapolis but it will be about the willingness to explore—
—Oh, we were just packed in there; it was too much; there were so many things I hated about it.
—If there was anything sinful about the Re-Imagining Conference, I think it was the gluttony, because that's what it felt like to me, there was so much offered.
—But, you know, it's understandable in a sense when we've been so held down and here we've got three days to just go do it! And we want to do this, oh, and we don't want to forget that, that's kind of what it was . . .
—Well, there were 150 organizers—
—And everyone of them had at least one idea, some probably even had two, or three! [all laugh] It's a miracle it didn't just go on all day and all night.
—Oh, it did! You just left for a while!
—That's right. I just left. I opted out. I just needed to be in a department store for a while!
—A little touch of reality, a little consumerism, a little materialism—[all laugh]
—Worship at another altar—
—But, seriously, I do think that the conference was a measure of our starvation for something real, something that connects with our lives.
—I think the Re-Imagining Conference was about women's experience. I was telling

about a sermon I did on Mother's Day, in which I talked about "weaning"—and what I realized about that is that women's experience is so absent in the liturgical worshipping life of the church.
—Absolutely.
—And that fits with what you were saying about starvation. Here was an opportunity for women to experience, to be in a liturgical, worshipful, educational setting—
—And validating all those women who were out there listening, who had never heard their experiences named or spoken in a religious setting.
—That's right. It isn't that women are alienated from the church. You look at any church and there are primarily women there, but we have been asked to be alienated from ourselves—
—That's right!
—In order to be in the church, we are expected to be and are alienated from some aspects of who we are—
—Exactly—
—Just put them aside and pretend to that asexuality we talked about in Elaine's other book.

The women read from a publication of the American Family Association, which went out to every Methodist church:

"Information about a pagan conference. . . . The Bible Renewal leaders in the Methodist church call for us to renounce the idolatrous worship, false teaching and syncretism of the ecumenical Re-Imagining Conference."
—Syncretism is now a bad word.
—This goes on: "We affirm the full and sufficient revelation of God in Christ through the Old and New Testament and that the Christian faith is a gift of God and not a human invention to be reformulated and re-imagined."
—It's always been reimagined.
—Look at the different images of Jesus through the centuries—
—Or in the Gospels!
—The whole Bible is full of disagreements, struggles to figure it out.
—That's why understanding "biblical literacy" is so important. Because if people don't know that simple reality of the Bible then they'll get caught up in that fear and the blaming and the alienation.
—It never ceases to amaze me how people who claim to know the Bible so well can be so blind to so much of the differences, [imitating a deep, authoritative voice]: "This is the authoritative word of God!" Except for the parts we don't like—Ha! How do they do that? Talk about syncretism. Isn't that what happened when you take, for example, the two stories of the nativity of Jesus and you weave them together as if it's one story and no conflict. Isn't that conflict?
—Or the resurrection.
—God knows we laughed at some of this stuff, but now I realize that there were actually spies sent there by their churches to report back what was going on!
—Well, so much of this is taken out of context. Like, who was it said we didn't need a bloody Jesus hanging on the cross—Well, I cheered when she said that, but it was in the context of her whole talk. It was great!
—At least you know what really went on.
—Really, if I just had to read this, I'd sure be in trouble, because you certainly cannot learn the truth by reading this stuff!

—If we had to rely just on this [referring to the reports they've been reading]—

—the worst is the taking it all out of context, because it was the whole experience that made it important and meaningful—

—And there was a reverence, a reverence about what happened in that whole conference and an honoring of everyone's right to try to explore their own spirituality.

—That's what I've been saying in public forums. I say, "Yes, I was there, and, no, I would not stand and say I agreed with everything that was being spoken"—

—Is there anyone who could?

—No, absolutely not.

—What I really appreciated was the mutual respect, the openness, the willingness to listen, and I think those are characteristics of the new paradigm. Because if we don't have those characteristics in our Christian lives as community, we can kiss it good-bye.

—That's right! It will just die.

—I did sense that there was a mutuality of respect and a willingness to allow for other people's experience.

—There was a gentleness and a caring that was really palpable. I mean people were trying to be so good to each other and so sensitive to each other's spiritual needs. So, if someone wanted to draw on the tablecloth, that didn't mean everybody had to. It was okay not to. I think there was something in that room that was really special at times.

—There was such wonderful music. There were so many really wonderful moments that aren't in any of these pieces of paper—

—Or it's in here but it's distorted, like they have quoted the words of the song by Sweet Honey in the Rock about the dead are not under the earth they are with us. It's quoted in here—

—as heresy!

—[Reading] "Sophia worship is theologically ignorant. Theology should start with God, not with women's lives." Well, then who can do theology?

—How can you know God if you don't start with your life? [here they are all talking at once. This comment has obviously struck a chord with them]

—How do we know that? Classical theology begins with the "I believe in God. Creator of all things."

—How do we know that but in our lives?

—Well, I think the Re-Imagining Conference was an experiment on the way to the new paradigm—and I think we need more experiments. But if this is the kind of response we're going to get, who's going to feel free to experiment?

—Opening some doors, moving into the future, and seeing what happens, and there's going to be a reaction.

—And the chaos you mention. It's important to see how the church responds to the conference and see what evolves from there. The new paradigm can't and won't be pure chaos. The response is important.

—At the time I really didn't realize just how courageous it was for some of those women to say what they did. In the midst of that conference it seemed like normal things to say. Of course, that's how all of us could connect with what we were hearing.

—What was important was speaking from your own experience or from the experience of women. That's not something you would hear in a typical theological conference. It's back to what you said earlier, that's not an experience that is allowed in the church.

—And what happens when it is allowed? You're very lucky if you can get away with it!

—You know when this first began appearing every single week in the Methodist publications, I would lie awake at night trying to figure out how to respond to it. I was so angry; they simply were not true. I thought about writing a letter to the editor, but it's so easy to write people off who do that.

—Right. My first reaction when all of this started happening was great! It shows that we're doing something right—it upset things. You can't get the toothpaste back in the tube, and that's what they're trying to do here. The momentum is on our side.

"A new church is being born," Loren Mead prophesied. In this book, I have offered concrete examples of how women's preaching, theology, and approach to reimagining what they "know" of God offer a clear and steady look at the new dialogic paradigm. I offer as well a theoretical model, the multi-stranded helix, to help us imagine with them the possibilities available when all the strands move together to collectively represent both human endeavor and divine essence. The dominant, or traditional, religious discourse is changing in women's pulpits and as a result of women's leadership in religion. Women's voices offer diverse approaches, reflective attitudes, different perspectives, and stimulating avenues for exploration. The women seem fearless to me, afraid of nothing. Speaking no longer only from the margins, they have broken through the fissures of the "old" Christendom paradigm and offer Christians new cooperative, reciprocal, and dialogic ways of being. Not surprisingly, however, they claim that many of their "new" ideas and approaches are not actually "new," but rather harken back to human concerns of compassion, community, inclusion, and empathy—the basics of the early teachings of the Christian church. Perhaps they suggest, the new paradigm is an older one come in new vestments. Just in time, they would say.

Notes

1. Loren Mead, *The Once and Future Church.*
2. Catherine Keller, "Inventing the Goddess," p. 340.
3. Keller, p. 341.
4. Keller, p. 340.
5. Keller, p. 340.
6. Keller, p. 341.
7. Keller, p. 341.
8. Keller, p. 342.
9. Keller, p. 342.
10. Keller, p. 342.
11. Rita Nakashima Brock, " 'Re-Imagining': One Year Later," p. 21.
12. Brock, p. 21.
13. Brock, p. 21.
14. Mead, p. 22 (emphasis mine).
15. Mead, p. 25 (emphasis mine).
16. Mead, p. 87 (emphasis in the original).
17. Mead, p. 48.
18. Mead, p. 30.
19. Mead, p. 31.

20. Sallie McFague, *Metaphorical Theology: Models of God in Religious Language.*

21. McFague, p. x.

22. McFague, pp. 8–10.

23. Ursula LeGuin, *The Language of the Night: Essays on Fantasy and Science Fiction,* ed. Susan Wood p. 159, as quoted by McFague.

24. McFague, p. 28.

25. McFague, p. 29.

26. McFague, p. 29.

27. *Inheriting Our Mothers' Gardens,* edited by Letty M. Russell, Kwok Pui-lan, Ada María Isasi-Díaz, and Katie Geneva Cannon.

28. Russell et al., p. 13.

29. Russell et al., p. 23.

30. Russell et al., p. 24.

31. Pui-lan, in Russell et al., p. 25.

32. Pui-lan in Russell et al., p. 32 (emphasis mine).

33. Kyung in Russell et al., pp. 54–72.

34. Kyung in Russell et al., p. 67.

35. Benavides in Russell et al., pp. 123–41.

36. Benavides in Russell et al., p. 123.

37. Russell in Russell et al., pp. 154–55.

38. Russell et al., p. 119.

39. Russell et al., p. 121.

40. Elizabeth A. Johnson, *She Who Is: The Mystery of God in Feminist Theological Discourse,* p. 269.

41. Unpublished manuscript provided to me by Rev. Kim Ryan. Dr. Hurty delivered three lectures for the "1993 Donohoe Forum," Arizona Ecumenical Council, Globe, Arizona Ecumenical Council, June 2–3, 1993, p. 2, Lecture #1.

42. Hurty, Lecture #1: "Power and Partnership," p. 1.

43. Hurty, Lecture #1, p. 4.

44. Hurty, Lecture #1, p. 6 (emphasis in the original).

45. Hurty, Lecture #2: "Conflict and the Collaborative Community," p. 1.

46. Hurty, Lecture #2, p. 2.

47. I am reminded here of Nelle Morton's *The Journey Is Home.*

When Two or More Are Gathered

CLARE AUSTEN
Unity Center, Columbia, Missouri
May 15, 1994

Lessons (read by members of the congregation).
Matthew 18: 18–20 (RSV): Truly I say to you, whatever you bind on earth shall be bound in heaven, and whatever you loose on earth shall be loosed in heaven. Again I say to you, if two of you on earth agree about anything they ask, it will be done for them by my father in heaven. For when two or three are gathered in my name, there am I in the midst of them.
Kahlil Gibran, *The Prophet*: When you pray, you rise up to meet in the air those who are praying at that very hour and whom save in prayer you have not met.*

Some of us probably go to church
out of habit.
That's certainly true for me.
My parents never missed a Sunday.
It was a very, very big deal in our house.
When I was about seven,
we had a minister that nobody liked,
and my parents—
stopped going to church!
And it was so strange
not to get up and go to church.
But my mom felt obligated to have church
   service anyway,
so I can remember sitting with our little
   hymnals
in our living room.
So it would not be unusual
for me to realize—
it's a habit.
My parents did it,
And I do it.
A lot of people go to church,
especially in the olden days,
out of that sense of
"God's gonna get me if I don't."
Now there may be just a little bit of that
   fear
still in us somewhere.
Some of us did grow up always going to
   church.

*Kahlil Gibran: *The Prophet* (reprint New York: Alfred Knopf, 1994), p. 67.

Even though we may have decided long
  ago
that we didn't believe in that kind of
  God—
that that wasn't our concept of God—
Yet there's a little guilt underneath there,
fear of God may make some of us come
  to church.
Sometimes in the past people went to
  church
because they had an image
in the community that they needed to
  uphold.
People have always gone to church to
  meet people,
to meet friends.
Did you ever have a parent who
told you that Church was the best place
  to meet your husband
or wife?
I did,
and I did meet my husband in church.
She was right!
People have always come to church
wanting to be part of something,
part of a community of people,
which is greater than just having friends.
It's being part of a sense of wholeness.
Even back when they may not have used
  those words
and nobody had read Scott Peck
and knew what "community building"
  was,
they still needed each other—
especially in small towns—
throughout the Middle Ages
and into America and the pioneers—
people had a need to come together.
Often in the belief systems back then,

you certainly didn't have as many
  choices.
Generally what you grew up with was
  what you knew—
the type of religion, the type of church
  you went to—
was what you would feel comfortable with
and continue with.
Now many of those
are reasons why we still come to church
  today,
to meet people.
And today,
there are so many choices,
and so many different kinds of belief
  systems,
that we tend to want
to come together with people of like mind
and there's nothing wrong with that.
That's good.
We want a dialogue;
we want to share openly
what we're thinking about
without being ridiculed.
And thankfully,
for something like Unity,
it's open enough
that we can have a lot of dialogue.
We have a lot of people
that believe very different things,
and we can rejoice in that.
That's good.
We don't have to feel afraid
to believe something different
than the person sitting next to us.
When my husband Jim and I were at the
  church growth conference
in Oregon in April,
we saw a survey which asked,

"Why do people come to new thought
   churches?"
New thought, for anyone who might be
   new,
or not know what that means,
is sort of a loose umbrella
terminology for Unity and many other
metaphysical movements that grew up in
   America
in the 1800s.
New thought believes in a divinity within,
we believe in the empowerment of the
   individual,
and the law of mind action.
These are things you don't usually hear
in your traditional Christian church.
The number one reason people go to
   church,
as mentioned in the survey,
was that people
really,
truly,
want a deeper sense of connection
with the divine.
They do not want to sit in church just to
know they are doing the right thing.
That connection with God, I think, calls
   to us.
It motivates us to ask the question what
   does it really mean
to feel God at work in my life?
The second reason that they go to
   church,
is to explore their spirituality
or explore their spiritual nature,
and I would add to that,
explore the meaning of being human.
We are both human and divine—
actually we're not two things

but that's how we've come to
   understand it.
We talk about ourselves as being human
and divine,
but it's really one thing—
the experience of being a human being
is also the experience of unfolding
that which God created us to be—
the divine essence of ourselves.
You really do have to
sort of explore and experiment with who
   you are,
because most of us
are not used to expressing our divine
   nature.
It gets covered up,
as we know,
with so many layers
of other things
and other beliefs,
especially limited ideas
that we hold about ourselves.
So exploration of our true nature with
   one another
is a reason that we come together.
We've left traditional beliefs behind in
   Unity,
we're tired of feeling bad about ourselves
and are searching for something
that will help us feel better.
Now,
I've had many, many joyous experiences
in the traditional church that I was
   brought up in,
but there was still always a sense of guilt
   and shame,
a sense of sin
and damnation,

and all those things that scare you
when you are a little kid.
I didn't want to feel bad about myself
    anymore,
and when I found a church
that told me that there was a spark
of the divine,
a spark of the Jesus Christ nature
    within me,
I really grabbed hold of that!
I really wanted to know
that I was part of God,
not just this unhappy little girl any longer.
I think people—
this was on the survey,
this was number four—
people come
to Unity,
to new thought movements,
because they have a true healing need.
This may be physical;
It may be emotional;
It may be mental.
We are all looking to find something
that we haven't found anywhere else.
We're seeking for answers
to our life challenges.
I don't know about you,
but the traditional Christian church
gave me answers, but they didn't always
    make sense to me;
they didn't always have depth,
so that I could take it home and really
    think about it.
It was just
"take this on faith."
When I came into Unity I realized
it gave me ideas that I could take home
and practice.

It is no coincidence that Charles Filmore
    called Unity
practical Christianity,
because you could walk out of the
    service,
or you could read a book,
and have something that could actually
change your life,
that day,
if you put it into action.
And last,
the reason that people have been drawn
to new thought churches
is because they're linked
with the positive thinking movement,
and the dreams that we want to have
    fulfilled—
and new thought churches and Unity
    have offered
a sense of that unlimited potential,
knowing that we're so much more than
    just human,
we're one with the Christ mind,
I can know anything,
do anything,
be anything,
and I want to know that because I have a
    dream
that's alive inside of me
and that's just as true today as it was
twenty years ago,
when I found Unity and began to go to
    church.
I called this talk today
"Where Two or More are Gathered."
To me it is essential that in church we
    come together.
Although being together is not always
    easy.

The twelve-step program says it's simple,
but it's not always easy.
That's true for us,
it's not always easy for us to come
    together
and be a spiritual community,
and reflect
and continue to learn
about the spiritual principles that we
    believe,
to continue to live them,
to see the Christ nature in each other,
and maybe even to call each other on
    some of our stuff.
Stuff that can be real painful.
Sometimes that's the reason that we stay
    home from church,
we're hoping nobody sees our pain,
or sees what we're dealing with
and thinks that we're not spiritual enough
to be in a Unity church.
I hope none of you ever feel that way.
This is where we come together to see
    the Christ
to love and celebrate—
that's why I like to call it a celebration
on Sunday morning.
Our celebration service.
We're not here to worship.
We're not here to worship a God that's
    up on a pedestal,
or out there somewhere.
Maybe we could say we're here to
    worship the Christ image,
but I would rather say we're here to
    celebrate it in each other,
to see it and mirror it back,
so that we all have an opportunity to
    grow.

I think that's why people come
and are attracted to Unity,
and I would add something else.
This is not on the survey list
but it's my sense,
it's part of my credo—
it's that we come together to be part of
    something bigger than we are.
Remember I said earlier how people
    came
and gathered in religious groups in order
    to feel part of something?
Well I think what we are craving.
I'll own it,
I think it is what I am craving.
I felt it as I came into Unity,
and still feel it today,
a sense
of being part
of the ongoing
evolution of human consciousness,
and that's happening,
and not just in this room,
but on a global scale.
And I want to come together with people
who believe,
who think,
who know,
that human thinking is changing.
You know,
there are a lot of mysteries
for us around human evolution.
Why on earth did
we come up out of the soupy seas?
As we celebrated on Earth Day,
we talked about the whole evolution of
    being.
Why did we come to have reflective
    minds

where we could think about things,
and talk about things,
and communicate the way we did?
We don't have the exact answer to that,
but I do know it's for good.
I do know that it's headed somewhere,
there's a divine Plan
and we're an exciting part of it,
and that's something that Unity
    represented for me.
Here's a group of people
willing to claim world peace.
It began in the seventies,
we began to know
we can claim it in consciousness
and know that it's gonna happen some
    day in the world.
And I've said this many times,
we have seen what's happened over the
    years,
since people in the quote
"new age movement"
began saying,
if we see it and affirm it,
it will happen.
So much has changed in the world,
and there's still a lot of war,
we still have a long ways to go.
There are people who have said
that the Earth would be better off
without human beings.
I don't think so;
I don't think so.
We've destroyed a lot it's true.
We continue to destroy important parts
    of it even today.
But I believe our thinking is changing
and evolving
and we're moving towards something

really profound and good.
I mentioned this a few weeks ago
when I talked about Barbara Marx
    Hubbard.
We truly are giving birth to something
and it's exciting for me
to be here in the midst of all of you
who hold that same vision.
To some of you that may be a new idea;
I know for many of you
it's what's been calling to your heart
for a long long time.
Yesterday the board of directors of this
    church and I
spent the whole afternoon
asking ourselves these same questions:
Why are we doing church?
Why are we here?
What is it that calls to each of us?
And everyone of us spoke to that—
what called us into Unity?
What's made a difference in our lives?
We're beginning a visioning process
for Unity Center of Columbia
that everyone of you will have an
    opportunity
to participate in,
because a vision cannot just be
my vision
or the board's vision.
If we're all going to do this together,
if we're all going to have an impact on
    our community,
first on our own
then on our community
and the world.
It's going to have to be a great vision
like world peace was on December 31,
    1986.

We're all going to have to hold
a similar vision.
Our parts in it can be different;
how we see it manifesting can be
   different;
but we have a dream for this center,
a way that we know
that Christ is being called
uniquely through us
in Columbia, Missouri.
Then it's going to happen,
and it's going to be exciting to be a part
   of it.
In that same church-growth workshop
in Oregon in April,
it gave me an idea about some of the
   things that were said.
If you want that kind of exciting ministry
with a lot of people involved
and lives being changed,
there's some things that need to happen:
involvement,
ownership of that vision was one of them.
But it also said:
the minister
has to work long hours
and be totally focused on the ministry.
Now I want to share with you today
that that's not my vision.
When I hear that,
I think about the ministers I know
that are very successful right now.
Most of them are single,
or they have adult children,
off doing their own thing in the world,
and I think—
is that the way it has to be?
Is that the only way to create ministry
is for me to pour my life into it

so that I don't have a life?
And I thought,
no, there's something wrong here.
That's not my vision.
And I talked about it with the board,
we asked what are all those things
that successful ministries are doing
that really fit us,
and what doesn't fit us?
And I want you to know that our vision
is going to be uniquely our vision.
It's going to come from us.
It's going to be about
what we want it to be about,
and we'll shout about it if we need to.
I know that if I'm a model of a workaholic,
then what are you going to do when you
   look at me?
What will you demonstrate in your lives
if I'm not having a balanced life
and taking care of my body,
my spirit,
my mind,
then what are we capable of creating
   together?
What are we going to manifest as a
   vision?
I want it to be for all of us,
and although I stand on a
pedestal up here,
I don't want to be on a pedestal in your
   minds,
because I'm human,
and I make mistakes.
But I am on a spiritual journey
and I'm excited to be part of this
spiritual community.
I believe we come together to do church,
because we're called to love one another,

to open our hearts to one another when
   we're hurting,
to help those wounds be healed.
And we have just begun
at Unity Center of Columbia
to help people heal.
In the vision that's coming forth now
throughout this summer and into the fall,
we're really going to take a look at that,
and I ask you today
to begin to form your vision.
If you had a mission statement for your
   life,
which we talked about,
for those of you who did the
effectiveness training with us this year,
we should have a mission statement,
and a vision statement for our life.
We should have a mission statement
for this church,
and for every sub-committee within it,
that all works together,
so that that vision that we hold
is one that we all agree upon,
and it's healthy,
and it's alive,
and we feel good about it.
Are you with me?
Yes?
Thank you, God.

Putting God's Blueprint into Action

CAROL MILLSPAUGH
Locust Grove United Methodist Church
Columbia, Missouri
September 26, 1993

Lessons.

Matthew 21:23–37 (NRSV): When he entered the temple, the chief priests and the elders of the people came to him as he was teaching, and said, "By what authority are you doing these things," and who gave you this authority?" Jesus said to them, "I will also ask you one question; if you tell me the answer, then I will also tell you by what authority I do these things. Did the baptism of John come from heaven, or was it of human origin?" . . . "What do you think? A man had two sons; he went to the first and said, 'Son, go work in the vineyard today.' He answered, 'I will not'; but later he changed his mind and went. The father went to the second and said the same; and he answered, 'I will go, sir'; but he did not go. Which of the two did the will of his father?" They said, "The first." Jesus said to them, "Truly I tell you, the tax collectors and the prostitutes are going into the kingdom of God ahead of you."

Whether it's a memory from a long-ago childhood,
or a more recent experience of yours,
most of us can recall more than one time when we said,
"Yes, I'll do that,"
but really it was just an occasion to put off doing something that we didn't want to do.
Maybe it was when we were asked to take out the garbage.
Maybe it was when we were being told for the *third* time to clean our room,
or please come in there and do the dishes.
And saying "yes," we still sat there,
wherever it was that we were,
watching TV or playing a game,
or doing something else.
And this procrastinating has probably happened
more than once

for everyone here today.
We really weren't being insincere when
we said yes,
and really didn't go,
we had just learned that that was a way
to get out of doing something we didn't
really want to do.
And for as many times as necessary to
put it off.
you might say,
"Yes, I'm coming" and, "yes, I will"
maybe we really meant to do it,
but we just never got around to it.
And this happens in adulthood a lot.
Two of the most frequent ways
we tend to postpone or avoid an
obligation
are
one, that phone message that's
"I'll call you back,"
and then they never do,
or the message that
"The check is in the mail,"
and of course it isn't.
Today's lesson reveals
that these are not just modern attitudes.
The second son in this story that Jesus
told
did the same thing.
When the father said,
"Son, I have some work I need your help
with outside.
Will you come out and help me?"
The son said "Okay, Dad,"
but then he never went.
Then the first son said, "No, I won't go,"
but then changed his mind and did go.
Jesus' question was,

"Which one of these did what the father
wanted?"
And the pharisees answered,
"Well, the one that first said no,
but then later changed his mind and did
go out to work."
Why did Jesus tell this story?
Well, he told this story to the religious
leaders of his day
who were pretty much like you and me,
and were considered the good church
people of that day.
The responsible people,
the ones who were following their faith.
And yet, these people were also rejecting
Jesus.
The people who followed Jesus, though,
were those who were drawn from the
people of the land.
These people did not heed the law,
they didn't dress well,
they didn't act well a lot of the times,
but they responded to Jesus' ministries,
and in fact became part of God's new
kingdom.
But those who were the keepers of the
temple,
who said that they *were* religious,
who had promised to obey God in their
worship,
yet did not obey God in their living.
The story is uncomfortably clear, really.
It's a direct challenge
to the so-called religious people of Jesus'
time,
to honestly look at themselves.
They are the ones who said,
"Yes, I'll obey you, God,"

and then they did not.
While the outcasts,
who were the tax collectors and
   prostitutes,
are those who said "No" to God at first,
they wanted to go their own way,
and then later took God's way
by following Jesus.
Both of these sons in this story
were children of the father,
and that's very clear.
Jesus' ministry was to both groups,
for God's claimed both as his children.
And I think if you and I look carefully at
   that story,
we might see some of ourselves in both
   of these sons.
The second son said "Yes,"
but then he didn't follow through.
And of course, you and I can relate to
   that easily.
You and I say many of the right things,
and more often than not, we really do
   mean it.
We say, "Yes, God, I want you to be the
   center of my life."
But then
so many other seemingly more important
   things
get in the way.
We say, "Yes, I accept the value system
that Jesus gave us in the Scriptures,"
but then that same gospel entails so
   many things,
and so much of life.
We are told to forgive,
but forgiving is difficult.
Especially when we don't think the other
   person

really deserves to be forgiven.
Feeding the hungry is important,
and we believe in that.
And yet, when it gets to a certain point,
when it gets inconvenient for us,
we somehow don't follow through.
Accepting other people is a good idea,
as long as the other person has learned
   his or her lesson.
Treating other people as brothers and
   sisters is fine,
but really if they're the kind of people
who are worthy of our friendship,
and only if they're not really
that different than we are.
Saying yes to the gospel, for all us,
is so much easier
than following through on what the
   gospel says.
Saying yes is so much less taxing,
than looking really at our own lives
and seeing what do we need to change
to follow that gospel.
Singing "Here I am Lord,"
is so much more satisfying,
to sing that song in worship on Sundays,
than to say, "Here I am Lord, now what
   shall I do?"
When we're home with our families,
or when we're at work,
or when we're listening to a community
   need,
it's always easy to say yes,
say yes to the gospel
as a blueprint for the life of a Christian.
But it's really hard to follow up on that
   yes,
especially when it flies in the face

of what's cost effective,
or socially comfortable.

This is a blueprint
for our new education building,
which we built three years ago. [she
    holds up the actual blueprints]
And on it, it's an actual blueprint,
I see some wonderful things on it.
It has on here, on this first page,
the layout for the upstairs part of our
    building,
and looking at this blueprint is really
    exciting.
You can see the classrooms there,
you can see where the doors and the
    windows are,
and the hallways.
It's just a wonderful thing to have this
    blueprint
and imagine what could come out of it.
So what if, three years ago,
when God was blessing
and continues to bless our church with
    growth,
and we knew we needed more room,
what if our plan was to come up with this
    blueprint?
And that's what we have now,
this wonderful blueprint.
But what if that's all we had done?
We couldn't be living in this blueprint,
we couldn't be meeting in the
    classrooms,
or studying for Sunday school,
or having committee meetings
for all the things that we do.
It wouldn't be as if we have a building,
all we would have would be this blueprint.

And that would be quite a bit less than
    what we do have.
We needed the blueprint,
to know how to build the building.
If we hadn't had it,
I can't imagine what we might have built!
But then we used this to build the
    building.
We're not living in this blueprint,
    obviously,
but we're living in the building that we
    built.
Jesus was saying to the church people of
    his day,
"You already have the blueprint,
you have a lot of things that are good,
you have a lot of it in me as a person,"
Jesus was saying.
You have the blueprint,
you know of your religious heritage and
    your beliefs,
and because you have that blueprint,
you think that you have the building,
but in fact you don't.
Knowing about your faith,
having this blueprint,
doesn't mean that you are practicing
    your faith.
Admiring God,
speaking well of God,
does not mean that you are following
    God's will.
I think you and I face this risk,
just as much as the people in Jesus' day
    did.
Because one of our dangers as
    Christians
is to think that it's enough to agree with
    God's will.

If we agree with what we hear in the
service,
if we agree with the hymns, the prayers,
the lessons,
but God's not asking only for our
agreement,
God's asking for us to put God's will into
action.
Jesus was surrounded with many people
who said the right things,
but he asked his followers not just to say
those things,
but to follow him,
to give their lives.
And you and I are challenged in this
Scripture
to consider not only what we believe
about what Jesus taught,
but how are we following,
how are we living out those beliefs.

Some time ago, on the Merv Griffin
television show,
Merv interviewed a person who was a
body builder.
"Why do you develop those particular
muscles," Merv asked.
And this body builder simply stepped out
in front of the camera,
and flexed this certain set of muscles.
And the audience all applauded.
"Well, what do you do with all those
muscles," Merv asked.
And again this muscular specimen flexed
his muscles,
the biceps, the triceps, swelled to
impressive proportions.
"But what do you use those muscles for,"
Merv persisted.

And this body builder was bewildered,
he didn't have an answer,
except to stand there and flex his
muscles.
Jesus' audience had fallen into that kind
of mistake
of thinking that words were enough,
of thinking they were pleasing God with
their religion,
when really they weren't following
through on it.
They have the blueprint right,
in fact, they knew the blueprint
backwards and forwards,
they knew their Bible.
But they were not building on it.
Their faith hadn't issued an action which
pleased God,
while many of the so-called
near-religious people
who heard Jesus,
had waked up to the fact that they
needed God,
and they were trying to practice what
they were learning.
That first son,
like the first followers of Jesus,
had first said "no"
when the father asked him to come and
work,
but later he changed his mind and went
out to help.
And that's really good news for us today,
because Jesus' story assures us
that even if we fail to respond to God at
other times in our lives,
God is reinviting us today.
How we responded yesterday isn't nearly
as important,

as how we respond from this moment on.
It may be that yesterday we were afraid,
or apathetic,
or in a lot of conflict, or something else
held us back.
But what about today?
We already have the blueprint.
We know what God's hopes and dreams
   are for us,
and for the world,
we have the new Scripture,
and as we see him in Jesus Christ.
We have that blueprint.
God asks us to build on that blueprint,
as we live our Monday through Saturday
   lives,
not only our Sunday lives.
As parents and children,
as employers and employees,
as students in school and teachers,
as choir members and Sunday school
   teachers,
neighbors,
all the different roles that we are in,
we are invited to put that blueprint plan
into the building of our lives,
and the lives of the world.

As we gave Bibles to our children today,
and in a few minutes as we baptize new
   infants,
we are beginning with the blueprint.
But God invites us not to stop with that
   blueprint,
but in fact to build on that for our lives
and for the lives of the world.
A building is what's intended to come
   from a blueprint,
and the new life and the new world
are what are intended to come
from our Christian faith in action.
Let us pray.
Lord, as you hear our words of worship
   and praise of you today,
inscribe in our thought, Lord,
the willingness to surround our words
   with faithful actions.
That in fact a wonderful build-ing,
a wonderful world,
may come from the blueprint
you have given us in Jesus Christ.
Amen.

The Gifts of God

TAMSEN WHISTLER
St. Barnabas Episcopal Church
Moberly, Missouri
October 17, 1993

The lessons read were Isaiah 25: 1–9; 1 Thessalonians 1: 1–10; and Matthew 22: 15–22. The Gospel lesson (NRSV) follows:

Then the Pharisees went and plotted to entrap him in what he said. So they sent their disciples to him, along with the Herodians, saying, "Teacher, we know that you are sincere, and teach the way of God in accordance with truth, and show deference to no one; for you do not regard people with partiality. Tell us, then, what you think. Is it lawful to pay taxes to the emperor, or not?" But Jesus, aware of their malice, said, "Why are you putting me to the test, you hypocrites? Show me the coin used for the tax." And they brought him a denarius. Then he said to them, "Whose head is this, and whose title?" They answered, "The emperor's." Then he said to them, "Give therefore to the emperor the things that are the emperor's, and to God the things that are God's." When they heard this, they were amazed; and they left him and went away.

When I was a child growing up in St. Louis,
the city was building new highways,
and the airport was expanding.
Both of those facilities
wanted land for their expansion,
and the land that they wanted
was within two miles of the high school
that I attended—
land on which stood three hundred
homes in our school district,
not to mention an amusement park and
two cemeteries.
The plan of the airport,
and the plan of the highway department,
was to offer homeowners
a percentage of the worth of the homes,
and then tear the homes down
and move people out
and anything that remained
would be taken over by the power of
eminent domain.

Now part of the plan
was that the agency,
the airport,
and the highway department
decided to assess the value of the
    homes
based on the fact that they were going to
    be torn down,
and so therefore they were worthless
and they technically had no value.
So, that was the "percentage"
they were going to offer the homeowners.
Now, this did not go over well with
    homeowners,
but most of them felt overwhelmed
by the fact it was the airport
and the highway department they were
    fighting
and so most people pretty much gave in,
except for Mrs. Courtney.
Mrs. Courtney is the mother
of one of my closest friends in high
    school,
and she was outraged
at the highhandedness of the airport
    authority
and the highway department,
so she and her husband refused to move
and they wrote letters to the newspapers,
and their commissioners,
and Congress,
that is, to state government authorities.
They organized some of the remaining
    neighbors
and friends
and they sat in their house with empty
    lots all around them,
until finally there was a lawsuit settled.

The airport did in fact have to pay all
    those homeowners,
including the Courtneys,
what their houses were actually worth.
They simply refused to leave
until they were paid a fair price.
So then one of the other things which
    happened,
as the result of this,
was that there was so much
controversy and
so much awareness
because of these three hundred homes,
that it occurred to some of the other
    people
that just tearing the houses down,
which was the idea of the airport
    authority
and the highway department,
was really a waste of resources,
and it would be better to move those
    houses,
those which could be moved,
and give them to people
who had never owned a home before.
And that's what happened, then,
with lots of the houses,
but it only happened
because Mrs. Courtney refused to move
and that gave enough people
enough time to figure out what was
    going on.
All of that took place more than twenty
    years ago.
Mrs. Courtney was made fun of
for her principles
and was called a variety of names,
including "un-American,"

an enemy of progress,
an obstructionist,
and other phrases less polite.
She wrote the newspapers so often
her family was embarrassed. [laughter]
But what she did
benefited three hundred other families,
a school district,
and eventually the airport.
And along with that,
every one of those agencies was
    reminded clearly
that their role is protection,
not oppression.
And everyone,
including those of us who were high
    school students at the time,
were reminded that even one person,
who is committed,
can make an immense difference.

Now, we're doing a variety of things here
    at church this morning.
We're participating in an ecumenical
    observance
of the children's Sabbath,
a day on which we recognize
what we already know to be true
that children and young people
are not only future participants
in our lives
and in the church,
but here and now they have
their own place with us,
and that they
and we together
have a commitment to a life beyond
    ourselves.

We are here to recognize that,
to state that commitment plainly,
to accept our own responsibilities
in the care and nurture of the children in
    our midst,
so they in turn
may be as St. Paul called each of us
    to be,
imitative of Christ,
models of the unique relationship
in the quality and commitment to the
    world.
Today, also,
we focus on stewardship,
which should begin our responsibility
    before God,
for the gifts and treasures
we have been given,
and for the time we use—
the way we use that time.
As the lessons point out for us this
    morning,
we have choices in our lives,
choices we can make
or allow others to make for us.
We choose
and we are chosen.
As chosen people,
we are committed to love,
to being in fact God's own love in the
    world,
through connection.
We choose
and are chosen
and to make the decisions
of our daily lives—
to make a lasting difference.
And we have committed

to something beyond the usual standards
and expectations of the world.
The gospel this morning is quite short,
but it is heavily loaded.
The religious authorities,
the Pharisees,
had aligned themselves with the
   Herodians.
That is a highly unusual combination,
because the Herodians were
   collaborating with the enemy.
They were the ones who courted King
   Herod,
who was a puppet monarch.
And he was preferring to be a puppet
   monarch
and enjoy his life of luxury
ignoring what his religion called him
   to do.
The Pharisees,
on the other hand,
were extremely religious.
They didn't want
to have anything much to do with Rome
   at all,
and they considered that their role
was to practice their religious beliefs,
in spite of the Roman Empire.
So for them to be in collusion with the
   Herodians
is completely, completely,
almost unbelievable.
These two groups, however,
see Jesus, himself,
as such a threat
that they form a plan together
and the design to trap him
into something that could be called
   sedition,

or undermining the government,
so that he could be arrested by Rome
and out of their way.
But Jesus, however,
sees through their little plot,
and he startles them both with his
   answers.
They're very clever answers.
He asks them for a coin,
and even in doing that
exposed the people questioning him
as treacherous hypocrites
because they are
inside the temple when they have this
   conversation
and it's a place where Jewish money can
   be used,
that's the whole point of the money
   changers
that Jesus rebuked
when he turned their tables over in
   another story.
The reason they're at the outskirts of the
   temple
is so that they can change the pagan
   money,
the Roman money,
into Jewish money,
which can be used in temple offering.
Roman money doesn't belong in the
   temple at all,
and yet when Jesus asked for a coin,
the coin that these people hand him
is a Roman coin,
that's pagan money.
Then he asks the question:
"Whose likeness is on the coin?"
"Whose picture is on this coin?"
If he were asking that of any of us,

we could look at any different number of
  our coins—
on one is Abraham Lincoln,
on another is George Washington,
and one, the eagle.
We have pictures on all our coins, too.
But the answer for this one is "Caesar,"
the emperor of the Roman Empire.
So, Jesus says,
"Then give Caesar what belongs to
  Caesar
and give God what belongs God."

Now, if we were listening Romans,
overhearing this conversation,
we would think that Jesus had given a
  very reasonable answer,
and we would not accuse him
of treason.
And the Herodians,
who were collaborating with Rome
would have thought the same thing.
It's okay to go along with Rome in this
  way.
The Pharisees, however, knew more than
  that,
and they knew that they were being
  particularly attacked,
with Jesus' answers.
Because the Pharisees believed
what Jesus believed,
which is that everything belongs to God,
even that Roman coin.
And so, while Jesus gave an answer that
  was,
we can say, "politically correct,"
it was also an answer that was a real
  threat to the Pharisees,
because it put them right back

in the place that they were supposed
  to be,
in terms of what they believed,
that absolutely everything belonged to
  God
and everything returns to God.

So while Jesus appears to have made a
  compromise,
he has, in fact, restated a basic Jewish
  belief:
all of creation is God's,
and belongs to God,
and no human being can claim
  ownership or control
over God's great gifts.
Our responsibility as human beings
is instead to be stewards,
caretakers,
nurturers,
not people lying in wait to trap somebody.
We are guardians of God's gifts,
not snatchers who use those gifts
to trick,
to trap,
to dominate,
or otherwise disturb other human beings.

Now, we have name for Jesus Christ,
in fact we call him often
as does Paul to the Thessalonians:
Jesus Christ the Lord,
a name we use so often
that we perhaps
cease to remember why it's important.
Jesus,
the name of the authentic human being,
who reveals his humanity in his
insistence on equality

and resistance to domination.
God is the divine authority in the world.
We talk about the divinity of Christ.
Jesus is the one who reminds us of the uniqueness
of our own beings as human beings,
of our own humanity,
the one the who calls always
to the outcasts of society.
And in Jesus' time
the outcasts of society included
tax collectors,
collaborators,
soldiers,
and women,
and children.
If you were a child in Jewish society,
you were unimportant.
You would have never gotten up
until you were at least twelve years old
and read the Torah in the service.
A child didn't count.
Jesus is the one, however,
who sat the child in the midst of his followers
and said, "This is the model.
This child is the one whom we entertain,
who we chose to share in the reign of God."
That is central
to our way of celebrating children—
that we choose,
we model,
we nurture and protect,
we honor the children in the room,
and in ourselves,
as children of God.
Christ, the second part
of the three part name for Jesus

that Paul uses—
the messiah, the savior.
Not the one who does everything for us,
but the one who calls into possibility,
in accepting and using the gifts God has given.
These are gifts of light,
and time,
and treasure,
talent and government coins—
gifts to share in Thanksgiving,
to offer in Thanksgiving.
We give back just a portion
of what we ourselves have been given.
The Christ, the Messiah,
is the chosen one,
and as the chosen, also chooses,
chooses love,
chooses commitment,
chooses something other than what's commonly expected.
And the chosen one lives life in response to that choice,
lives death in response to that choice,
lives in us as the chosen,
who chooses that same commitment,
to love where love seems useless,
or impossible.
Lord, the third part of the title,
is the title actually of the emperor on the coin.
That's what everybody was supposed to call Caesar,
call the emperor "Lord."
The Jewish people did not do that
because they believed
that "Lord" was connected with God's name,

and the followers of Jesus used the word
  "Lord,"
to point out that the ruler of the world
is somebody other than the Roman ruler.
The ruler of the world dies on a cross,
calls the outcasts into the center,
and calls us to understand that rule
in terms of domination,
is not what "rule" is.
"Rule" instead is found
in terms of commitment,
choice and love.
We are, in fact, we believe,
stewards of creation,
with the choice to build up or destroy.
We're called to build
to use and share our talents.
And this day, in particular,
to share our treasure,
what we might otherwise hoard
or keep to ourselves.
We are called to be imitators of Christ,
models of the light,
and responsibility,
and commitment,
models for our children
and protectors of them
who recognize also
that the children in this room

and everywhere in the world
are models for us
as well.
And we are called to take for them,
and for ourselves,
the kinds of risks
that many others took—
like my friend's mother,
because we believe what she believed,
what she proved, in fact, to be true:
one person,
one ordinary person,
no matter how young or no matter how
  old,
who responds to being chosen,
by choosing commitment,
and love,
can make all the difference in the world.
Talk about Sabbath as a time of rest and
  prayer,
and talk about Sabbath signs of
  stewardship,
love and commitment,
about our responsibility as chosen
  people.
and the choices every single one of us in
  this room
has an opportunity to make.
Amen.

What Should I Do?

MARGARET ANN CRAIN
Peachtree Road United Methodist Church
Atlanta, Georgia
April 25, 1993

Lessons. Acts 2: 36–47; Luke 24: 12–35.

We have a tradition in this church
of being very faithful to the lectionary
   readings,
at this 8:30 service, and I have done that
   as well.
It's a fine discipline
because it makes sure that we get
   through the whole Bible
every three years,
as I know you know.
I have appreciated the readings for
   today.
They turned out to be very meaningful
and appropriate for the place where I am
in my faith journey.
And I'll share my thoughts with you.
Today's gospel,
is the story of those two people
making a journey to the town called
   Emmaus,
and they discover that a man they meet
   on the road is Jesus.

It wouldn't be so amazing,
if it weren't that three days earlier,
they had seen Jesus die on a cross.
You probably remember this story,
it's in the last chapter of Luke.
As they walk along, the stranger
   interprets
the scriptures to these followers of Jesus,
who were saying all of these terrible
   things have happened.
And when he joins them finally for
   supper,
they realize who he is,
and at that moment
he vanishes from them.

Now we might say,
"How foolish you are,
why in the world didn't you recognize him
   at once?
We thought you knew him.
We thought you'd been with him.

This is the man you put so much
hope in."
Part of the answer to that, of course,
lies in the effect of expectation on our
perceptions.
We usually see, you know,
what we think we're going to see.
And our experiences shape that
expectation.
Take for instance the little boy
who,
when asked to describe the famous
painting of Whistler's mother—
you know the one I mean,
she's sitting in the rocking chair, she
looks very old—
when he was asked to describe that
painting, he said:
"It shows a nice little lady
sitting in a chair,
waiting for the repairman to bring back
the TV set."

The gospel we call Luke doesn't tell us
why they don't recognize Jesus.
All we know is that, quote:
"When he was at the table with them, he
took bread,
blessed and broke it, and gave it to them.
Then their eyes were opened and they
recognized Him."

What a rich story!
One of my favorites,
probably one of yours.

Both the Emmaus story in Luke
and the account of Peter's sermon in
Acts,
are records of us,
of humans,
and how God acts toward us,
and then what we do.
And what we do
is the place I'm going to focus this
morning,
but first we have to deal with those first
things.
And in both these stories,
the first thing
is God's action.
God alone is able to overcome the
human death that Jesus experienced;
God's action makes Jesus available
to us;
God's action through Christ's death and
resurrection
placed Jesus with his sorrowing followers
on that road to Emmaus.
Likewise, in the reading that Mike shared
with us a minute ago,
Peter tells us,
through the writer of Acts,
that God has made Jesus both Lord and
Christ.
God has made Jesus both Lord and
Christ.
And that this is the same Jesus whom
we crucified.

John's gospel tells us, "In the beginning
was the word and the word was with
God,
and the word became flesh and dwelt
among us."
So we begin always with God's actions.
The whole
of the biblical witness testifies to that.

God is there before us,
from creation to the present.
And what do we do?
We crucify him.

We reject the gracious act which God
  has done.
That's what Peter tells us in today's
  lectionary reading.
"Now wait a minute," you say to me.
"I didn't crucify Jesus. I wasn't there!
I didn't have anything to do with that
  action!
You can't blame me for that!"
But that's a cop-out and I know it.
I know that a crowd can be swayed by a
  voice which speaks out.
In response to Pilate's question,
remember he asked,
"Do you want me to release for you the
  King of the Jews?"
And someone had to be the first to shout,
"No, Barabbas."
And I doubt
that I could have been the one,
the courageous voice which said,
"Yes, free Jesus, God's anointed one."

So, in an ambiguous,
I admit—in a roundabout impersonal sort
  of way—
I am guilty.
I crucified Jesus.
Even more, I think,
I crucify Jesus every day
as I make choices
which are not really consistent
with God's will for the earth
and for creation.

I crucify Jesus
when I use more than my share of the
  world's resources.
And I may leave some child to starve in
  Somalia,
or downtown Atlanta.
I crucify Jesus
when I don't hear the cry of my family
  member
who is hurting and needs a hug.
You might say,
"She's being a little melodramatic to say
  she crucifies Jesus,"
and I probably am.
I don't always do what God wants me
  to do,
but I'm not driving any nails.
And I suppose you're right,
I'm not really driving any nails,
but my guilt is real,
just the same.
A lot of pop psychology
which has tried to overcome a huge
  deficit in self-esteem,
has adopted that "I'm okay, you're okay"
  attitude.
Guilt is out of fashion.
Guilt is not healthy,
psychologically,
and I do agree with that.
Women,
especially,
have lost themselves in that endless
  struggle to do more,
to make everyone happy,
to fix the family,
to nurture and care
for everything and everyone.
And since, my friends,

no one can make another person happy
because happiness comes from inside,
we're doomed to failure in that whole
   project.
Hence,
guilt.
But you know,
guilt as a step on the way to something
   else
can be kind of helpful,
even necessary.
We do have responsibility.
Peter's sermon says it pretty bluntly.
He says, "This Jesus whom *you*
   crucified."
The people listening to Peter knew he
   was right,
and they responded with the critical
   question,
"What should we do?"

That's where the good news comes in,
thank goodness.
Remember who took the first step in this
   situation?
Not Peter,
but God.
God took the first step,
by becoming human in the person of
   Jesus,
the baby
helpless in his mother's womb.
The good news is that even in the face of
   our active resistance,
God is greater than we are.
God continues to act first.

So what should we do?

Well, I want to suggest several things to
   you this morning.
Kind of a straightforward "How-to for
   Christians."
Let me hasten to say that I'm preaching
   to myself as much,
and probably more,
than I'm preaching to you.
I'm still trying to discover what all of this
   means,
and I suspect most of us are.
So the first step in my little "How-to for
   Christians" is,
do something.
Take one action
which clearly puts God first in your life.
Not just a little thought or a prayer,
although those are perfectly nice things.
No, *do* something,
something concrete.
I might suggest,
now this is really simple,
but when you get your paycheck,
you sit down and you write the first check
   to the church.
Don't pay Visa,
or the mortgage,
or the car payment, or whatever,
all those urgent things first.
No, but write the first check,
give the first fruits to God.
Make up your mind
what portion is God's
and give it to God first.
I used to throw all my bills in a pile,
and just pay them in the order that they
   came up,
I'd work from the top down.

And the envelope for the church was
   always there way ahead,
because they mailed it out at the
   beginning of the year,
so, it was at the bottom of the pile.
I paid it last,
and by the time I got to it,
I don't know about you,
you probably have all the money in the
   world,
but I was feeling abused sometimes
as I watched the money disappear out of
   the checking account.
I didn't feel very good, by the time I got to
   that church check,
about writing it.
And I would think,
maybe I can just do a little less this
   month.
But you know, when I write the check to
   the church first,
I really feel differently about it.

Or maybe your action needs to relate to
   the use of your time.
Is there something you've been called to,
but you haven't said yes to yet?
Maybe singing in the choir,
or teaching Sunday School.
Maybe starting a small group with friends
for intentional talk about your lives and
   God's presence.
Or how about enrolling in a Disciple Bible
   Class for next fall
to really find out what's in the Bible.
What's important here
is to give the time as your *first* priority,
instead of the last gasp of your energy.

I was so touched by the story
that some of our members shared with
   us last week,
at lunch,
about a prayer group they used to
   belong to.
The group, all working professional
   people,
with a lot of demands on their time,
convened together to meet every
   Monday morning at 6:30.
That's a.m.!
For prayer and breakfast.
They all admitted that Mondays are
   always kind of hard,
but they seemed to go so much better,
when they started the week in that way.

Putting God first.

So number one is to take an action.
Do something which puts God first in
   your life.

And number two,
is to reflect on that action.
I don't mean just sit back and give
   yourself strokes for being such a good
   person,
although that's all right,
because you are.
But I mean critical reflection,
which asks the hard questions
about what effect the action has had on
   your understanding of yourself,
and your understanding of God.
I'm talking about reflecting theologically
   about the action.

Well, how do you do that? you say,
I'm not a theologian,
I don't know how to do that stuff.
But you do.
Because to reflect theologically
is simply to tell our stories.
In the telling,
we discover God's presence.
That's what theology is.
"Theo" meaning God,
"logy" meaning word,
theology,
God talk.
Frederick Buechner,
a very popular and very provocative
   author,
wrote about the importance of our stories
   in a recent book of his
called *Telling Secrets*.
Here's what Buechner says:
"I talk about my life,
because if,
on the one hand,
hardly anything could be less important,
on the other hand,
hardly anything could be more important.
My story is important not because it is
   mine, God knows,
but because if I tell it, anything like right,
the chances are you will recognize it,
in many ways it is also yours.
Maybe nothing is more important than
   that we keep track, you and I,
of these stories of who we are and where
   we have come from,
and the people we have met along the
   way.

Because it is precisely through these
   stories,
in all their particularity,
as I have long believed and often said,
that God becomes known to each of us,
most powerfully and personally.
If this is true,
it means that to lose track of our stories
is to be profoundly impoverished,
not only humanly,
but also spiritually."*

Our stories
are probably our most accessible
   resource
for coming to know God.
Buechner's book argues that we in fact
   have to tell our stories
authentically and truthfully.
Without the truth of our failures,
as well as our successes,
our wounds as well as our strengths,
our doubts as well as our faith,
the stories cannot reveal God's
   presence.

What we hunger for, I think,
more than anything else,
is to be known in our full humanness,
and yet paradoxically
that's probably what we fear the most as
   well.
What we can do for each other as
   Christians
is to offer to listen to each other's stories.

And we listen with awe,

*Frederick Buechner, *Telling Secrets* (San Francisco: HarperCollins, 1991), p. 30.

and respect,
for these are sacred stories,
stories which reveal God's actions
and God's presence.

I am impoverished,
humanly and spiritually,
as Buechner says,
when I don't hear your story.
I am humanly and spiritually
    impoverished, too,
when I don't keep track of my own story,
for it tells me who I am,
and points to where I must go next.
It clarifies the turning points in my life,
and the gracious gifts
which can only be attributed to God.

In my opinion
the most powerful spiritual organization
in the United States today is
unfortunately not the United Methodist
    Church,
not even the Southern Baptist Church,
or the Roman Catholic Church,
but AA,
Alcoholics Anonymous.

AA is a church in all the best sense of
    the term.
AA understands
how telling our stories reveals God's
    grace and leads to healing.
Nearly a year ago, someone very close
    to me asked for their help.
Her life was in shambles and that's
    putting it mildly.
Alcohol had taken control,
she was in debt,

locked out of her home,
thrown on the mercy of friends,
and the friends were out of patience.
She called AA,
and within ten minutes,
help was there.
Eleven months later, she's still sober,
and her life is turning around.
And the key to that turning around—
the theological term by the way is
    repentance—
the key to that turning around was telling
    her story.

"I'm addicted to alcohol,
it's ruined my life,
here's how it happened,
I want to free myself."
AA knows that in the telling,
in the entering of the wound,
in the sharing of the secret that's been
    kept for so long,
in the empathetic entering of the wound
    is the healing power of God.
And as we listen,
as we enter the wounds along with that
    person,
as we bear the secrets,
God's healing power is loosed:
For God's healing power works
    through us,
you and me as we share our stories.

So that's the second thing we should do,
reflect theologically by telling our stories.

And number three on the "How to" list
is to live authentically from those stories
into the future.

Jesus walked with the disciples on the
  road to Emmaus,
and when he was gone,
they *ran* to tell their story.
Likewise
when Peter's hearers asked "what should
  we do?"
he told them to repent.
Our repentance,
our turning around
requires that we know our stories
for they tell us who we are,
how God is present in our lives,
and thereby direct us into the future.
It's God's first action which empowers,
frees us to move towards the future.
For God was there before us,
and will continue to be there before us.
Peter's sermon tells us that in a didactic
  sort of way,
and the story of the disciples who walked
  to Emmaus,
tells us through story.
God's grace can be trusted,
my friends,
to be there first.

And that's the good news.

Would you join me in prayer?

Creator God,
you know our stories often better than we
  do ourselves.
But this morning, in the beauty of this
  sanctuary,
we ask you to gentle us,
quiet us
into an unclenched moment.
A deep breath,
[takes an audible deep breath]
a letting go of heavy expectancies,
a letting go of the shriveling anxieties,
a letting go of dead certainties.
Softened by this silence,
surrounded by your light,
and open now to the mystery,
we pray that we may be found by
  wholeness,
surprised by recognition, (whispered)
and transformed by healing,
trusting in your grace
we pray,
Holy One,
Amen.

Bibliography

Abu-Lughod, Lila. "Can There Be a Feminist Ethnography?" *Women and Performance* 5, 1 (1990): 7–27.

Ackermann, Robert John. *Religion as Critique*. Amherst: University of Massachusetts Press, 1985.

Alan of Lille. *The Art of Preaching*. Trans. Gillian R. Evans. Kalamazoo, MI: Cistercian Publications, 1981.

Allen, Paula Gunn. *The Sacred Hoop: Recovering the Feminine in American Indian Traditions*. Boston: Beacon Press, 1986; 1992.

———, ed. *Spider Woman's Granddaughters: Traditional Tales and Contemporary Writing by Native American Women*. New York: Ballantine Books, 1989.

Anderson, Sherry Ruth and Patricia Hopkins. *The Feminine Face of God: The Unfolding of the Sacred in Women*. New York: Bantam Books, 1991.

Anshen, Ruth Nanda. "Introduction" to Liebe F. Cavalieri, *The Double-Edged Helix: Science in the Real World*. New York: Columbia University Press, 1981, pp. 1–11.

Aristotle. *Rhetoric*. Trans. W. Rhys Roberts. New York: Modern Library, 1954.

Baldwin, Karen. "'Woof!' A Word on Women's Roles in Family Storytelling." In Rosan A. Jordan and Susan J. Kalčik, eds., *Women's Folklore, Women's Culture*. Philadelphia: University of Pennsylvania Press, 1985, pp. 149–62.

Bascom, William. "The Four Functions of Folklore." In Alan Dundes, ed., *The Study of Folklore*. Englewood Cliffs, NJ: Prentice-Hall, pp. 279–98.

Bauman, Richard. *Verbal Art as Performance*. Rowley, MA: Newbury House, 1977.

Belenky, Mary Field, Blythe McVicker Clinchy, Nancy Rule Goldberger, and Jill Mattuck Tarule. *Women's Ways of Knowing: The Development of Self, Voice, and Mind*. New York: Basic Books, 1986.

Bennett, Gillian. "'And I turned round to her and said . . .': A Preliminary Analysis of Shape and Structure in Women's Storytelling." *Folklore* 100, 2 (1989): 167–83.

———. "Heavenly Protection and Family Unite: The Concept of the Revenant Among Elderly Urban Women." *Folklore* 96, 1(1985): 87–97.

Birkerts, Sven P., ed. *Literature: The Evolving Canon*. Boston: Allyn and Bacon, 1993.

Brock, Rita Nakashima. "And a Little Child Will Lead Us: Christology and Child Abuse." In Carol Bohm and Joann Brown, eds., *Christianity, Patriarchy, and Abuse*. New York: Pilgrim Press, 1989, pp. 42–61.

———. *Journeys by Heart: A Christology of Erotic Power*. New York: Crossroad, 1989.

———. "'Re-Imagining': One Year Later." *The Disciples* 132 (October 1994): 21.

Buttrick, David. *A Captive Voice: The Liberation of Preaching*. Louisville, KY: Westminster/John Knox Press, 1994.

Campbell, Joan and David Polk, eds. *Bread Afresh, Wine Anew: Sermons by Disciples Women.* St. Louis: Chalis Press, 1991.

Campbell, Karlyn Kohrs. *Man Cannot Speak for Her.* Vol. 1. *A Critical Study of Early Feminist Rhetoric.* New York: Greenwood Press, 1989.

Christ, Carol P. and Judith Plaskow, eds. *Womanspirit Rising: A Feminist Reader in Religion.* San Francisco: Harper and Row, 1979.

———. *Weaving the Visions: New Patterns in Feminist Spirituality.* San Francisco: Harper and Row, 1989.

Clark, Elizabeth and Herbert Richardson. *Women and Religion: A Feminist Sourcebook of Christian Thought.* New York: Harper and Row, 1977.

Clements, William. "The Rhetoric of the Radio Ministry." *Journal of American Folklore* 87 (1974): 318–27.

———. "The American Folk Church in Northeast Arkansas." *Journal of the Folklore Institute* 15 (1978): 60–80.

Clifford, James. *The Predicament of Culture: Twentieth-Century Ethnography, Literature, and Art.* Cambridge, MA: Harvard University Press, 1988.

Clifford James and George E. Marcus, eds. *Writing Culture: The Poetics and Politics of Ethnography.* Berkeley and Los Angeles: University of California Press, 1986.

Coffin, William Sloane. *The Courage to Love.* San Francisco: Harper and Row, 1982.

Cooey, Paula M., Sharon A. Farmer, and Mary Ellen Ross, eds. *Embodied Love: Sensuality and Relationship as Feminist Values.* San Francisco: Harper and Row, 1987.

Craddock, Fred B. "Narrative: Distance and Participation." In Richard Lischer, ed., *Theories of Preaching: Selected Readings in the Homiletical Tradition.* Durham, NC: Labyrinth Press, 1987, pp. 250–58.

Crapanzano, Vincent. *Tuhami: Portrait of a Moroccan.* Chicago: University of Chicago Press, 1980.

Crotwell, Helen Gray, ed. *Women and the Word: Sermons.* Philadelphia: Fortress Press, 1978.

Crawford, James W. *Worthy to Raise Issues: Preaching and Public Responsibility.* New York: Pilgrim Press, 1991.

Daly, Mary. *Beyond God the Father: Toward a Philosophy of Women's Liberation.* Boston: Beacon Press, 1973.

Davis, Gerald. *"I got the Word in me and I can sing it, you know": A Study of the Performed African-American Sermon.* Philadelphia: University of Pennsylvania Press, 1985.

Dudley, Carl S. and Earle Hilgert. *New Testament Tensions and the Contemporary Church.* Augsburg: Fortress Press, 1987.

Elkins, Heather Murray. *Worshiping Women: Re-Forming God's People for Praise.* Nashville, TN: Abingdon Press, 1994.

Farrer, Claire R., ed. *Women and Folklore: Images and Genres.* Prospect Heights, IL: Waveland Press, 1975.

Ferrero, Pat et al. *Hearts and Hands: The Influence of Women and Quilts on American Society.* San Francisco: Quilt Digest Press, 1987.

Fine, Elizabeth C. and Jean Haskell Speer, eds. *Performance, Culture and Identity.* Westport, CT: Praeger, 1992.

Fiorenza, Elisabeth Schüssler. *In Memory of Her: A Feminist Theological Reconstruction of Christian Origins.* New York: Crossroad, 1983.

Fishbane, Michael A. *Text and Texture: Close Readings of Selected Biblical Texts.* New York: Schocken Books, 1979.

Flake, Carol. *Redemptorama: Culture, Politics, and the New Evangelicalism.* New York: Anchor Press, 1984.

Foss, Karen A. and Sonja K. Foss. *Women Speak: The Eloquence of Women's Lives*. Prospect Heights, IL: Waveland Press, 1991.

Friedman, Ellen G. and Miriam Fuchs, eds. *Breaking the Sequence: Women's Experimental Fiction*. Princeton, NJ: Princeton University Press, 1989.

Fulkerson, Mary McClintock. *Changing the Subject: Women's Discourses and Feminist Theology*. Minneapolis: Fortress Press, 1994.

Gilligan, Carol. *In a Different Voice: Psychological Theory and Women's Development*. Cambridge, MA: Harvard University Press, 1982.

Geertz, Clifford. "Thick Description: Toward an Interpretive Theory of Culture." In Geertz, *Interpretation of Cultures: Selected Essays*. New York: Basic Books, 1973.

Gillespie, Joanna Bowen. *Women Speak: Of God, Congregations, and Change*. Valley Forge, PA: Trinity Press International, 1995.

Gluck, Sherna Berger and Daphne Patai. *Women's Words: The Feminist Practice of Oral History*. New York: Routledge, 1991.

Green, Rayna. "Magnolias Grow in Dirt: The Bawdy Lore of Southern Women." *Southern Exposure* 4 (1977): 29–33.

Hagen, June Steffensen, ed. *Rattling Those Dry Bones: Women Changing the Church*. San Diego: LuraMedia, 1995.

Hampson, Daphne. *Theology and Feminism*. Oxford: Blackwell, 1990.

Heyward, Carter. *Touching Our Strength: The Erotic as Power and the Love of God*. San Francisco: Harper and Row, 1989.

Hillard, Van E. "Census, Consensus, and the Commodification of Form: The NAMES Project Quilt." In Cheryl B. Torsney and Judy Elsley, eds., *Quilt Culture: Tracing the Pattern*. Columbia: University of Missouri Press, 1994.

Hillman, James. *Re-Visioning Psychology*. New York: Harper and Row, 1975.

Holland, Dewitte, ed. *Preaching in American History: Selected Issues in the American Pulpit, 1630–1967*. Nashville, TN: Abingdon Press, 1969.

Hollis, Susan Tower, Linda Pershing, and M. Jane Young, eds. *Feminist Theory and the Study of Folklore*. Urbana: University of Illinois Press, 1993.

Hunter, James D. *Culture Wars: The Struggle to Define America*. New York: Basic Books, 1991.

Hurty, Kathleen S. "Collaborative Leadership in Chaotic Times, Nos. 1, 2 and 3." Arizona Ecumenical Council, Globe, Arizona. 2–3 June 1993. Unpublished manuscript.

Irigaray, Luce (trans. Robert L. Mazzola). "Equal to Whom?" (a response to Fiorenza, *In Memory of Her*). *differences* 1, 2 (summer 1989): 60–76.

Johnson, Elizabeth A. *She Who Is: The Mystery of God in Feminist Theological Discourse*. New York: Crossroad, 1992.

Jordan, Rosan A. and Susan J. Kalčik, eds. *Women's Folklore, Women's Culture*. Philadelphia: University of Pennsylvania Press and Publications of the American Folklore Society, 1985.

Kalčik, Susan. " '. . . like Ann's gynecologist or the time I was almost raped': Personal Narratives in Women's Rap Groups." *Journal of American Folklore* 88, 347 (1975): 3–11.

Kaufman, Gordon D. *The Theological Imagination: Constructing the Concept of God*. Philadelphia: Westminster Press, 1981.

Keller, Catherine. *From a Broken Web: Separation, Sexism, and Self*. Boston: Beacon Press, 1986.

———. "Inventing the Goddess: A Study in Ecclesiastical Backlash." *Christian Century* (April 6, 1994): 340.

Kelley, Margot Anne. "Sisters' Choices: Quilting Aesthetics in Contemporary African-American Women's Fiction." In Cheryl B. Torsney and Judy Elsley, eds., *Quilt Culture: Tracing the Pattern.* Columbia: University of Missouri Press, 1994, pp. 49–67.

Kennedy, Rodney. *The Creative Power of Metaphor: A Rhetorical Homiletics.* Lanham, MD: University Press of America, 1993.

Kim, C. W. Maggie, Susan M. St. Ville, and Susan M. Simonaitis, eds. *Transfigurations: Theology and the French Feminists.* Minneapolis: Fortress Press, 1993.

King, Martin Luther, Jr. *Strength to Love.* Philadelphia: Fortress Press, 1981.

Krieger, Susan. *The Mirror Dance: Identity in a Women's Community.* Philadelphia: Temple University Press, 1983.

Langellier, Kristin M. and Eric E. Peterson, "Spinstorying: An Analysis of Women Storytelling." In Elizabeth C. Fine and Jean Haskell Speer, eds., *Performance, Culture, and Identity.* Westport, CT: Praeger, 1992.

Lawless, Elaine J. "Writing the Body in the Pulpit: Female-Sexed Texts." *Journal of American Folklore* 107, 423 (Winter 1994), pp. 55–82.

———. *Handmaidens of the Lord: Pentecostal Women Preachers and Traditional Religion.* Philadelphia: University of Pennsylvania Press and Publications of the American Folklore Society, 1988.

———. *Holy Women, Wholly Women: Sharing Ministries of Wholeness Through Life Stories and Reciprocal Ethnography.* Philadelphia: University of Pennsylvania Press and Publications of the American Folklore Society, 1993.

———. "I was afraid someone like you would . . . an outsider . . . would misunderstand": Negotiating Interpretive Differences Between Ethnographers and Subjects." *Journal of American Folklore* 105, 417 (1992): 302–14.

———. "Narrative in the Pulpit: Persistent Use of *Exempla* in Vernacular Religious Contexts." *Journal of the Midwest Modern Language Association* 21, 1 (Spring 1988): 48–64.

———. "Women's Life Stories and Reciprocal Ethnography as Feminist and Emergent." *Journal of Folklore Research* 28, 1 (1991): 35–60.

LeGuin, Ursula and Susan Wood. *The Language of the Night: Essays on Fantasy and Science Fiction.* New York: Putnam, 1979.

Lischer, Richard. *Theories of Preaching: Selected Readings in the Homiletical Tradition.* Durham, NC: Labyrinth Press, 1987.

Llosa, Mario Vargas. *The Storyteller.* Trans. Helen Lane. New York: Farrar, Straus, Giroux, 1989.

Long, Thomas. *Preaching and the Literary Forms of the Bible.* Augsburg: Fortress Press, 1988.

Lowry, Eugene. *The Homiletical Plot: The Sermon as Narrative Art Form.* Louisville, KY: Westminster/John Knox Press, 1980.

Marcus, George E. and Michael M. J. Fischer. *Anthropology as Cultural Critique: An Experimental Moment in the Human Sciences.* Chicago and London: University of Chicago Press, 1986.

Mascia-Lees, Frances E., Patricia Sharpe, and Colleen Ballerino Cohen. "The Postmodernist Turn in Anthropology: Cautions from a Feminist Perspective." *Signs* 15 (1989): 7–33.

McAdams, Dan P. *The Stories We Live By: Personal Myths and the Making of the Self.* New York: Wm. Morrow, 1993.

McFague, Sallie. *The Body of God: An Ecological Theology.* Minneapolis: Fortress Press, 1993.

———. *Metaphorical Theology: Models of God in Religious Language*. Philadelphia: Fortress Press, 1982.

———. *Models of God: Theology for an Ecological, Nuclear Age*. Philadelphia: Fortress Press, 1987.

Mead, Loren. *The Once and Future Church*. New York: Alban Institute, 1991.

Meese, Elizabeth A. *Crossing the Double-Cross: The Practice of Feminist Criticism*. Chapel Hill: University of North Carolina Press, 1986.

Minh-Ha, Trinh T. *Woman, Native, Other: Writing, Postcoloniality, and Feminism*. Bloomington: Indiana University Press, 1989.

Mitchell, Carol. "Some Differences in Male and Female Joke Telling." In Rosan A. Jordan and Susan J. Kalčik, eds., *Women's Folklore, Women's Culture*. Philadelphia: University of Pennsylvania Press, 1985, pp. 163–86.

Mitchell, Henry H. *Celebration and Experience in Preaching*. Nashville, TN: Abingdon Press, 1990.

Moir, Anne and David Jessel. *Brain Sex: The Real Difference Between Men and Women*. New York: Carol Publishing Group, 1989.

Moltmann-Wendel, Elisabeth. *A Land Flowing with Milk and Honey: Perspectives on Feminist Theology*. Trans. John Bowden. New York: Crossroad Press, 1989.

Morton, Nelle. *The Journey Is Home*. Boston: Beacon Press, 1985.

Mraz, Barbara, ed. *Sacred Strands: Sermons by Minnesota Women*. Rochester, MN: Lone Oak Press, 1991.

Muto, Susan. *Womanspirit: Reclaiming the Deep Feminine in Our Human Spirituality*. New York: Crossroad Press, 1991.

Noren, Carol M. *The Woman in the Pulpit*. Nashville: Abingdon Press, 1992.

O'Brien, Theresa King, ed. *The Spiral Path: Essays and Interviews on Women's Spirituality*. St. Paul, MN: YES International Press, 1988.

O'Day, Gail R. and Thomas G. Long, eds. *Listening to the Word: Studies in Honor of Fred B. Craddock*. Nashville, TN: Abingdon Press, 1993.

Oden, Thomas C. *Minstry Through Word and Sacrament*. New York: Crossroad, 1989.

Ochshorn, Judith. *The Female Experience and the Nature of the Divine*. Bloomington: Indiana University Press, 1981.

Peacock, James L. "Ethnographic Notes on Sacred and Profane Performance." In Richard Schechner and Willa Appel, eds., *By Means of Performance: Intercultural Studies in Theatre and Ritual*. Cambridge; New York: Cambridge University Press, 1990, pp. 208–35.

Peck, Catherine. "Your Daughters Shall Prophesy: Women in the Afro-American Preaching Tradition." MA Thesis, University of North Carolina, 1983.

Peppers, Cathy, "Fabricating a Reading of Toni Morrison's *Beloved* as a Quilt of Memory and Identity." In Cheryl B. Torsney and Judy Elsley, eds. *Quilt Culture: Tracing the Pattern*. Columbia: University of Missouri Press, 1994, pp. 84–95.

Pershing, Linda. " 'She Really Wanted to Be Her Own Woman': Scandalous Sunbonnet Sue." In Joan Radner, ed., *Feminist Messages: Coding in Women's Folk Culture*. Urbana: University of Illinois Press, 1993, pp. 98–125.

———. *They Tied a Ribbon Around the Pentagon: Women's Contemporary Fabric Arts as Social Critique*. Knoxville: University of Tennessee Press and Publications of the American Folklore Society, 1995.

Petroff, Elizabeth Alvilda. *Medieval Women's Visionary Literature*. New York: Oxford University Press, 1985.

Proctor, Samuel D. *Preaching about Crises in the Community*. Louisville, KY: Westminster/John Knox Press, 1988.

Radner, Joan Newlon, ed. *Feminist Messages: Coding in Women's Folk Culture.* Urbana: University of Illinois Press, 1993.

Radner, Joan Newlon with Susan Lanser. "Strategies of Coding in Women's Cultures." In Joan Radner, ed., *Feminist Messages: Coding in Women's Folk Culture.* Urbana: University of Illinois Press, 1993, pp. 1–29.

Raitt, Jill. "Strictures and Structures: Relational Theology and a Woman's Contribution to Theological Conversation." *Journal of the American Academy of Religion* 50, 1 (March 1982): 3–17.

Ratcliffe, Krista. *Anglo-American Feminist Challenges to the Rhetorical Traditions: Virginia Woolf, Mary Daly, and Adrienne Rich.* Carbondale: Southern Illinois University Press, 1995.

Regan, Helen. "Not for Women Only: School Administration as a Feminist Activity." *Teachers College Board* 91, 4 (Summer 1990): 565–77.

Rohrbach, Peter-Thomas. *The Art of Dynamic Preaching: A Practical Guide to Better Preaching.* New York: Doubleday, 1965.

Roof, Wade Clark and William McKinney. *American Mainline Religion: Its Changing Shape and Future.* New Brunswick, NJ: Rutgers University Press, 1987.

Rosenberg, Bruce. *The Art of the American Folk Preacher.* New York: Oxford University Press, 1970. Reissued as *Can These Bones Live?*

Ruby, Jay, ed. *A Crack in the Mirror: Reflexive Perspectives in Anthropology.* Philadelphia: University of Pennsylvania Press, 1982.

Ruether, Rosemary Radford. *Sexism and God-Talk: Toward a Feminist Theology.* Boston: Beacon Press, 1983.

———. *Women-Church: Theology and Practice of Feminist Liturgical Communities.* San Francisco: Harper and Row, 1986.

Ruskin, Cindy. *The Quilt: Stories from the NAMES Project.* New York: PocketBooks, 1988.

Russell, Letty. *Human Liberation in a Feminist Perspective.* Philadelphia: Westminster Press, 1974.

Russell, Letty with Kwok Puilan, Ada Maria Isasi-Diaz, and Katie Geneva Cannon. *Inheriting Our Mothers' Gardens: Feminist Theology in Third World Perspective.* Louisville, KY: Westminster/John Knox Press, 1988.

Schaef, Anne Wilson. *Women's Reality: An Emerging Female System in a White Male Society.* San Francisco: Harper and Row, 1981.

Sered, Susan Starr. *Priestess, Mother, Sacred Sister: Religions Dominated by Women.* New York: Oxford University Press, 1994.

Seymour, Jack L., Margaret Ann Crain, and Joseph V. Crockett. *Educating Christians: The Intersection of Meaning, Learning and Vocation.* Nashville, TN: Abingdon Press, 1993.

Shepherd, Linda Jean. *Lifting the Veil: The Feminine Face of Science.* Boston: Shambhala, 1993.

Shoemaker, Nancy, ed. *Negotiators of Change: Historical Perspectives on Native American Women.* New York: Routledge, 1995.

Showalter, Elaine. *Sister's Choice: Tradition and Change in American Women's Writing.* New York: Oxford University Press, 1991.

———. "Piecing and Writing." In Nancy K. Miller, ed., *The Poetics of Gender.* New York: Columbia University Press, 1986, pp. 222–47.

Sleevi, Mary Lou. *Women of the Word.* Notre Dame, IN: Ave Maria Press, 1989.

Smith, Christine M. *Weaving the Sermon: Preaching in a Feminist Perspective.* Louisville, KY: Westminster/John Knox Press, 1989.

————. *Preaching as Weeping, Confession, and Resistance: Radical Responses to Radical Evil.* Louisville, KY: Westminster/John Knox Press, 1992.

Spinning a Sacred Yarn: Women Speak from the Pulpit. New York: Pilgrim Press, 1982.

Spivak, Gayatri Chakravorty. *In Other Worlds: Essays in Cultural Politics.* New York: Methuen, 1987.

Spretnak, Carol, ed. *The Politics of Women's Spirituality: Essays on the Rise of Spiritual Power Within the Feminist Movement.* New York: Anchor Doubleday, 1982.

Stacey, Judith. "Can There Be a Feminist Ethnography?" *Women's Studies International Forum* 11, 1 (1988): 21–27.

Starcke, Walter. *The Double Thread.* New York: Harper and Row, 1967.

Suchocki, Marjorie Hewitt. "Friends in the Family: Church, Seminary and Theological Educators." In Joseph C. Hough, Jr. and Barbara G. Wheeler, eds., *Beyond Clericalism: The Congregation as a Focus for Theological Education.* Atlanta: Scholars Press, 1988, pp. 49–60.

Tannen, Deborah. *You Just Don't Understand: Women and Men in Conversation.* New York: Ballantine Books, 1990.

Taylor, Barbara Brown, *Gospel Medicine.* Cambridge, MA: Cowley, 1995.

————. *The Preaching Life.* Cambridge, MA: Cowley 1993.

Tedlock, Dennis. *The Spoken Word and the Work of Interpretation.* Philadelphia: University of Pennsylvania Press, 1983.

Thistlewaite, Susan and Mary Potter Engel, eds. *Lift Every Voice: Constructing Christian Theologies from the Underside.* San Francisco: Harper and Row, 1990.

Tickle, Phyllis A. *Re-Discovering the Sacred: Spirituality in America.* New York: Crossroad Press, 1995.

Titon, Jeff Todd. *Powerhouse for God: Speech, Chant, and Song in an Appalachian Baptist Church.* Austin: University of Texas Press, 1988.

Torsney, Cheryl B. and Judy Elsley, eds. *Quilt Culture: Tracing the Pattern.* Columbia: University of Missouri Press, 1994.

Trible, Phyllis. "Feminist Hermeneutics." In Richard Lischer, ed., *Theories of Preaching: Selected Readings in the Homiletical Tradition.* Durham, NC: Labyrinth Press, 1987, pp. 199–206.

————. *God and the Rhetoric of Sexuality.* Philadelphia: Fortress Press, 1978.

Tyler, Stephen A. *The Unspeakable: Discourse, Dialogue, and Rhetoric in the Postmodern World.* Madison: University of Wisconsin Press, 1987.

Valentine, Kristin B. and Eugene Valentine. "Performing Culture Through Narrative: A Galician Woman Storyteller." In Elizabeth C. Fine and Jean Haskell Speer, eds., *Performance, Culture, and Identity.* Westport, CT: Praeger, 1992.

Van Harn, Roger E. *Pew Rights: For People Who Listen to Sermons.* Grand Rapids, MI: Eerdmans, 1992.

Walker, Alice. *In Search of Our Mothers' Gardens: Womanist Prose.* San Diego: Harcourt Brace Jovanovich, 1983.

Warner, Stephen R. *New Wine in Old Wineskins: Evangelicals and Liberals in a Small-Town Church.* Berkeley: University of California Press, 1987.

Watson, James D. *The Double Helix: A Personal Account of the Discovery of the Structure of DNA.* ed. Gunther S. Stent. New York: Norton, 1980.

Weigle, Marta. "Women as Verbal Artists: Reclaiming the Sisters of Enheduanna." *Frontiers* 3, 3 (1977–78): 1–9.

Welsh, Clement. *Preaching in a New Key: Studies in the Psychology of Thinking and Listening.* Philadelphia: United Church Press, 1974.

Willimon, William H. *Peculiar Speech: Preaching to the Baptized.* Grand Rapids, MI: Eerdmans, 1992.

Wingren, Gustaf. *The Living Word: A Theological Study of Preaching and the Church.* Trans. Victor C. Pogue. Philadelphia: Fortress Press, 1960.

Zikmund, Barbara Brown. "Women as Preachers: Adding New Dimensions to Worship." *Journal of Women and Religion*, 3, 2 (Summer 1984): 12–16.

Index

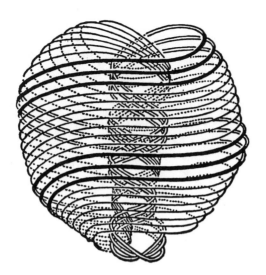